Lammas Magic

The Celtic festival of Lughnasa (from the Gaelic *násad*, meaning "games or assembly" of Lugh, a Celtic deity and hero) survived the rise of Christianity by becoming Lammas (from the Anglo-Saxon *hlaef-mass*, meaning "loaf-mass"). It marks the start of the harvest when the first grain is gathered, ground, and baked into a loaf of bread. The Lammas loaf is still traditional in many parts of the British Isles. It is a wonderful way for the modern kitchen witch to work magic.

Lammas Bread Wish Spell

Make a loaf of bread at Lammas and before you put the loaf into the oven, dip a paintbrush in milk and write on the crust what you most desire. Bake the bread, then eat it while still warm.

Lammas Bread Protection Spell

A book of Anglo-Saxon charms advised the crumbling of the Lammas loaf into four pieces and the burying of them in the four corners of the barn to make it safe for all the grain that would be stored there. You can use this old spellcraft in a protection spell for your home.

Bake a Lammas loaf, and when it is cool break it into four pieces — don't cut it with a knife—and take one to each corner of your property with the words:

I call on the spirits
Of north and south, east and west
Protect this place
Now, at the time of the Blessing.

Leave the bread for the birds to eat or bury the pieces.

D1637078

ABOUT THE AUTHORS

Anna Franklin is a well-known English Pagan author and witch who runs the Hearth of Arianrhod as its High Priestess and director. She collaborated with Paul Mason on the popular *The Sacred Circle Tarot*. She lives in England where she also illustrates books and works as a professional photographer.

Paul Mason is an English Pagan artist, photographer, and illustrator best known for his stunning photomontage images and book jacket designs. He has illustrated several of Anna Franklin's books and is making his debut as a writer in co-authoring this book. Paul lives in the English Midlands.

TO WRITE TO THE AUTHORS

Lammas

Celebrating Fruits of the First Harvest

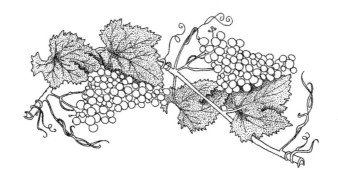

ANNA FRANKLIN AND PAUL MASON

2001
Llewellyn Publications
St. Paul, Minnesota 55164-0383

FIRST EDITION
First printing, 2001

Cover art by Kate Thomssen
Cover design by Lynne Menturweck
Editing and book design by Christine Snow
Illustrations by Anna Franklin: pages iii, 3, 20, 29, 31, 32, 37, 43, 47, 69, 71, 80, 85, 98, 112, 127, 137, 179, 181, 183, 197, 198, 217, 229, 233, 235, 253
Illustrations by Paul Mason : pages 8, 13, 17, 50, 58, 59, 89, 91, 92, 94, 102, 103, 140, 143, 155, 167

Library of Congress Cataloging-in-Publication Data
Franklin, Anna.
    Lammas: celebrating fruits of the first harvest / Anna Franklin and Paul Mason.–1st ed.
      p. cm.
    Includes bibliographical references and index.
    ISBN 0-7387-0094-0
    1. Lammas. 2. Cookery. 3. Rites and ceremonies. I. Mason, Paul, 1952– II. Title.
    BF1572.L35F73 2001
    299–dc21   00-069431

Llewellyn Publications
A Division of Llewellyn Worldwide, Ltd.
P.O. Box 64383, Dept. 0-7387-0094-0
St. Paul, MN 55164-0383
www.llewellyn.com

Printed in the United States of America

Other Works by Anna Franklin and Paul Mason

Fairy Lore
(Capall Bann, 2000)

The Sacred Circle Tarot: A Celtic Pagan Journey
(Llewellyn, 1998)

Familiars
(Capall Bann, 1997)

Herbcraft
(Capall Bann, 1995)

Other Works by Anna Franklin

Ritual Incenses and Oils
(Capall Bann, 2000)

The Wellspring
(Capall Bann, 2000)

Personal Power
(Capall Bann, 1998)

Pagan Feasts
(Capall Bann, 1997)

Upcoming Books by Anna Franklin

Midsummer Magic
(Llewellyn, 2002)

DEDICATION

To Eric, Flake, and Rick, the warrior kings of Lughnasa.

CONTENTS

Part 1:
History, Customs, and Lore of Lughnasa and Lammas

Part 2: Celebrating Lughnasa

Part 1

History, Customs, and Lore
of Lughnasa and Lammas

Chapter 1

The Forgotten Festival

It was upon a Lammas night,
When corn rigs are bonnie,
Beneath the moon's unclouded light,
I held awa to Annie.[1]

Although Lughnasa has an ancient and fascinating history, nowadays it is a rather obscure festival. Unlike Halloween, for example, the average person outside of the Pagan community has probably never heard of it — even in Ireland, where the name of the festival survives in modern Gaelic as Lúnasa, the month of August.

Lughnasa is Irish Gaelic and means "the *násad* (games or an assembly) of Lugh," a leading Celtic deity and hero. Lughnasa was one of the quarter festivals of the Celtic year, the others being Samhain on November 1, Imbolc on February 1, and Beltane on May 1. The festival seems to have included tribal assemblies and activities extending over two to four weeks. It was celebrated only in Britain, Ireland, France (ancient Gaul), and possibly northern Spain.

Pagans celebrate Lughnasa as one of the eight festivals in the witches' Wheel of the Year,[2] but many know little about it beyond the fact that it marks the beginning of harvest. Unlike May Day, Yule, or Midsummer, relatively few of Lughnasa's customs survive either in folklore or historical record. Nevertheless, even in these times of all-year-round imported crops, its presence can still be felt. If we dig deep, we can find its traces.

While on the one hand Lughnasa is little-known, on the other its influence is still felt on our modern patterns of both work and leisure. Factory and school holidays were timed to coincide with the start of the harvest so that more people would be free to help with the harvesting. Even in today's post-industrial age, early August remains the traditional time for summer holidays and fairs. There are some traditional Lughnasa customs that are still practiced today, but these tend to be confined to specific localities and cultures. There are no practices as widespread as those celebrated at Yule or Easter, although there are several clearly defined themes that underlie the traditional Lughnasa celebrations and rites.

LAMMAS

Lughnasa is also called Lammas, from the Anglo-Saxon *hlaef-mass,* meaning "loaf-mass." The *Anglo-Saxon Chronicle* of 921 C.E. mentions it as "the feast of first fruits," as does the *Red Book of Derby.* It was a popular ceremony during the Middle Ages but died out after the Reformation, though the custom is being revived in places. It marks the first harvest, when the first grain is gathered in, ground in a mill, and baked into a loaf. This first loaf was offered up as part of the Christian Eucharist ritual.

There was a Lamb's Mass held at the cathedral of St. Peter in York for feudal tenants, and some say this may have given rise to the name since fresh baked bread and lamb are traditionally eaten at Lammas. This seems unlikely. Since Lammas was celebrated only in Britain — no other Germanic or Nordic peoples observed Lammas or held any other feasts on August 1 — it seems more likely that it was merely a renaming of the Celtic Lughnasa. (However, important festivals were celebrated elsewhere around this time, and these throw new light on the meaning of Lughnasa. We shall be looking at some of these in the next chapter.)

Lammas was a rent day, and land tenure and pasture rights were often settled at Lammas. Some grazing lands were given over to common use from Lammas to Candlemas. Stock was put to pasture on the hay meadows, which then remained common through spring until the Enclosure Acts of the early nineteenth century. It was a time of sheep and cattle fairs accompanied by games.

LUGHNASA NEW STYLE OR OLD STYLE

One of the main reasons for the obscurity of Lammas/Lughnasa is the confusion caused by its variety of names and the differing dates on which it is celebrated. In 1582 Pope Gregory XIII wiped out ten days from the old Julian calendar to make it astronomically correct. However, the Gregorian calendar was not adopted in Britain until 1752 and Ireland until 1782, by which time eleven days had to be dropped. This led to the festival being celebrated on either August 1 or 12 called, respectively, New Style and Old Style Lughnasa, or New and Old Lughnasa. As a general rule, most celebrations gradually moved to the New Style calendar. The Calendar Act of 1751 excluded markets, fairs, and courts; these were held on the natural date, August 12. To add to the confusion, many Lammas/Lughnasa celebrations were traditionally held on either the previous or the following Sunday. Further complicating matters, many Lammas/Lughnasa festivities became appropriated to Christian saints' days or the nearest Sunday.

TRADITIONAL LUGHNASA/LAMMAS CUSTOMS

There is very little historical evidence of what actually took place at a Celtic Lughnasa gathering. We know that it was celebrated around August 1 and included a tribal gathering. From the date it seems likely that Lughnasa marked the beginning of the harvest, but this is not recorded; it was the Anglo-Saxons that titled it a feast of first fruits. It is possible that Lughnasa initially marked a summer roundup of flocks and herds and only later became a feast of first fruits.

Most of the clues as to the real nature and practices of Lughnasa come from folklore survivals. From these we can tell that the celebrations took place on a hilltop or near a holy well. There were games and contests, a bull sacrifice and feast, and trial marriages were entered into.

Folklore survivals of Lughnasa are celebrated under a wide variety of names, such as Bilberry Sunday, Garland Sunday, and Domhnach Crom Dubh ("Crom Dubh Sunday"), depending on the locality, at various dates between mid-July and mid-August. To begin our investigation into this ancient festival, we should begin by looking at some of these.

HILLTOP GATHERINGS AND PILGRIMAGES

Assemblies on hilltops are a traditional part of the proceedings. In Ireland and the Isle of Man, many of these hilltop gatherings have survived to the present day. Some have become associated with the local Christian saint and many more with St. Patrick. These Christianized forms of an earlier tradition are typically a strange combination of the sacred and the profane. A pilgrimage, often barefoot, accompanied by a great deal of praying, would often be followed by drinking, dancing, fighting, and very unruly behavior. Such pilgrimages were undertaken as a penance for past sins and to gain remission in purgatory in the afterlife. Nineteenth-century Protestant observers were horrified by what they considered to be idolatry and gross immorality on the part of the Catholic peasants.

Yet other hilltop assemblies show no sign of having been taken over by the Christian religion. These survivors of Pagan Lughnasa celebrations were considered by the country people to have no particular religious significance. Over the years they had gradually become an excuse for a festive outing to mark the start of the harvest.

Croagh Patrick

Rising to 2,510 feet (765 meters), Croagh Patrick, near Westport in County Meath, is the most famous pilgrimage mountain in the whole of Ireland. Although it has long been associated with St. Patrick, it was originally venerated by the ancient Irish as the dwelling place of Crom Dubh and was one of the main sites for Lughnasa celebrations and rituals. The mountain and its surrounding area were, however, a site of ritual purpose long before the coming of the Celts. The spectacular nature of the mountain has drawn pilgrims since Neolithic times, an unbroken tradition of religious activity that has lasted for over 6,000 years.

The earliest evidence of human activity at the site is a single flake of shaped stone, a type used by the nomadic hunters of the pre-agricultural Mesolithic period, dating from between 6,000 and 4,000 B.C.E. More impressive archaeological remains at Croagh Patrick date from the Neolithic Age (4,000–2,000 B.C.E.). These include a partially buried tomb on its western slope and some impressive rock art on its eastern approach. This latter site became known as St. Patrick's Chair and was incorporated into the Christian pilgrimage to the mountain's summit. A survey revealed an important solar alignment between St. Patrick's Chair and the sacred peak. This takes the form of a "rolling sun phenomenon," during which the sun appears to rest on the ridge of the mountain before rolling down its side at sunset. This happens twice a year — in early April and again for a few days in August, around the time of Lughnasa. There are also important Bronze Age (2,000–600 B.C.E.) remains at Croagh Patrick, consisting of standing stones, alignments, and cairns. Several of these ancient artifacts have also become part of the Christian pilgrimage. Excavations in the 1990s discovered the remains of a fort encircling the summit, dating from between 1,000 and 500 B.C.E. Early churchmen had previously assumed that St. Patrick spent forty days praying and fasting on a bare mountaintop, but now it has been proved that Croagh Patrick was an important religious center in ancient Pagan times.

A local tale relates how Patrick confined demon-birds in a hollow below the mountain's summit called Log na nDeamhan. He then had to face an even more fearsome adversary in the devil's mother, or Corra (Caoirthineach in Gaelic). These later developments of the story introduced the traditional Lughnasa theme of an epic battle between the forces of light and darkness.

Before 1113 C.E., Lent or St. Patrick's Day (March 17) was the accepted time of year to make a pilgrimage to Croagh Patrick, but in this year a thunderbolt is said to have killed thirty of the pilgrims, and the pilgrimage period was changed to summer, the most popular dates being the last Friday or Sunday of July. This story can be seen as an example of the old Pagan gods gaining revenge on their Christian

usurpers. Until 1838, an ancient relic, the Clog Dubh, which was said to be the original black bell with which Patrick banished the demon-birds from the mountain, played an important part in the pilgrimage ritual. It was placed in a chapel at the summit. Each pilgrim was to kiss a cross engraved on the bell and then pass it three times sunwise around their body. The Clog Dubh is now displayed in the National Museum in Dublin. Another custom with a clear Pagan origin was the placing of a nail or piece of rag in the stonework of the ruined chapel at the summit as an offering.

Although Croagh Patrick was originally a Pagan sanctuary for the celebration of life's abundance, under Christianity it became the scene of penance for supposed sinfulness. Many of the Christian pilgrims ascended the mountain barefoot, or even on their knees, as an act of atonement.

Although the penances of the earlier Christians were severe, they still retained much of the ancient appetite for celebration — with drinking, dancing, and music — once they had descended the mountain. Many of the eighteenth and nineteenth-century accounts of the pilgrimage were written by Protestants who were horrified by the mixture of extreme piety and rough high spirits displayed by the Irish Catholic peasants.

In the present day, around one million pilgrims climb Croagh Patrick each year, including 40,000 or so on the last Sunday in July.

Lhuany's Day (Isle of Man)

Lhuany was the Manx version of the god Lugh. On the first Sunday after Old Lammas, the Manx inhabitants would climb to the top of Snaefell, the highest mountain on the Isle of Man. Their festivities must have been rather unruly, as one nineteenth-century observer described them as behaving "very rudely and indecently" — an intriguing but somewhat vague description. There is a local story that the custom died out when a clergyman started to take a collection on the summit.

As elsewhere in the British Isles, this was a day for visiting wells. Those on the Isle of Man were said to be at the peak of their healing powers on this date. For example, St. Maugold Well near Ramsey is reputed to cure sterility if the sufferer throws a pin in the well or dips their heel into it. This was still a popular practice right up to the beginning of the twentieth century.

Lammas Towers (Scotland)

In Lothian until the 1790s, young herdsmen would gather together in bands of up to 1,000 strong and build towers of turves (pieces of sod) seven to eight feet high, topped with flagstaffs and ribbons. They would sally forth from their towers and fight rival groups with cudgels, or those with no local rivals would march to the village at noon and hold footraces.[3]

HOLY WELLS

Water is also associated with Lughnasa. Assemblies at wells would often be held on the feast day of the local saint, but many of these gatherings were moved from the saint's day to late July and early August; probably evidence of an earlier Pagan custom reasserting itself.

Britain and Ireland have a large number of holy wells — over 1,000 in England, 1,000 in Wales, 600 in Scotland, and at least 3,000 in Ireland. Many of the wells shown on maps are those that have been popularized as "wishing wells." Coins are thrown into them or strips of cloth are attached to adjacent thornbushes for good luck or healing, a remnant of offering sacrifices or leaving votive offerings to a Celtic or Roman deity.

The Celtic festivals were thought to be among the best times to visit wells, especially during Beltane, Midsummer, and Lughnasa. Dawn or just before was considered to be the most appropriate time of day to go there. As well as leaving an offering, the method and direction of approach to the well was also important. Some wells have specific rites that have to be observed to ensure an efficacious cure, such as circling it three times sunwise.

The traditional offering varies from place to place and from time to time. Throwing coins into the water was very common in Roman times, and we still practice this today. Other wells were known as "rag" or, in Scotland, as "cloutie" wells. A piece of cloth would be tied to an overhanging tree or bush with the wish that the illness would gradually fade away as the cloth rotted into the well. This practice is still widespread today, although some of the offerings are a little bizarre. These include audiotapes, plastic materials, and synthetic cloth — all materials that do not easily degrade, showing a lack of the proper understanding of this ancient practice.

A relatively painless form of blood sacrifice was customary at some wells. Those seeking a cure would prick a finger to draw blood and then throw the pin into the well. In other cases, specific offerings were required for specific cures. At St. Columba's Well (Donegal, Ireland), which is said to cure the lame, it is customary to leave a crutch in hopes that it would no longer be needed.

Leaving offerings at wells and waterways is a very ancient practice, and there is archeological evidence of this from early Bronze Age sites; a considerable amount of helmets, swords, and shields have been excavated.

Well Dressing (England)

In many English villages, especially those in Derbyshire, wells are decorated with elaborate floral tributes, a custom known as well dressing. This practice dates back thousands of years in one form or another but is not a continuous tradition; in many cases, the custom died out and was revived in Victorian times or even more recently.

Well dressing takes place on various dates in different localities, usually around Beltane, Midsummer, and the Feast of the Assumption. Also known as Marymass, the Feast of the Assumption is celebrated on August 15, four days after Old Lammas Eve. The Assumption is the main feast of the Virgin Mary in the Catholic calendar and commemorates the day in 45 c.e. when Mary's body ascended into heaven. Bearing in mind the date and that many sacred Pagan wells were renamed after Mary, this festival and its customs are clearly yet another example of the Christianization of earlier traditions and beliefs.

Along with Lammas, it marked the period of harvest festivities. In more northern parts of Scotland, where the harvest was later, Marymass replaced Lammas as the festival of the first harvest. Mary took on the characteristics of harvest goddesses from many earlier cultures and is sometimes depicted in robes decorated with ears of grain.

Originally wells would have been adorned with simple garlands. Nowadays, well dressing has developed into a highly ornate folk art, with a strong element of friendly competition between neighboring villages. A wooden framework is erected and covered with clay into which flower petals, leaves, moss, berry seeds, and pine cones are pressed to produce elaborate pictures, usually of biblical subjects.

FAIRS AND WAKES

Are you going to Scarborough Fair,
Parsley, sage, rosemary, and thyme,
Remember me to one who lived there,
She once was a true love of mine.[4]

Late July and the month of August were traditionally times for fairs. The weather would usually be mild and the ground suitable for traveling. Many traditional Lammas/Lughnasa fairs are still celebrated today. They are especially devoted to enjoyment and entertainment, with the trading of farm animals being a less important element of the fairs. In bygone times, a visit to the Lammas Fair was the main public social event of the year, and for young people it was an exciting opportunity to meet prospective romantic partners.

Puck Fair (Ireland)

This is one of the best-known traditional fairs. It is held at Killorglin, County Kerry, on August 10, 11, and 12. These dates are known as Gathering Day, Fair Day, and Scattering Day, respectively. There are several legends about the fair's ancient origins but no written records stating when the Puck Fair was first celebrated. A charter from King James I giving official legal status to the fair was granted in 1603.

The most famous and interesting aspect of the fair is the important role that a male goat plays in the proceedings. Several accounts of the fair suggest a link between a pre-Christian deity and the goat, known as "King Puck" (from the Gaelic *puc*, meaning "he-goat"). Its origins may be ancient, though there are various local legends to explain it. One concerns a goat that is said to have warned the inhabitants of the approach of Cromwell's army. No matter what its exact origins, the fair has remained the most culturally, economically, and socially important event in the Killorglin calendar right up to the present day, attracting thousands of visitors from around the world.

On the first day of the fair, Gathering Day, a wild mountain goat is paraded through the colorfully decorated streets. This parade features a queen of the fair along with carnival floats from local cultural and business organizations. The parade ends in the town square where the coronation ceremony is enacted. A three-tiered stand is erected in the square, and the goat is placed on the lowest tier. The queen of the fair reads a proclamation to the assembled crowds and places a crown on the head of the goat; everyone then salutes the new King Puck. After this investiture ceremony is completed, the goat is elevated to the highest tier of the stand. For the next three days, the "king," fed on a diet of cabbages, looks down on his loyal and pleasure-seeking subjects from a height of fifty feet. It is said that Killorglin is the only place where a goat acts as king and the people act the goat.

There is also a horse fair on Gathering Day, which was famous throughout Europe; several armies once sent buyers to the Puck Fair to purchase mounts for their cavalry.

August 11 is called Fair Day and is the traditional date for the buying and selling of cattle and sheep. Nowadays, this is also the occasion for Comórtas Na nAmhrán Nuachumtha Gaeilge, an Irish song competition.

The final day of the fair is Scattering Day. In the evening, the noble King Puck is dethroned and brought down from his stand. He is paraded once more through the town, this time on the shoulders of four men who collect his "expenses" from the local tradespeople. In the past he was sold at auction, but is nowadays released into the wild mountains of Kerry. Traditional music and dancing continues throughout the night, and the Puck Fair is over until the following year.

There were once several other Irish fairs during which male animals were enthroned. These customs took place on a variety of dates in addition to Lughnasa, but have many similarities with the festivities at Killorglin. At Cappawhite in County Tipperary, a white horse was paraded through the town and put on top of a local fort for the fair's duration.

At Lammas and Lughnasa fairs throughout Britain and Ireland, various other symbols were displayed, such as a white glove, or the rods and wands of office belonging to the local sheriffs and bailiffs. At the St. James' Fair in Limerick, which lasted for a fortnight, a white glove was hung out at the prison. During this time, no one could be arrested for debt.

Muff Fair (Ireland)

First the Fair of Muff and then the holiday:
We'll meet him on the road and well he knows the way.

This is a horse fair held on August 12 (or August 13, if the twelfth falls on a Sunday) close to a rise in the ground called the Rock of Muff in County Cavan. It is undoubtedly a survival of an ancient Celtic celebration. A mile to the west is the Hill of Loughinlay, which is the site of a festive outing on the Sunday before the fair itself. Such assemblies on hilltops are, of course, a feature of traditional Lughnasa activities. Although horse-trading at the fair is serious, the main crowds attending are drawn there for drinking and dancing. Faction-fighting (see later in the chapter) was once a feature of Muff Fair. Although such fights were usually regarded as fairly good-natured exercises of strength and skill, matters sometimes got out of hand. The local farming community is divided on sectarian religious lines, and 1830 was the date of a particularly brutal encounter in which shots were fired and two of the participants killed.

Ram Fair (Ireland)

This was also known as the Lammas Fair and was an occasion for great festivity. Its most notable feature was the enthroning of a white ram high on top of the old Green Castle's walls. He presided over the greatest sheep fair in South Down and was called the "King of the Bens." It had all the traditional amusements of a country fair—stalls and sideshows, wrestling and boxing bouts, dancing and music. Faction-fighting was once common at the Ram Fair, but this became ritualized as the Shillelagh Dance, which was performed to the music of Uillean pipes.

Royal National Eisteddfod (Wales)

Every year in August this festival is held in Wales, alternating between the northern and southern parts of the country. There are displays of songs, poetry, dancing, rhetoric, and all aspects of Welsh culture; everything is conducted in the Welsh language. In addition, there are various contests, the most important of which is for the bards, who have to compose a verse on a set topic according to complicated traditional poetic structures. The climax of the event is "the chairing of the bard" when the winner is crowned and seated on a specially constructed chair. Should the poems be deemed unworthy, no chairing takes place.

Wake Fairs (England)

Many traditional summer fairs are called wake fairs. Why a summer fair should be described as a wake may seem puzzling. A wake is a vigil kept in the presence of the body of the deceased in the period between the death and the burial. Traditionally, games, feasting, and drinking play a large part in the proceedings. It was also the custom to hold a wake with a vigil and prayers on the eve of the feast day of the local saint, and follow it with a fair on the next day. Over a period of time, this custom died out, and all that usually remained was a purely secular occasion with much feasting and merrymaking.

It seems likely that the original deity honored with a summer wake would have been the corn god, who dies with the cutting of the corn.

SPORTS AND GAMES

Lugh is said to have founded annual games to commemorate Tailtiu, his foster mother, and games are a common feature of Lughnasa festivals.

Highland Games (Scotland)

The various Scottish games are probably a descendant of the Lughnasa games. Various rulers prohibited sporting events, either because they were considered an immoral and unruly waste of time, or in an attempt to encourage the practice of military skills instead. Such bans proved unenforceable in Scotland, and the heavy events (as such games are called) have remained a widespread tradition in Scotland up until the present day. With the mass migration of the Scots, these sports have spread throughout the world, especially to the United States, Canada, and Australia. In England, they are much less common, being confined to northern areas such as the Border Counties and the Lake District.

Some Scottish games are still held around the traditional time of Lughnasa, but nowadays they may be held at any time during the summer or autumn, allowing champion sportsmen to compete at several different venues.

Grasmere Sports (England)

These games take place on the Thursday nearest August 20. Activities include fell races (running up and down the local hills), field and track events, and hound trails. The highlight for many visitors is the rare opportunity to watch Cumberland and Westmorland wrestling. This ancient sport is a ritualized form of the hand-to-hand combat that was once prevalent in more turbulent times. The competitors dress in vests and long, silky underpants beneath embroidered trunks, somewhat like Superman. All the contestants are amateurs, and one fall is required to find the winner.

Herri Kilorak (Spain)

These are the rural games of the Basque people of France and Spain and are one of the many traditional activities held in the area between late July and early August. The Herri Kilorak is similar in character to other rural sports festivals, such as the English Lakeland and Scottish Highland games. They take place in Bilbao during mid-August. Activities include corn races, log-chopping, stone-lifting, hay-bale tossing, and tug-o-war. The stone-lifting event involves contestants hoisting weights ranging from 220 pounds to over 700 pounds onto their shoulders. In the corn races, each of the competitors has to run with a 200-pound sack of grain on his shoulder.

The Basques claim to be the bravest and strongest people in the world and have been great sailors since very early times. Their folklore tells of them reaching America long before Columbus. The Basques are a unique people with a language and folklore unlike any other in Europe. One of their chief deities was Mari, a goddess who lived in deep caves. She could take on many forms, especially that of an extremely beautiful woman who moved from mountaintop to mountaintop, crossing the sky like a ball of fire. Several mountains in the Basque region have a shrine to Mari on their summit. The similarity of her name to that of the Christian Mary probably explains the popularity of La Blanca fiestas, festivals in honor of the "White Virgin" on August 4, and the Semana Grande fiestas, which celebrate the Assumption of the Virgin Mary on August 15.

Grand Wardmote (England)

The first week in August sees the Woodmen of Arden's Grand Wardmote at Meriden in Warwickshire. This is a four-day archery contest with contestants using yew longbows. It is said that this is the very contest that Robin Hood attended and won. The present company is a revived one, formed in 1785.

Horseracing (Ireland)

Even today the Irish still associate equine activities with this time of the year. It can surely be no coincidence that such famous and long-established events as the Dublin Horse Show, the Connemara Pony Show, and the Galway Races take place in late July and early August. The connection between horses and water lives on in the Irish tradition of racing along beaches at low tide. The Laytown Strand races are unique, being the only official race meeting in Europe to be held on a beach. The meeting is held in late July or early August, the precise date being dependent on the height of the tides.

Horse-swimming (Ireland)

Horse-swimming was an activity particularly associated with Lughnasa and is recorded as having taken place throughout Ireland. It was once a widespread custom. Horses were made to swim through lakes and streams at Lughnasa or on the nearest Sunday. In some parts of the country, Westmeath for example, cattle were also made to swim. It was thought that no animal would survive the year unless they were so drenched, and that the swimming ensured the good health of the beasts.

Ridings (England and Scotland)

"Riding" is the term given to the practice of asserting territorial rights to an area of land by riding over it on horseback. The practice was particularly common in the counties of southern Scotland and northern England where the borders were in dispute. The custom was also used to maintain the rights to graze animals and forage for wood on areas of common land known as "Lammas lands." Until the Enclosures Acts of the eighteenth and nineteenth centuries (which put common lands into private ownership), these lands were let to farmers from spring until the end of July. The haymaking had to be completed by Lammas as the lands reverted back to common grazing land from Lammas until the following Candlemas.

In their present form, ridings are mainly colorful nineteenth-century reinventions of the earlier tradition, ceremonial and recreational in character and having no legal significance. Ridings take place between mid-June and early August and are often accompanied by fairs and feasts.

LAMMAS BATTLES

Faction-Fighting

Faction-fighting was a customary feature of many Lughnasa assemblies. Groups of young men from rival villages would gather and fight. Faction-fights could be fierce and lead to injuries and, rarely, death. It was the observance of the custom that was considered important rather than winning at all costs. Fights would last around ten to fifteen minutes and were fought with sticks or shillelaghs (blackthorn clubs). The opposing teams would kiss or shake hands as friends afterward.

There is a strongly held belief in Irish folklore that the success or failure of the harvest was dependent on the fairies, and it was decided by a battle between two troops from neighboring areas. This idea that success in battle bought fruitfulness to the crops of the winning side is probably the origin of faction-fighting. Máire Mac-Neill suggests that these fights were symbolic reenactments of these fairy battles.[5]

Battle of the Flowers (United Kingdom)

This event takes place on Jersey, one of the Channel Islands, in mid-August. The "battle" is between groups of islanders who compete to see who can make the most original picture from flowers. Since the nineteenth century, these have been paraded on flat trucks like a carnival float, but the local tradition of making floral patterns and pictures dates much earlier. Exhibits can be up to forty-five feet long and contain 100,000 or more fresh flowers; hundreds of volunteers spend all night cutting heads off flower stems and sticking them to the framework. It also features an illuminated moonlight parade. The parade consists of massive floats with marching bands and dancers. The Battle of the Flowers festival attracts an audience in the region of 40,000 people. This is also the traditional time for the Channel Islands' agricultural shows, similar to the county fairs.

OTHER LUGHNASA/LAMMAS CUSTOMS

Quarter Day Legalities (England and Scotland)

Lammas was one of the quarter days on which criminal and civil courts were convened, contracts were signed, legal and marital agreements entered into, and rent payments due. Such significant dates were often printed in red on calendars, hence the expression "red-letter day" to denote an important event or special occasion.

The other old quarter days were Whitsuntide, Martinmas, and Candlemas. In later times, there was a different set of quarter days: Lady-Day, Midsummer, Michaelmas, and Christmas. In these two sets of quarter days, witches might recognize their eight festivals.

Rush-Bearing (England)

The custom of rush-bearing takes place all over England in late July. Processions of people bearing rushes or accompanying ornately decorated carts carrying rushes proceed to the local church. The rushes are blessed and scattered over the floors of the church.

Telltown Marriages, Handfasting, and Wife-selling

Telltown, Teltown, or Tailtean marriages were temporary unions entered into at Lughnasa. At Larganeeny (Lag an Aonaigh, "the hollow of the fair") there was an oral tradition recorded in the nineteenth century that a form of marriage was held there in Pagan times. A number of young men went into a hollow at the north side of the wall and an equal number of marriageable young women went to the south side of the wall, which was so high as to prevent them from seeing the men. One of the women put her hand through the hole in the wall, and a man took hold of it from the other side, being guided in his choice only by the appearance of the hand. The two who joined hands by blind chance were obliged to live together for a year and a day. At the end of that time, they appeared together at the Rath of Telton and, if they were not satisfied, they obtained a deed of separation and were entitled to go to Larganeeny again to find a new partner.

One of the largest Lammas fairs was held at Kirkwall, in the Orkney Islands off the coast of Scotland. The fair lasted eleven days, and taking a sexual partner for its

duration was a common practice. Such couples were known as "Lammas brothers and sisters." For couples thinking of a slightly longer commitment, this was a traditional time for handfasting. Couples would join hands through a holed stone, such as the ancient Stone of Odin at Stenness, and plight their troth for a year and a day. Many such temporary unions became permanent arrangements.

Another marital custom was the widespread belief that a man could legally divorce his wife by putting a halter around her neck and leading her to the marketplace to be sold on a fair day. In some cases, this was a relatively civilized arrangement between the husband, wife, and her lover — all three meeting amicably afterward for a drink. In other cases, the wife would be "sold" to a stranger.

The practice still went on in rural areas as late as the midnineteenth century. In 1855, at Chipping Norton in the English Cotswolds, a man sold his wife for £25 ($40), a generous amount, as half a crown (25¢) was all that custom required. This arrangement was no longer considered respectable by the townspeople. For three nights running, the purchaser and his new "bride" were subjected to "rough music," a traditional rural punishment for sexual misdemeanors where the victims would be assailed by a cacophony of discordant noise and ribald verses. On the third night, a straw effigy of the man was burnt outside his house. He eventually gave in and paid the original husband to take his wife back.

Queensferry Burryman and Ferry Fair (Scotland)

The Burryman makes his appearance in Queensferry around Lammas. He has a surreal appearance, like an alien from a science fiction movie. His whole head and body are covered in burrs (hooked seed pods). He wears a garland headdress and carries two staffs covered with flowers. He is paraded around the local area to collect alms on the second Friday in August. As the town of Queensferry has expanded, so has the Burryman's route, which now takes around nine hours to complete. Having survived an exhausting day on little more than water sipped through a straw, the Burryman's final duty is to open the Ferry Fair.

The origins of this custom are obscure. He may be a representative of the harvest spirit or, alternatively, a scapegoat paraded through the town to remove the sins of the populace or decoy blight from the harvest — after which he would be thrown in the sea or otherwise abused. Other accounts associate him with the local fisheries, suggesting that his function was to propitiate a sea god.

Bilberry Sunday (Ireland)

Lughnasa is known as Bilberry Sunday in many districts of Ireland, and it is traditional to climb the mountainsides to collect these fruits for the first time on this day. The association between bilberry-picking and Lughnasa is widespread and has given rise to a variety of names for the festival: Blaeberry Sunday, Domhnach na bhFraochóg, Heatherberry Sunday, and Whort Sunday. The size and quantity of berries at Lughnasa was taken as a sign of whether the harvest would be good or not.

A typical example of these fruit-gathering traditions used to take place at Croc na Béaltaine in County Donegal. On the first Sunday in August, the young people would set off after lunch to pick bilberries and not return until nightfall. Often the bilberry collecting was an excuse for the young men and women to pair off. When the fruits had been collected, the boys would thread the berries into bracelets for the girls, competing to make the prettiest for their partners. There would then be singing and dancing. Before returning home, it was traditional for the girls to remove their bracelets and leave them on the hillside. After climbing back down the hill, the young men indulged in sporting contests, such as horseracing, hurling, and weight-throwing.

At Ganimore, also in Donegal, there were some interesting customs associated with the occasion. Everyone climbing the hill wore a flower, and at the summit, these were all put in a hole and buried as a sign that summer was over. The young men held dancing competitions with the winner being able to choose any of the girls as his wife. Fighting often broke out as a result, and the parish priest finally put an end to this custom.

Throughout Ireland, Bilberry Sunday was very much a festival for children and young people. In some cases, old people were not allowed to climb the hills.

Cally Sunday

In parts of Ireland, the nearest Sunday to Lughnasa was known as Cally Sunday. It was the traditional day to lift the first new potatoes.[6] The man of the house would go out to dig the first stalk while the woman of the house would don a new white apron and prepare to cook them, covering the kitchen floor with green rushes in their honor. In some localities, the first potatoes were eaten with cabbage and bacon; in others, with fish. But for most of the cottagers of the west, the favored dish was one known variously as *ceallaigh*, cally, colcannon, *bráightin*, or poundy. This dish consists of boiled potatoes, mashed and mixed with butter or milk, and then seasoned with onion, garlic, or cabbage.

The family would give thanks that the "Hungry Month" of July was over, as the harvest had begun. It was believed that if you ate a good meal on Cally Sunday, then you would not go hungry for the next twelve months.

The farmer who failed to provide his family with a meal of new potatoes on Cally Sunday was derided as a Felenmuir Gaoithe, or "wind farmer." It was considered to be a sign of bad management to have to lift potatoes before Cally Sunday.

It seems likely that the custom of first fruits would once have applied to grain. In later days, when grain crops were the province of large landowners, the custom was transferred to the introduced potatoes, grown by everyone with a patch of ground as a subsistence crop.

Blessing of First Fruits (France)

In France, July 25 was celebrated as either St. James' Day or St. Christopher's Day. This is when the first fruits of the harvest were blessed, often in the form of token baskets of apples brought into the church and then distributed by the priest and eaten by the congregation.

Marie au Blé (France)

A custom known as Marie au Blé was celebrated at Valenciennes until 1823. The festival began on the third Monday of July and lasted eight days. A girl was chosen, dressed in white, and led in a dancing procession through the streets. A youth carried a tin plate covered with a white napkin on which were put the first ears of grain.

Marymass or La Feille Moire (Scotland)

Marymass, sometimes known as Murmass, is the Scottish name for the Feast of the Assumption on August 15. It replaced the earlier festival of Lughnasa in these northern regions where the harvest was later. The Lammas bannock (a traditional Scottish loaf) made from the new corn would be dedicated to Mary, Mother of God. There were sundry customs surrounding these celebrations, many of which survived well into the nineteenth century, owing to the isolation of the islands and highlands of Scotland. A collection of this lore was published in the midnineteenth century as the *Carmina Gadelica*, and although various Christian saints are praised in the traditional songs and prayers, these rituals show their Pagan Celtic origins explicitly.[7]

Beannachadh Buana is the Scottish Gaelic name given to the start of reaping. It was a day of celebration and ritual. Whole families would go to the fields dressed in their best clothes to hail the god of the harvest. The father of each family would lay his hat on the ground and face the sun. Taking up his sickle, he would cut a handful of corn, which he passed three times around his head while chanting the "Iolach Buana," or "Reaping Salutation" (see appendix 5 for the full verse). The rest of the family would join in, in praise of the god of the harvest who provided bread, corn, flocks, wool, health, strength, and prosperity.

When the reaping was completed, it was time for the *cur nan corran* (casting of the sickles) and the *deuchain chorran* (trial of hooks). These traditions included throwing the sickles high in the air and observing how each came down, how it struck the ground, and how it lay. These omens foretold such outcomes as who was to marry or remain single, and who was going to be ill or die, before the next season's reaping came around.

In past centuries, elaborate rituals surrounded the preparation of the first bannock, which was called, in Gaelic, the Moilean Moire. Early in the morning, the people would go out into the fields to pluck the ears of the new grain. These would be spread over rocks to dry and then husked by hand. After being winnowed and ground in a quern (mill), the flour was made into dough and kneaded in a sheepskin. It was then traditional to cook the bannock before a fire of rowan or other sacred wood. When it was cooked, the father of the family broke the Moilean Moire into pieces to be shared with his wife and children. They would sing the "Ioch Mhoric

Mhather," or "Paean of Praise to the Holy Mother," while walking in a procession sunwise around the fire, with the father in the lead and the rest of the family following in order of seniority.

Ioch Mhoric Mhather
("Paean of Praise to the Holy Mother")

Mother of the Shepherd of the flocks,
I cut me a handful of the new corn,
I dried it gently in the sun,
I rubbed it sharply from the husk with mine own palms.

I ground it in a quern on Friday,
I baked it on a fan of sheepskin,
I toasted it to a fire of rowan,
And I shared it round my people.

I went sunways round my dwelling,
In name of the Mary Mother,
Who promised to preserve me,
Who did preserve me,
In peace, in flocks,
In righteousness of heart,

In labor, in love,
In wisdom, in mercy,
For the sake of Thy Passion.
Thou Christ of grace,
Who till the day of my death wilt never forsake me!
Oh, till the day of my death wilt never forsake me!

The man would then put the embers of the fire into a pot, along with bits of old iron. The family then proceeded sunwise around the outside of their house and, sometimes, around the fields and flocks. It was also traditional on this date to make pilgrimages to wells dedicated to Mary.

Many of these traditions have died out, but there are still two remaining as Marymass fairs in Scotland. One, at Inverness, is a 1986 revival of an event first recorded in 1591. There are a variety of processions, shows, and stalls throughout the day. The Marymass fair at Irvine near Kilmarnock lasts for twelve days and starts on the Thursday nearest August 15. The fair dates back to the twelfth century and possibly much earlier. It originally featured a parade with a Marymass Queen, in which a girl was chosen to represent the Virgin Mary. Following a visit to the fair in 1563 by Mary Queen of Scots, the Marymass Queen was dressed as Queen Mary rather than the Virgin Mary. A similar change of identity took place at Inverness after Mary Queen of Scots visited in 1562. Two of the major features of the fair are horseraces and a festival of traditional music.

Crom Dubh Sunday (Ireland)

The Sunday nearest to August 1 is known as Domhnach Crom Dubh, or Crom Dubh Sunday, in many parts of Ireland. Crom Dubh was a Pagan deity of whom little is known, though in Christian myth he is portrayed as an archetypal Pagan overcome by a Christian saint. In many accounts, he is said to have been a Pagan chieftain who was converted to Christianity by St. Patrick.

A central motif in many of these tales is that of a fearsome bull. The bull was important to Celtic culture as a symbol of aggression, strength, and virility. In the story, St. Patrick asks for food, and Crom Dubh sends his bull in the hope that it will kill the saint, but instead it submits meekly to Patrick, allowing itself to be slaughtered and eaten. Crom Dubh is enraged by the failure of his plan and asks Patrick to return his bull, knowing the impossibility of his request. To his surprise, the saint has the animal's bones and hide put together and brings the beast back to life.

There are two different endings to the story. In some accounts, Crom is so impressed by Patrick's powers that he willingly converts to Christianity; in others, the resuscitated bull kills the Pagan chief. This myth is probably a folk-memory of the custom of sacrificing an animal at Lughnasa. At Loch Maree, Scotland, and Cois Fhairrge, Ireland, bulls were sacrificed at Lughnasa as late as the eighteenth century.

Notes

1. Robert Burns, *The Rigs O'Barley*, 1783.
2. The other festivals in the Wheel of the Year are Imbolc (February 1), spring equinox or Ostara March 21), Beltane (May 1), summer solstice (June 21), autumn equinox (September 21), Samhain/Halloween (November 1), and the winter solstice or Yule (December 21).
3. William Hone, *The Every Day Book and Table Book*, 1832.
4. Traditional English folk song.
5. Máire MacNeill, *The Festival of Lughnasa* (Amen House, London: Oxford University Press, 1962).
6. Older varieties matured later than modern ones when new potatoes are lifted in June.
7. Alexander Carmichael, *Carmina Gadelica*, 1928.

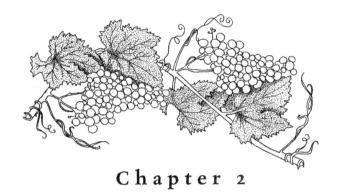

Chapter 2

Around the World

At his vanishing away she lifts up a lament,
"O my child," at his vanishing away she lifts up a lament
"My Damu," at his vanishing away she lifts up a lament
"My enchanter and priest!" at his vanishing away she lifts up a lament.[1]

Though the festival of Lughnasa, or Lammas, was celebrated only in Ireland, Britain, Gaul, and perhaps northern Spain, this time of year marked important festivals in other parts of the world. Before we look more closely at Lughnasa itself, it will pay us to look at some of these.

ANCIENT GREECE

The festival of Adonis was held during late July. The cult of this vegetation god is generally thought to have originated in Syria, and his name is a variation on the Semitic Adonai, simply meaning "Lord."

According to the most complete version of his story, the mortal King Cinyras boasted that his daughter Myrrha ("Myrrh") was more beautiful than Aphrodite, the goddess of love. As a punishment, the gods caused the unfortunate Myrrha to fall in love with her father. By a trick, she inveigled him into sleeping with her and getting her pregnant. When the king discovered what had happened, he was overcome with disgust and guilt and took up his sword to kill her.

She fled from the palace, but he caught up with her on the brow of a hill. Just as he lifted the blade to strike her, the goddess Aphrodite took pity on the girl and instantly changed her into a myrrh tree, which the sword cleaved in two.[2] Out tumbled the infant Adonis. Aphrodite caught him and concealed the lovely boy inside a chest, which she asked Persephone, the queen of the Underworld, to look after.

Overwhelmed with curiosity, Persephone peeped inside the chest and instantly fell in love with the handsome youth she found there. When Aphrodite demanded that she return Adonis to her, Persephone refused, wanting to keep him for herself. Eventually, the two goddesses appealed to Zeus, the king of the gods, to settle the quarrel. He appointed the muse Calliope to make the ruling, and she decided that Aphrodite should have Adonis for one-third of the year, Persephone for another third, and that he should have one-third to himself.

However, Aphrodite was not happy with this and decided to cheat. She donned her magic girdle, which caused all that looked upon her beauty to fall hopelessly in love with her; as a result, Adonis wanted to be with her all the time. Persephone reported this to Aphrodite's usual lover, the war god Ares, who flared into a jealous rage. He transformed himself into a wild boar and tore Adonis to pieces.[3] From each drop of blood that fell, a red flower bloomed.[4]

Zeus resolved to put an end to the squabbling and mayhem and decreed that Adonis must spend the winter with Persephone but could spend the summer with Aphrodite. When Adonis was with his beloved Aphrodite, the land bloomed and the people rejoiced, but when he was with Persephone in the Underworld, winter came and the people mourned. As in other fertility religions, it was the mating of the young god and goddess that made the earth blossom and fruit.

The rising of the Dog Star, Sirius, on July 27, marked the beginning of the "Dog Days," when the sun burns at its most fiercest.[5] The Dog Star follows Orion the Hunter about the sky. The ancient Greeks and Romans thought that it was a distant sun (the central sun of the Milky Way) that at this time of year rose with our sun to add its own heat, making the weather unbearable. Its influence was considered baneful and malign. Pliny said that Sirius burned with "a bright fire and sheds a killing light." He went on to say that "this is the constellation which has the most widespread effects on earth. At its rise the seas are rough, wine in the cellars bubbles, marshes are stirred."[6] Aristotle said, "This is a period of great upheaval when the sea is extremely rough and amazing catches are made, when fish and mud rise to the surface."[7]

Hesiod described it as "a desiccating sun," burning up plants and making the seeds in the earth sterile by depriving them of food. Animals died of thirst, vines burned, and humans were prostrate with fevers and illness, especially siriasis (a type of meningitis that attacks young children). According to these ancients, the Dog Days are a time of cruel heat when men's skins are burned and their throats parched with thirst. Those afflicted with hydrophobia were said to have been driven mad by Sirius.[8] In fact, the Greeks imagined the constellation of Canis Major in the form of a rabid dog, with its tongue lolling and its eyes bulging. It was during this time that the Adonia Festival was celebrated,[9] as Theophrastus said, "when the sun is at its most powerful."

During the festival, women would plant small gardens — called Gardens of Adonis — in clay pots or wicker baskets. These were composed of wheat, barley, fennel, and lettuce. The women would climb ladders up to their rooftops, thereby placing the little gardens as close to the sun as they could. During this time of year, the great heat gives an impetus to plant growth, but the plant can become leggy and spindly, outgrowing its strength, while

young shoots wither in dryness. The gardens were left to grow for only eight days — in contrast to the eight months taken by the cereal crop to come to maturity. At the culmination of the festival, the gardens were then taken from the roofs and cast into the sea or into springs.

Thereafter, beginning of August was sacred to the goddess Demeter and her daughter, Persephone. Demeter is the goddess of the grain, and her bounty is all the harvest.

ANCIENT ROME

The ancient Romans associated the hottest part of the year with the rising of the Dog Star, calling it the *dies cani cultriac*. This survives in the modern phrase "Dog Days." The astronomer Manilius said of Sirius:

> *It barks forth flame, raves with its fire, and doubles the burning heat of the sun. When it puts its torch to the earth and discharges its rays, the earth foresees its conflagration and tastes its ultimate fate. Neptune lies motionless in the midst of his waters and the green blood is drained from leaves and grass. . . . beset by temperatures too great to bear, nature is afflicted with a sickness of its own making, alive but on a funeral pyre: such is the heat diffused among the constellations, and everything is brought to a halt by a single star.*[10]

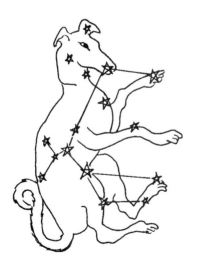

He went on to relate how the heat brought out the worst in people, with anger, hatred, fear, impetuosity, frayed tempers, and arguments — all fanned by alcohol. At such times, he said, people would go out hunting to take things out on "all legitimate prey," without any caution or fear, since the rage engendered by Sirius drove them to it. The Romans also called Sirius *Janitor Lethasus*, the "Keeper of Hell," a type of Cerberus figure guarding the lower heavens, the abode of demons.

Also held in Rome this month was the Heracleia, held to honor the hero-god Hercules, sometimes compared to Lugh. Like Lughnasa, this festival was celebrated with games and contests.

The ancient earth goddess Ops was honored as Lady Bountiful and planter of the seeds. Celebrants sat on the earth to be close to her.

ASSYRIA

The ancient Assyrians called the Dog Star "Dog of the Sun," or "Star Dog of the Sun." The Assyrian month of Abu meant "fiery hot," because the sun was in Leo and, therefore, raging and hot like a lion. It coincided with July/August and the Lughnasa period. Ancient Assyrian physicians thought that while the sun was in Leo, medicines became poisonous and baths were equally harmful.

AKKADIA

Tammuz is the Akkadian or Assyro-Babylonian equivalent to the Sumerian Dumuzi and the Syrian Adonis, a vegetation god of death and resurrection. He was the lover of the goddess Ishtar and died every year during the hot month of Tammuz (July/August), gored by a boar. His soul was taken to the Underworld, and the goddess Ishtar led the lamentation as the world mourned Tammuz's death with the keening of women. She then descended to the Underworld and retrieved his soul from the clutches of the queen of the Underworld, her sister Ereshkigal. To reach her, she had to pass through the seven gates of the Underworld, divesting herself of her clothes and jewels at each gate until finally she was naked and vulnerable. Ereshkigal was unmoved and would not give up the young god. She ordered Namtar, the plague bringer, to imprison Ishtar and inflict threescore plagues upon her.

Meanwhile, the earth was arid, barren, and joyless. Sin, the moon god, and Shamash, the sun god, decided that something had to be done. They asked Ea, god of water, magic, and wisdom, to help. He sent a messenger into the Underworld with a powerful spell, and the goddess of the Underworld was forced to release her prisoners. Ishtar was purified by Ea's waters and passed back through the seven gates, regaining her raiment and jewels. Joy returned to earth.[11] Echoes of this myth are found throughout North Africa and the Near East.

The women mourned Tammuz every year during July/August (coinciding with the Lughnasa period), making little gardens like those of Adonis. After the gardens had been thrown into the sea, they rejoiced, for the god had been reborn.

MESOPOTAMIA

The Babylonian equivalent of Tammuz is Dumuzi, or rather *dumu.zi*, meaning "rightful son." He was the consort of the goddess Inanna and a prominent fertility god of the death and resurrection type. He was called "the shepherd," who helped the sheepfolds to multiply, and was also the shepherd of the stars, the farmer who made the fields fertile. Under his rule there was plentiful vegetation and grain. He was also the god of streams and fresh running water. Dumuzi was lamented when the dry heat of summer caused the pasture land to brown and wither and lambing, calving, and milking to come to an end.[12] He was called the Wild Bull, who was sacrificed; who laid down and lived no more. As he is called the god of the abyss (Dumuzzi-Absu), it may be assumed that the sacrificed god became King of the Underworld, like the Egyptian Osiris.

According to the story, the young god courted the goddess of love and war, Inanna. She was at first unwilling to see him, but after being persuaded by the sun god Utu (her brother) and the moon goddess Ningal (her mother), the young couple met and fell in love. Their mating caused the earth to blossom and fruit. Then the heat of high summer dried up the grasslands and the milk within the cattle. The young god was dying, and he was lamented and mourned. As the grain was cut and stored or made into beer, the god was said to go into the Underworld to return next year when the sap rose in the trees and vegetation returned to the earth. His sister was Geshtinanna, the wine goddess, who consented to take his place in the Underworld for six months of every year, so that he might return to earth.

He was the sacrificed sacred king. He was the Bull of Heaven, Taurus, which disappears for six weeks from the Sumerian horizon from January to March.

NORSE

The Dog Star, Sirius, is called Lokabrenna ("the Burning of Loki" or "Loki's Brand"). Sif ("Relative") was the wife of Thor, the god of thunder. She had beautiful golden hair until Loki cut it all off for a prank. Thor was so angry that he wanted to kill the trickster, but Loki was able to persuade the dwarves to make some magical hair for Sif, which once it touched her head would grow like her own hair. It is clear that Sif's hair is the golden corn that is cut and regrown with the next year, making her a corn or harvest goddess. Her husband is the thunder god who brings the fertilizing rain to the earth in the summer to make it grow. Loki, usually described as a god of wildfire and heat, is associated here with Sirius and the heat of the Dog Days, which causes the ripening (and therefore subsequent cutting) of the grain. Perhaps his role in the change of the seasons is also commemorated in the story of how he tricks blind Hoder (who represents darkness) into killing his brother Baldur (the sun god) with a small dart made from mistletoe.

As the name of Lugh is often said to be, Loki's name is related to the Latin *lux,* meaning "light," and also the Old English *leoht,* "light," and *liechan,* "to enlighten."

It was also in August that the god Odin sacrificed himself on the World Tree to gain knowledge of the runes. He hung there for nine days and nights, staring into the abyss, pierced by a lance and losing one of his eyes in the process.

ANCIENT EGYPT

In late July, the first heliacal (i.e., just before sunrise) rising of the Dog Star occurs in Egypt. Unlike other parts of the world, the effects of Sirius were considered beneficial, and its appearance was thought to cause the yearly rising of the flood waters in the Nile Delta. The star is titled "the Water Bringer." It was this inundation of the great river that provided the rich alluvial deposits for the cultivation of crops and marked a time when the country, parched by intense heat and drought, would be brought back to life. This was the greatest festival in the Egyptian calendar.

Egyptians called the star Septit, or Sothis in the Greek form of the name, and identified it with the goddess Isis.[13] She appeared in the Pyramid texts as the chief mourner for her husband, the vegetation god Osiris, whom she brought back to life with magic. She was represented in hieroglyphs as a woman with a headdress in the shape of a throne, often depicted holding her son Horus or kneeling on a coffin. The rising of Sothis was considered to be the goddess coming to mourn her husband and bring him back to life (as corn god) with the flooding of the Nile. It was called the Festival of Isis Seeking Osiris in the Darkness.

Isis and Osiris, together with their siblings Set and Nepthys, were the children of the earth god Geb and the sky goddess Nut. Set married his sister Nepthys, while Osiris married Isis, and the latter pair became rulers of Egypt. Thoth the Scribe acted as their chief advisor. Osiris taught humankind how to plant and harvest grain, how to make tools, and how to make bread and beer. Isis taught them how to make wine. Together they built temples and reformed the religion of Egypt. After a few years, Osiris traveled abroad and introduced these ideas into other countries, leaving the wise Isis to act as regent.

Then, in the twenty-eighth year of his reign, Osiris was murdered by his jealous brother, Set. Set is generally seen as an evil figure, the personification of the dry desert that surrounds the thin strip of fertile Nile Valley. Set and his followers tricked Osiris into getting into a coffin, then they nailed down the lid and threw it into the Nile. It washed up in Byblos, but Set found it and cut his brother's body into fourteen pieces, which he scattered across Egypt.

Isis searched the whole land until she found the pieces, leaving a funeral inscription at each site — all but the fourteenth part, the phallus, which had been eaten by a crab.[14] The jackal-headed god Anubis, son of Osiris and Nepthys, mummified the body, and this was the first mummy. Isis formed a new phallus by magic and, transforming herself into a kite, mated with the corpse and conceived Horus, the falcon-headed god. Isis was forced to hide from Set until Horus was old enough to avenge his father. As a baby in the marshes, he was watched over by the goddesses Nepthys, Sekhat-Hor, Neith, and Selkis. He was also guarded by "the seven cows of Hathor," identified with the Pleides cluster of stars. Horus is sometimes said to be Osiris reborn.

Osiris chose to remain in Amenti ("West"), the Land of the Dead, to act as the judge of souls. He is usually depicted as a mummy. Much of the lore of Osiris and Isis was appropriated by the Christian religion. Osiris was a god who chose to become a man to guide his people. As such he was called "the Good Shepherd" and

was depicted with a shepherd's crook. As a corn god, he
died, was buried, and was brought back to life when Isis, as
Sothis, caused the Nile to flood. As corn, he fed his people
and was called the "Resurrection and the Life." His flesh
was eaten in the form of wheaten cakes. Like Mary, Isis
was called "the Star of the Sea" and "Queen of Heaven," a
virgin who brought forth a son titled "the Savior of the
World"— the hero who brings order back into the universe. The pair was forced to hide from an evil king until
the son became a man.

The Osiris cult merged with the sacred Apis Bull early
on. A real bull was honored as his living image. The bull
was also identified with Horus who was called "the bull of
the mother," perhaps as his father's reborn self. The bull is
an ancient symbol of strength and virility.

Isis is called "Mistress of the Year's beginning," who
causes the Nile to swell. She revives the Nile just as she
revives Osiris. She gives birth to Horus, as Sothis gives birth to the Nile. Horus is
the New Year child.[15] It was from the womb of Isis-Sothis that Horus was born.
One inscription says, "It is Horus the intrepid that will come forth from Osiris, in
his name of Horus who is within Sothis."[16]

Isis, hiding from Set, is symbolized by the seventy-day absence of Sothis from
the sky.

The ancient Egyptians believed that Sothis was the home of departed spirits.
Several people have theorized that the tunnels of the great pyramid of Cheops
function as telescopes, orientated to give a view of the southern sky, including the
stars Orion and Sirius (Osiris and Isis) and their yearly cycles.[17] The Egyptian representation of Sothis was a five-pointed star, a half-circle, and a small triangle or
pyramid. In very ancient times, Sirius could not be seen in Egypt, but then,
because of the precession of the equinoxes, it appeared in the night sky around
10,500 B.C.E. To the ancient Egyptians it would seem that a new, very bright star
had just been born. Perhaps because it appeared when Virgo was rising in the east,
it became the symbol of the virgin goddess Isis.[18]

The Egyptian calendar was based on Sirius, with the heliacal rising marking the New Year. In fact, of all the stars, only the heliacal rising of Sirius coincides with the length of our solar year of 365.25 days. However, this year was twelve minutes shorter than the true year, and the Egyptians had no leap year, so at the end of each year, extra time accrued. This time was "saved up" until after 1,460 years there would be a whole year of extra time, called a Sothic Year, or the "Year of the Phoenix." This was a year of festivities and featured the burning alive of a phoenix-eagle (representative of the sun) on a bed of frankincense and myrrh. From the ashes a worm was said to form, which would eventually become a new phoenix. The worm was, in fact, the six hours left over at the end of a phoenix year, and after four years there would be a whole day accrued — a phoenix chick. It would take 1,460 years for the whole phoenix to form.[19] The emperor Augustus "killed the phoenix" when he reformed the Egyptian calendar.

The Egyptians also had a civil year of 365 days, with three seasons of four months with thirty days, leaving five extra days. Five chief gods of the Egyptians were born during these "five days out of time," which were calculated according to the rising of Sirius and dated between July 30 and August 3.[20] According to Plutarch, the Goddess of Nature was married to the God of Time but fell in love with the sun and mated with him. Her husband cursed her and said that she should not give birth during any month of the year. Later she fell in love with another god (Plutarch calls him Hermes), and this god won from the moon a seventieth part of her light, or five days. He placed them outside the lunar months, so the goddess was able to have her children: Osiris, Horus the Elder, Set, Isis, and Nepthys.

CANAAN

The Canaanite god Baal was the son of the supreme god El and a death and resurrection god of the Adonis/Dumuzi/Tammuz type. He was also described as a god of thunder and rain who brought fertility to the earth. His cult animal was a bull. His sister was an earth and battle goddess called Anat.

His chief enemy was Mot, the god of sterility and death, and the representative of the desiccating summer. The two fought and Baal was killed, but before he died, he became a bull and mated with a cow so that he could ensure the continuation of the world. He descended to the Underworld, and his sister set out to recover his body, calling on the sun goddess Shapash for help. She traveled to the Underworld and pleaded with Mot for his return; when he refused, she drew her sword and killed him. Then with a shovel she winnowed him, with fire she parched him, with a millstone she ground him, and in a field she scattered him; the birds then ate his remains, and the wild beasts consumed the fragments. This is an obvious reference to the grain harvested at the end of the fertile season, winnowed and ground. In this case, Mot, the god of the Dog Days, is winnowed as corn.

The Canaanites offered the first fruits of the crop, fire-dried, to the gods. The Israelites followed this custom and, according to the Bible, "Thou shalt offer for the meat offering of thy first fruits green ears of corn dried by the fire, even corn beaten out of its full ears."[21]

With the spring, Baal was reborn and the earth rejoiced. Thus, alternatively, come the seasons of mourning, sacrifice, and rejoicing to the ancient Canaanites.

ISRAEL

Shavout, the Festival of Weeks, also referred to in the Bible as Hag HaBikkurim ("Festival of First Fruits"), is the Jewish festival that commemorates the giving of the Torah to Moses on Mount Sinai. It also celebrates the beginning of the harvest, when the first fruits were bought to the Temple in Jerusalem to be offered to God. It falls around late June or early July, earlier than Lammas, but the crops ripen earlier farther south. One sheaf is taken from the standing crops and brought to the priest, who says: "And he shall wave the sheaf before the Lord for you to be accepted: on the day after the Sabbath the priest shall wave it."[22]

Shavout, with its offering of wheat, marked the end of a cycle that began when the barley crop was offered at the earlier festival of Pesach. Pesach is associated with the Hebrew experience as slaves in Egypt, while Shavout represents their becoming a liberated people created in the image of Jehovah.

It is customary to decorate synagogues and homes with flowers and greenery and eat a celebratory meal comprised of new fruits, vegetables, and a dairy dish. The Torah prohibited the cooking of meat and milk together; the pots and pans that had been used for both were forbidden. It was necessary for the early Jewish people to prepare a meal that required no cooking, so milk or cheese were eaten instead.

North America

The Green Corn Festival (also called the Green Corn Ceremony or Dance) is a Native American celebration and religious ceremony that has many similarities to Lammas. The Cherokee, Iroquois, Muskogee, Seminole, Yuchi, and several other Native American tribes celebrate the festival, though the actual rites vary from tribe to tribe. It is the most important festivity of the Muskogee (Creek) and Hopi nations, where it typically lasts for about eight days. As with Lammas/Lughnasa, it is a celebration of the ripening corn, in this case maize rather than wheat, and is also the start of the new year known as Hiyuce. The date and length of the festival varies as well.

Maize, which is thought to have been introduced from Mexico in about 200 C.E., quickly became the most important staple foodstuff of these nations and was accorded great significance in the life of each tribe. Games were played and songs and dances were performed. It was the time for religious renewal. The camp sites and the circle (or "stomp dance ground") would be cleaned, and a new fire would be lit. To build the new fire, four logs would be arranged in a cross by a specially appointed fire-maker. This sacred fire was thought to have considerable power, representing a physical link between humankind and the Great Spirit. Among the Creek, the sacred fire is identified with the sun; both are masculine forces and part of the male ritual domain. The "Black Drink"—a potent herb mixture containing button-snake root that induced vomiting—was drunk for cleansing and purification. This was followed by a period of fasting before the new corn was eaten for the first time. After these rituals, preparations were made for the feasting and dancing.

The rites of the Green Corn Ceremony are divided into day and night activities. One of the most important day ceremonies is the Ribbon Dance, performed by the women of the tribe. The dance lasts for about three hours and usually takes place around midday on a Friday. Three or four leaders chosen from the tribal elders are appointed for life. They carry sticks or knives painted red at the ends that are waved in rhythm to the dance. The dancers are decorated with ribbons and rattles, and terrapin shells are tied around their lower legs. Male singers and gourd players provide the musical accompaniment. The women dance counterclockwise in a single file around the stomping ground.

Thanks are given for sun, rain, corn, and the successful outcome of a bountiful harvest. Storytellers relate folktales about what happens when this thanksgiving is not performed; some creation myths tell of how the people of the tribe were made from corn by the Great Spirit. Ballgames are played; the rules varying according to the tribe. The Yuchi has teams of boys versus girls who play a form of basketball; the boys are allowed to throw and catch the ball but forbidden to run with it. The girls are allowed to throw, catch, or run with the ball in order to score. The Iroquois compete by throwing a ball at a pole to see who can reach the highest.

Council meetings, although not part of the ceremony, are also held at this time. Minor crimes are forgiven and problems resolved. There are also naming ceremonies, for youths who come of age and for babies.

RUSSIA AND EASTERN EUROPE

Throughout Eastern Europe there are a multitude of traditions associated with harvest time. Harvest holidays were celebrated between late July/early August and the autumn equinox. Many of these holidays were more practical than ritual, and the traditional songs were often concerned with the work at hand and praise for the host and hostess of the celebrations. Nevertheless, a variety of otherworldly beings appear in Slavic folklore and mythology at harvest time. These vary from good-natured helpers, rather like hobgoblins, to more dangerous supernatural creatures best treated with caution or avoided altogether. Some of these harvest spirits are very similar to those of other cultures. Others are less closely linked with the harvest, such associations being only one part of their characteristics as household or nature spirits.

In ancient days on July 20, a human sacrifice was offered to the thunder god Perun. This was necessary to placate the deity and prevent him from sending late summer storms to destroy the crops. The victim was chosen by ballot. On one occasion, a Viking's son was chosen, and his father refused to give him up. As a result, both father and son were sacrificed to Perun. The priest said a traditional prayer:

> *Perun! Father! Thy children lead this faultless victim to thy altar. Bestow,*
> *O Father, thy blessing on the plow and on the corn. May golden straw*
> *with great well-filled ears rise abundantly as rushes. Drive away all*
> *black hail-clouds to the great moors, forests, and large deserts, where*
> *they will not frighten mankind: and give sunshine and rain,*
> *gentle falling rain, in order that the crops may thrive!*

A bull would also be sacrificed and eaten during a communal feast.

At a later period, the Ukrainian people celebrated the start of autumn on St. Illia's Day, August 2. Like many other Christian saints, Illia was originally a Pagan deity associated with Perun, and this date probably originated as one of the Pagan god's holy days. Here is a traditional saying of St. Illia's Day: "Until dinner, it's summer. After dinner, it's autumn." Illia would curse anyone swimming after this feast day.

Yablochnyi, or Medovoy Spas, is a cross-quarter holiday between the summer solstice and the autumn equinox. Also known as "Apple Honey Savior," it celebrates the start of the harvest when fruit and honey are ready to be gathered. The beehives would also be blessed.

The festival of Zaziuki is celebrated on or about August 7 and may have originally been part of the same holiday as the Yablochnyi/Medovoy Spas. The first sheaf of corn, the *zazhinochnyl* or *zazhinnyi*, was taken into the farmhouse and threshed separately. In some areas, it would be blessed and mixed in with the seed corn.

The peasants of the Lublin region of Poland gather together a week before the harvest celebration, or Dozynki, to make the *przepiorka*, a three-dimensional wreath decorated with ribbons and flowers. This wreath is then presented to the owners of the land known as the revered Lord and Lady. The Lord oversees the progress of the harvest and is hailed with chants: "That he may live and prosper for a hundred years!" A female harvester is then chosen to become the Przodownica ("Harvest Queen"). She is selected on the basis of a combination of beauty, hard work, and eloquence. The Harvest Queen is encircled by the whole of the community and honored with a crown made of wheat, rye, oats, and wildflowers.

The Dozynki celebration itself is held on or near the Feast of the Assumption, August 15. The harvesters dress up in their traditional ornately embroidered Sunday clothes and march in a procession to the farmhouse singing, "*Plon mamy plon, ze wszystkich stron*" ("We have gathered the harvest for you from all sides of the field"). The Harvest Queen removes her crown of grains and flowers, gives a speech in praise of the workers, and bestows a blessing on the Lord and Lady, offering her crown as a symbolic sacrifice. The fruits of the new harvest are then presented, including bread made from the fresh wheat, wine from the new grapes, and baskets of fruits and vegetables. The Lord and Lady offer vodka and other drinks to celebrate the occasion and are thanked for their hospitality and goodwill. The festival continues until the early hours with traditional music, dancing, and songs.

The last sheaf (the *dozhinochnyi orotzhinnyi*) would also be decorated with flowers, ribbons, or women's clothing and placed in the entrance corner of the home until October 1, when it would be fed to the cattle. Sometimes this ceremony would be combined with that of a small patch of corn, which was left uncut. The spirit of the harvest was said to hide from the reapers in this uncut patch of wheat, which was known as the "Beard of Velos" (or Veles). Velos was the god of animals and wealth. The uncut sheaves were decorated with ribbons and bent toward the ground in a ritual known as "curling the beard." The harvest spirit was thus believed to be sent back to the earth to ensure fertility in the following year. Bread and salt, the traditional symbols of hospitality, were left as offerings.

The Poludnica ("Midday Spirit") are rather mischievous and malign female spirits of Slavic mythology, which occur throughout eastern Europe under a variety of names and guises: Poednica, Poludniówka, or Przypoldnica. She usually appears at harvest time and may have the appearance of a graceful white lady, a slim teenage girl, or an old hag who haunts fields and houses at noon, sometimes floating high in the air amid violent gusts of wind. If a woman leaves her child alone in the fields at harvest time, the Poludnica may steal him or her. Naughty or crying children are quieted and told to behave or the Poludnica will carry them off.

In Poland, she manifests herself as a tall woman wearing a long, white robe and carrying a sickle. Throughout the summer, she haunts the woods and fields, giving chase to anyone who is working there. She may ask difficult questions of them, visiting misfortune on those unable to answer. Sometimes she has a whip with which she strikes anyone who crosses her path, any of her victims being doomed to an early death. Women who have recently had children or who go out at midday are particularly at risk. She sometimes appears during a storm or as a wind or other natural phenomena. In Moravi, the Poludnica is an old woman with slanting eyes, disheveled hair, an ugly face, and horses' hooves instead of feet.

In Russia, the Poludnica appears as a tall, beautiful girl dressed in a white gown. She walks around the fields at harvest time, seizing and twisting the heads of anyone she finds working there at midday, causing severe pain to her unfortunate victims. She also lures small children into the corn. In Siberia, she is described as a scantily clothed old woman with thick curly hair, who lives among nettles or reedbeds and is fond of kidnapping naughty children. In some other parts of Russia, she is seen as a more benign guardian of the crops and fields.

There are many stories about the Poludnica that are associated with the harvest. She comes out of the woods at midday; anyone working in the fields at that time must talk with her about one subject. Failure to do so results in illness or the forfeiting of one's head. The Poludnica often asks questions about the growing of wheat or hemp, punishing those who are unable to answer correctly. In her role as a guardian of the corn, she protects it from thieves and punishes children who tread upon it.

Another harvest spirit of the Russians is the Polevik, or Polevoy. He is as tall as a corn stalk until harvest time, when he shrivels down to the height of the stubble. He runs away from the scythes of the harvesters and hides in the remaining corn. He is brought into the barn with the last sheaf to be cut. As with the Poludnica, he appears at noon but also at sunset. At these times it is dangerous to fall asleep in the fields, for the Polevik roams about on horseback, sending illness to those he rides over.

The Russians also have a more helpful spirit, the Belun, a little old man with a long white beard and gown. The Belun helps the reapers and is said to bestow fine gifts upon them. He only appears during the day and guides anyone who has lost his or her way.

INDIA

This Hindu harvest festival of Onam is celebrated throughout the state of Kerala, in the southwestern tip of the Indian subcontinent, during late July and early August. People dress up in new clothes and decorate their homes with flowers. Elaborate feasts are prepared, and food is given to the poor and to the Brahmins (priestly caste).

According to legend, Vishnu, one of the Hindu holy trinity, was jealous of King Mahabali, a popular and benevolent ruler of Kerala. Vishnu appeared before Mahabali disguised as a Brahmin dwarf and begged for as much land as he could cover in three strides. King Mahabali agreed to this request and begged the dwarf to take more land. Vishnu could not be tempted by this and took his first step, which covered the entire heavens. His second step covered the whole of the earth, and for his third, Vishnu placed his foot on Mahabali's head and forced him down into the earth. The unfortunate king had by now realized the true identity of his adversary. He requested and was granted the wish of being allowed to return once a year to visit his subjects. The story of Mahabali's forced burial and return each year symbolizes the planting of seed and the annual cycle resulting in the fruits of the earth.

Notes

1. Ancient lament for Adonis.
2. Myrrh was a well-known aphrodisiac, and the birth of Adonis from myrrh indicates the orgiastic nature of his rites. The drops of gum shed by the myrrh represent the tears shed for him during the Adonia.
3. In some versions of the tale, it is Artemis, the goddess of the hunt and moon, who causes his death.
4. Identified as anemones or red roses.

5. According to Marcel Detienne (*Gardens of Adonis*, p. 100), the Athenian astronomer Meton dated the heliacal rising of Sirius to July 20, but his contemporaries dated it to July 23 or 27, depending on whether the real or apparent rise was referred to.

6. Pliny, *Natural History* II.

7. Aristotle, *History of Animals*, 350 B.C.E.

8. Hydrophobia is better known as rabies, one of the symptoms of which is a blazing thirst but a fear of water.

9. Marcel Detienne, *The Gardens of Adonis*, 1977.

10. Manilus, Book 5 of the *Astonomica*.

11. Witches will recognize this story as the descent of the goddess into the Underworld.

12. Thorkild Jacobson, *The Treasures of Darkness*, 1976.

13. A Greek form of her Egyptian name Aset or Eset, meaning "throne."

14. Possibly the constellation of the Crab, which precedes the inundation.

15. Robert Bauval and Adrian Gilbert, *The Orion Mystery*, 1998.

16. R. T. Rundle Clark, *Myth and Symbol in Ancient Egypt*, 1959.

17. Robert Bauval, *The Orion Mystery*; Philip Vandenburg, *The Curse of the Pharaohs*; Robert Anton Wilson, *Cosmic Trigger*; Lucy Lamie, *Egyptian Mysteries*.

18. Because of the precession of the equinoxes, the rising of Sirius occurred at the summer solstice in 3300 B.C.E., on July 19 at 0 C.E., but now occurs around August 5 — it moves forward by 8.5 days every 1,000 years.

19. Robert Graves, *The White Goddess*, 1961.

20. John Opsopaus, *Five Days Out of Time*, http://www.cs.utk.edu/~mclennan/BA/OM/BA/PT/BA/FDOT.html.

21. Lev. 2:4.

22. Lev. 23:9–14.

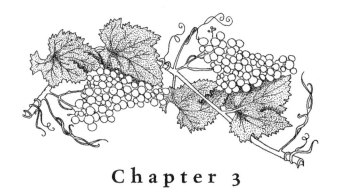

Chapter 3

Lugh

I stand in the front line of battle,
King and leader of the land
Long-armed with spear and armor
I stand in the front line of battle.[1]

The word Lughnasa translates as "the games, or assembly, of Lugh." Classical writers attest to a great festival held at Lyon ("Lugh's Fort") on the first day of August in ancient Gaul. It seems that festivals connected with the god Lugh were held throughout the Celtic lands of Britain, Gaul, and Ireland at the end of July and beginning of August, stretching over a period of up to two weeks or longer. These gatherings included the settling of tribal business matters, horseracing, athletic contests, martial contests, and rituals to ensure a plentiful harvest and to open the season of the hunt and the traditional time for collecting oysters and the fruits of the sea.

There is plenty of evidence that in Ireland tribal gatherings were held at Lughnasa. The most important of these was the Tailtiu, or Telltown, associated with the High King of Ireland, whose seat at Tara was only fifteen miles away.

Lugh is said to have instituted the Tailtiu games in honor of his foster mother, the earth goddess Tailtiu, though the games predate the introduction of the Lugh cult into Ireland by at least 2,000 years. It is more likely that the new Lugh cult usurped an earlier harvest festival of an earth/harvest goddess. Events included throwing the dart (the *gaelbolga*), high-jumping, pole-vaulting, stone-throwing, triple-jumping (the *geal-ruith*), and throwing the wheel (the *roth-cleas*). Also included were elements of the *óenach*, an Irish tribal gathering that was a mixture of business, ritual, horseracing, and a bull sacrifice and feast. The last games were held at Telltown on August 1, 1169, during the reign of Ruraigh Ó Conchobar, the last of the high kings of Ireland.

THE CULT OF LUGH

As the festival is named after the god Lugh, it is necessary to look at his origins and mythology. Now this is where it starts to get complicated. While some writers state, without hesitation, that Lugh was a sun god,[2] others, with equal force, argue that he was neither a god of the sun nor harvest.[3]

Lugh's adventures are related in the *Irish Mythological Cycle*, a collection of stories that describe the exploits of a variety of gods and heroes. These stories were initially passed on as an oral tradition, and scholarly monks wrote down the earliest versions we know in the eighth and ninth centuries, when elements from biblical sources and Greek and Roman myth frequently crept in. It was often the case that the Celtic stories were embroidered with extra details or were subtly altered to conform to the recorder's preconceived idea of a good story. It is difficult now to pick out the threads of the original myth, but we do have some earlier evidence. Writing about the Gauls circa 52 B.C.E., the Roman emperor Julius Caesar said:

*The god they reverence most is Mercury. They have very many images of him
and regard him as the inventor of all arts, the god who directs men upon
their journeys, and their most powerful helper in trade and getting money.*[4]

Though Caesar equated this paragon with the Roman deity Mercury, the evidence suggests that Lugh was the object of their veneration.

The continental Celts knew him as Lugus, and his cult rose to prominence and became widespread throughout the Celtic world from the middle of the Iron Age onward. There are some inscriptions to Lugoves, a plural of Lugus, which may mean that the god may have occasionally appeared as a Trinity.[5] He was known as Lud in England, Llew or Lleu in Wales, and Lugh or Lugaidh in Ireland. Many place-names throughout the central and western parts of Europe provide evidence of his importance to the Celts. Lyons in France was once the capital of Gaul and was called Lugdunum, "the Fort of Lugus," while Carlisle in Britain was Caer Lugubalion. It is possible that London, the capital of England, was named after Lud, meaning "the Fortress of Lud." Other examples include Leiden, Laon, Loudon, Leiden, Laon, Lauzun, and Liegnitz — all meaning "Fortress of Lud."[6] In the Celtic world, a fort may indeed be a fortified place, but it can also refer to an earthwork, mound, or hill associated with Otherworldly characters. There is a Ludgate Hill near St. Paul's Cathedral in London where, according to one tale, the god is buried.[7]

The cult of Lugh was a latecomer in Ireland, introduced around the time of Christ by Gaulish or British refugees fleeing from the advancing Roman armies; there was a great migration of British Celts into Ireland at that time.[8] Lugh and his festival soon supplanted the earlier harvest lore, becoming one of the four focal points of the year in the early Irish calendar.

Lugh is said to have held a festival at the beginning of the harvest every year at Tailtiu (modern Telltown). The festival was held at an ancient burial mound — not unusual for the ancient Celts, who liked their ancestors to be included in their festivities. The renowned Irish scholar Dr. Dáithí Ó hÓgáin states that the name Tailtiu is not Irish in origin and is probably a borrowing of the Welsh *telediw*, which means "well-formed." It would tend to indicate a settlement of British Celts connected with the site.[9]

LUGH'S NAME

Lugh's name has presented a translation problem for scholars. Robert Graves believed that it was connected with the Latin *lux*, meaning "light," or with *lucus*, meaning "grove."[10] Dr. Ó hÓgáin argues that the name is more likely to be derived from a Celtic word *lugio*, meaning "oath," making him the patron of sworn contracts.[11] There is some evidence that the cult of Lugh originated much farther east. Lugh's name may be connected with ancient Mesopotamia where the title of the sacred king was *lugal*. There is a Sumerian god called Ninurta, titled Lugalbanda, whose exploits are detailed in the *Lugal-e*. He was lord of the plow and master of the fields, the young warrior and champion of the gods, as well as being an ancient thunder god who brought the storms that gave life to the land. The *Farmer's Almanac* (1700 B.C.E.), an instructive manual on how to grow barley, praises him as "the life giving semen."[12]

Lugh has several titles, including Lámhfhada ("long-armed"), referring to his magical spear, which flashed or roared when used in battles. This seems to be a clear reference to lightning and thunder. According to one Irish saying, during thunderstorms:

> *Lugh Long-arm's wind is flying in the air tonight*
> *Yes, and the sparks of his father Balor Béimann.*

The Welsh Llew was equally called Llaw Gyffes, or "accurate arm." It is possible that Lugh had aspects as a thunder god. This connection is born out in the naming of Ludchurch in Staffordshire (England) on the River Dane.[13] Ludchurch, indicating the chapel of the god Lud, is a rocky chasm hidden in the forest. The river rushing into the chasm causes a noise like thunder. It is said to be an entrance to fairyland, and stones taken from nearby rocks were carved as protective amulets.[14] This would seem to equate Lugh/Llew with a number of other sky gods who are armed with thunder and lightning, and who are associated with the

Earth Mother; in Lugh's case, she is named as Tailtiu. In the earlier myth, it is likely that Lugh was the fertilizer of the Earth Mother with his summer rains. The shocked Christian myth recorders would have changed the son and lover of the mother to platonic foster son.

Lugh is also titled Samhioldánach, "equally skilled in all the arts," a supreme craftsman. The Welsh Llew is called "the one with the skilful hand."

THE STORY OF LUGH LONGARM

According to Irish mythology, there were a series of invasions of the island by several different races. The first conquerors were from Spain, but all of them perished in a plague.[15] A second wave of Spanish invaders succeeded in colonizing the country, although another invading group called the Formori, or Formorians, continually harassed them.[16] Next to arrive were the Fir Bolg, the Fir Gálion, the Fir Domnann, and then, eventually, the godlike Tuatha Dé Danann ("People of the Goddess Danu").

The Formorian tyrant Balor lived on Tory Island and had one daughter called Eithne. It was foretold that if she should give birth to a son, he would kill his grandfather. Balor locked her in a tower so that no man could come near her. However, Cian of the Tuatha Dé Danann fell in love with Eithne, and the pair contrived to meet and make love. The offspring of this liaison was Lugh. His existence was at first kept secret, but, inevitably, Balor discovered the deception. He ordered that Cian be put to death while Eithne and her son were set adrift in a boat to perish.

According to one version of the tale, mother and son were saved by the kindness of Goibhleann, or Goibhniu, the smith. He forged Lugh a great spear, which gave the boy his sobriquet *lámhfhada*, or "long arm." Another version, recorded in a twelfth-century poem, says that Lugh was raised in the otherworld Eamhain Abhlach, or "apple land." He was first fostered with the sea god Manannán Mac Lir, who taught Lugh the multitude of skills that earned him the title of *ildánach*, or "many gifted."

Lugh was fostered for a second time with Tailtiu, queen of the Fir Bolg. Tailtiu died while clearing the central plain of Ireland for the cultivation of crops. The place of her death in the Boyne Valley of County Meath became the site of a great assembly at the end of July or beginning of August. Known as the Oenach Tailtenn, this gathering was said to be instituted by Lugh in memory of her, though we know that it predates the arrival of the Lugh cult and the Celts by hundreds of years.

The most comprehensive account of Lugh is found in *Cath Maige Tuired* ("the Battle of Moytirra"), an eleventh-century Irish text that includes material originally recorded at an earlier date. It is the story of a struggle for supremacy between two of the early races, the Formorians and the Tuatha Dé Danann. It relates how the Dagdá (the "good god")[17] led the Tuatha Dé Danann into Ireland and into battle against the Fir Bolg. After this, the First Battle of Moytirra, the Fir Bolg entered into a treaty with the Tuatha Dé Danann and the Formorians, and from then onward occupied the province of Connaught and its outer islands.

During the battle, the high king Nuada lost his right arm, and since a maimed king could not rule, Bres ("Beautiful") became king of the Irish. Bres was of mixed descent — Formorian on his father's side and Tuatha Dé Danann on his mother's — but he proved to be a bad ruler. Under his leadership the Irish were oppressed, with the unfortunate Tuatha Dé Danann forced into menial servitude under the Formorians. He was also mean; he offered poor hospitality to visitors and neglected his poets and artists. The Tuatha Dé Danann finally demanded his abdication and reinstated Nuada, thus breaking the treaty and declaring war on the Formorians.

It is at this point that Lugh enters the story; an unknown newcomer who arrived at the court of the Tuatha Dé Danann at the Hill of Tara in the Boyne Valley, just as Nuada was celebrating his return to the throne. Lugh marched up to the door and demanded entrance. The astonished gatekeeper stared at the young man dressed like a king and demanded his name and purpose.

"My name is Lugh. I am the son of Cian and the grandson of Balor by Eithne, my mother."

"But what is your craft?" asked the gatekeeper, "For no one enters Tara without an art."

"I am a carpenter," replied Lugh.

"We don't need a carpenter; we already have one. He's called Luchtainé."

"I am a clever smith."

"We have one of those, too. His name is Goibhniu."

"I am a warrior."

"Ogma is our champion."

"I am a harpist, a poet from the Land of Apples, rich in swans and yew trees."

"We've already got an excellent bard."

"I am a sorcerer."

"We've got plenty of druids."

"I am a healer."

"Our healer is Diancécht."

"I am a cup bearer."

"We've got nine of those already."

"I am a worker in bronze."

"We have one called Crední. And he's a very good one, too."

"Then go and ask the king if he has a single man that can do all of these things. If he has then there is no need for me in Tara."

The gatekeeper went inside and told the assembly that a young man was at the gates who called himself Lugh, Master of all the Arts. The king sent out his best chess player to test the cunning of this stranger. Lugh invented a new move called "Lugh's Enclosure" and won the game. Nuada invited him in, and Lugh went straight to the chair called "the sage's seat," reserved for the king's wisest advisor. The king did not upbraid him, but watched with the rest of the court while Ogma demonstrated his strength. Ogma pushed a huge stone out of the door that would have needed scores of oxen to move it. The court applauded, but Lugh got up, picked up the rock, and put it back in its place. The court then begged him to play his harp for them, so he played the magical sleep tune, which sent them all to sleep for a whole day and night. Next he played such a sad song that they all wept, then a lively measure that had them all laughing with joy. He also performed amazing feats of dexterity, such as leaping on a bubble without bursting it.

Nuada began to think that such a man as this would be very helpful against the Formorians. After speaking with his advisors, he decided to lend his throne to Lugh for thirteen days while he took the sage's seat. Lugh was then entrusted with leading the Tuatha into battle. He asked each of the gods what they would contribute to the struggle.

Crední, the bronzesmith, promised to manufacture sword hilts, rivets for spears, and bosses and rims for the shields. Diancécht, the physician, made a replacement arm of silver for Nuada and promised to cure all the wounded, while Goibhniu, the smith, offered to make magical lances that could never fail in battle. Luchtainé, the carpenter, promised to provide all the shields and lance-shafts. The champion, Ogma, boasted that he would kill the king of the Formorians with thrice nine of his followers. The Dagdá asserted that the bones of the Formorians would be crushed beneath his club like hailstones under the hooves of horses. Cairpré said that he would curse them and take away their honor and morale with his satires. The head magician, Mathgan, said that by his magical arts the twelve mountains of Ireland would be hurled at the enemy. The cupbearers said that they would hide the twelve lakes and twelve chief rivers of Ireland from the Formorians, so that they would not be able to quench their thirst. Figol, the druid, promised to send three streams of fire into the faces of the enemy and take away two-thirds of their strength. The Morrigan declared that she would chase all those that fled from the battlefield.

In the ensuing battle at Moytirra,[18] Lugh circled around the warriors on one foot and with one eye closed to chant a spell to weaken the enemy. Now Lugh's grandfather and enemy, Balor, had a baleful eye that was only open during battle, because anyone on whom it gazed would be destroyed by its poison. A well-aimed stone from Lugh's slingshot knocked this lethal eye of Balor's right out the back of his head, killing twenty-seven of his followers in the process. Lugh chased Balor to the hilltop of Mizen Head with the intention of beheading him. Balor cunningly told Lugh that he could gain his power by placing his head on top of Lugh's own. However, when Lugh had decapitated Balor, he suspected a trick and placed the head on a large rock, which immediately shattered.

After the battle, the Formorian dead were as numerous as the stars of heaven, the sands of the sea, the flakes of a snowstorm, dewdrops upon grass, and the waves of a storm at sea.[19] Those surviving ran to their ships and fled to their islands, leaving the Irish mainland to the Tuatha Dé Danann. Lugh spared the life of Bres on condition that he would teach them how to plow, sow, and reap the harvest. To placate the victors, Bres offered to ensure that the cows should always be with milk, and that there should be four harvests a year in Ireland, but the people refused this. "This has suited us," they said:

Spring for plowing and sowing,
Summer for strengthening the corn,
Autumn for the ripeness of corn and reaping,
Winter for consuming it.[20]

A tenth-century manuscript says that after the death of Nuada, Lugh became the king of the Tuatha Dé Danann. He was consecrated at the hill of Tailtiu and ruled Ireland for forty years. He appears in another story that began when his father turned himself into a lap dog and went into Newgrange (Brugh na Bóinne) in County Meath. He was killed there by the sons of Tuirell (or Tuireann): Brian, Iuchair, and Iucharba. Lugh demanded compensation and asked the three men to procure seven nearly impossible things for him. The three brothers did this, but returned injured and dying. Their father asked Lugh to lend them his mantle of healing, but Lugh refused and let them die.

Lugh died at the hill of Uisneach, killed by three more brothers. These were the sons of Cearmaid whom Lugh had killed so that he could possess his wife. One of the men thrust a spear through Lugh's foot, and Lugh retreated into the lake and drowned. It is now called Loch Lughbhorta.

A later work states that after death he ruled in the Otherworld.[21] When Conn of the Hundred Battles (a mythical Irish hero) made a journey to the Otherworld, he came across a golden tree and a house with a ridgepole of gold. Inside were a king and queen seated on golden thrones. The woman was the sovereign goddess of Ireland, while the king told Conn that he was Lugh. The queen gave Conn a drink to demonstrate that he was the approved king of Ireland.

LUGH AND BALOR

The central part of the story is the rivalry between Lugh and his grandfather, Balor (also known as Balar or Bolor). The pattern of this tale is a common one, though it more commonly occurs in Mediterranean myth than Celtic lore. The basic outline begins with a prophecy that the grandson (or son) of the king will overthrow him. The king takes the precaution of locking his daughter up in a tower, but she manages to meet a lover and give birth to a son. The king then sets his daughter and grandson adrift in a basket or chest in a river or the sea, expecting both to die or, alternatively, exposes the baby on a hillside to die. However, the two are saved and, after some time in exile, the young prince returns to overthrow the old king. There are many examples of myths conforming to this pattern: Oedipus, who was exposed as a baby and returned to kill his father; Auge and her son, Telephus, were set adrift on the sea in a chest, as were Semele and Dionysus, Danae and Perseus. The Welsh poet Taliesin was cast adrift on the sea only to be rescued by Elphin. In another fable, Tyro fell in love with the river god Enipeus, but he was indifferent. Poseidon disguised himself as the river god and ravished her. She bore twin sons in secret and set them afloat down the river in an alder wood ark, just like the one in which Romulus and Remus were set afloat.

Scholars have put forward several possible explanations of the youth and father/grandfather myth pattern. The stories may illustrate how the cult of a new god supplanted that of an old one. Alternatively, the old grandfather may be the setting sun or the dying sun of winter or autumn, while the young man represents the dawn sun or spring-summer sun. The old king may be the old year and the young prince the new. They may represent seasonal gods, when one season grows old and a new season succeeds it. The old god may represent the forces of blight and winter that have to be overcome by the spring and so on.

THE STORY OF THE WELSH LLEW

The *Mabinogion* is a collection of stories that contains a Welsh variant of Lugh's history. Though the tales are obviously ones with ancient Pagan themes, they were not recorded in written form until the medieval period. Here the hero of the *Mabinogion* is called Llew Llaw Gyffes ("Llew of the Skilful Hand") and is obviously the Brythonic (British) equivalent of the Gaelic Lugh. Laud Llaw Ereint ("Llud of the Silver Hand") replaces Nuada.

In this Welsh version of the myth, Arianrhod ("Silver Wheel") was the daughter of the goddess Dôn and niece of King Math of Gwynedd. Math couldn't sleep unless he rested his feet in a virgin's lap. When his usual virgin was deflowered, Arianrhod was suggested as her replacement. To test her purity, Arianrhod had to step over Math's wand, but as soon as she had done so, she gave birth to Llew and his brother Dylan. Arianrhod refused to have anything to do with the boys. Dylan ("Son of the Wave") jumped into the sea and swam away.

Llew was brought up by his magician uncle, Gwydion ap Dôn. His growth was rapid; when he was but a child of one year, he seemed like a child of two. When he was two, he traveled about by himself. When he was four years old, he was as tall as a boy of eight.

Arianrhod refused to recognize him as her son but placed several taboos on him. When Gwydion took the boy to her castle, she placed a curse on him, saying that he should never have a name until she gave him one. This was a serious thing; to be without a name was to be nothing in this world or the next. Gwydion came up with a plan to trick Arianrhod into naming her son. By magic he formed a boat from seaweed and rushes and some beautiful leather from sedge. Disguised as shoemakers, Gwydion and Llew sailed up to Arianrhod's castle and began to sew the leather. Arianrhod looked down from her balcony and thought that she would like some new shoes, so she sent her maid down to the shore with her measurements. Gwydion knew that he must force her to come out and first made some shoes too big, then some too small, though both pairs were exquisite. Eventually, Arianrhod went down to the boat to be fitted in person. While Gwydion was fitting the shoes, a wren came and perched on the boat. The boy took out his bow and shot the wren through the leg. Arianrhod was impressed. "Truly," she said, "he is one with a steady hand!"

"Thank you," Gwydion said, "The boy now has his name, Llew Llaw Gyffes!"

At this, the goddess cried angrily that the boy should never have arms unless she should bestow them on him. Nevertheless, Gwydion took Llew home to Dinas Dinllev and brought him up as a warrior. When he was ready, the two returned to Caer Arianrhod disguised as bards. The goddess received them kindly, pleased to hear their songs and stories. The next morning, Gwydion cast a powerful spell that made it appear as though a vast army was descending on the castle. The air rang with shouts and trumpets, and the bay seemed full of enemy ships. Arianrhod became afraid and asked Gwydion what she should do.

"Give us arms," he replied, "and we will defend you." While her maidens armed Gwydion, Arianrhod herself strapped armor onto Llew. Instantly the glamour ended, and it was seen that no army threatened. Realizing that she had been tricked, Arianrhod laid a further taboo on Llew — that he should never marry a woman born of the race of men. Gwydion and his fellow magician, Math ap Mathonwy, gathered the flowers of oak, broom, and meadowsweet to fashion a lovely maiden as a bride for Llew. She was called Blodeuwedd ("Flower Face").

Llew and his "flower bride" lived happily until one day Llew was away and a hunting party arrived, led by Gronw Pebyr. Gronw and Blodeuwedd immediately fell in love and plotted to rid themselves of her husband. The problem was that he could be killed neither by day nor by night, indoors or out of doors, clothed or naked, riding or walking, nor by any lawfully made weapon. Blodeuwedd tricked Llew into revealing to her that he could only be killed at twilight when on the bank of a river with one foot on the back of a he-goat and the other on the rim of a bath under a canopy. The spear needed to kill him would take a year to make, working only on Sundays. Armed with this information, Gronw set about making preparations.

When all was ready, Blodeuwedd asked Llew to show her how he could balance on a goat and bath at the same time. Llew was more than ready to indulge his young wife's curiosity and took up his position with one foot on the rim of a bath, the other on the he-goat. As he teetered there, Gronw emerged from the trees and hurled the magical javelin at him, wounding him in the thigh.[22] However, instead of dying, Llew turned into an eagle and flew away.

When Gwydion ap Dôn learned what had happened, he set off to find his poor nephew. He searched far and wide until one day he discovered a sow behaving very strangely. It was devouring the maggots and gobbets of flesh that fell from an eagle perched in an oak tree. Gwydion immediately recognized that the eagle was the mortally wounded Llew. Using his magical powers, he transformed his nephew back into human shape and took him home to nurse him back to health.

When news of Llew's recovery reached Blodeuwedd and Gronw, they realized that all was up and took flight. With her servants, Blodeuwedd tried to cross the river, but her maids were in such a panic that they all drowned in the swift-flowing waters. Left alone, Blodeuwedd was soon discovered by Gwydion, who avenged his nephew by changing her into an owl, the most hated of all birds.

Gronw tried to treat with Llew and offered him land and money in reparation. Llew refused and demanded that Gronw meet him in the place of his treacherous act and allow him to return the favor under the exact same circumstances. The two came to the bank of the river, and Gronw took up his position on the goat and cauldron, but pleaded with Llew that since he had come to this pass through the wiles of a woman, Llew should allow him the boon of placing a stone between himself and the blow. This Llew granted, but when he hurled his spear, it pierced through the stone and through Gronw, too, breaking his back. The stone still lies on the banks of the river Cynfael, with the hole through it, and it is called Llech Gronw, or "Gronw's Stone."

The Meaning of Llew's Story

At first the story seems to be merely the tale of an unfaithful wife or, to take a more enlightened view, a woman rebelling against a role decided for her by the men who created her. However, it is an ancient tale of the changing roles of the gods and goddesses of the seasons.

Blodeuwedd is the blossoming earth goddess of the summer; her name means "Flower Face." She is the sovereign goddess of the land, whom the sacred king must marry in order to rule. Her two lovers are seasonal gods or annual sacred kings, rivals for her hand.

Arianrhod means "Silver Wheel" and denotes that she has an aspect as a moon goddess. She is also a weaver and spinning goddess, and with her wheel spins the cosmos and all the life that is in it. While she claims to be a virgin, she gives birth to two sons. The story of a birth of a god from a virgin mother is a common one in mythology. In ancient times, the goddess did not need the agency of a fertilizing god to bring forth life. The god son of a virgin mother is usually a sacrificial death and resurrection god, as here Llew clearly is. The twin sons are fairly common in myth and represent the two gods, the light and dark twins, who fight for rulership of the year.

Llew's bride, Blodeuwedd, is described as having fingers that are "whiter than the ninth wave of the sea," proving that she is also a moon goddess — an aspect of Arianrhod herself. Gronw is Lord of Pebyr ("Lord of the Lake"), another metaphorical twin and rival of Llew. When he is struck by his rival's spear, Llew becomes an eagle, as the soul of the sacred king or ruler is said to do. Later, when the "fight" is restaged under exactly the same circumstances, Llew becomes the victor. This is obviously a biannual or annual fight for rulership of the year and the hand of the goddess. Blodeuwedd becomes the owl, the autumn/death goddess with the changing of the year. Owls are very vocal in November (the death time of the year) and then fall silent until February. As such, they are the heralds of the goddess in her death and winter aspect. Blodeuwedd is a Welsh name for the owl, and some say the face of an owl resembles a flower.

PARALLELS IN THE WELSH AND IRISH ACCOUNTS

Though there are obvious differences between the Welsh and the Irish accounts, they do have several themes in common. Lugh is the grandson of the Irish mother of the gods, Danu, while Llew is the grandson of her Welsh equivalent, Dôn. Lugh and Llew have to be hidden away from close relatives who will do them harm. Both are fostered by mentor-figures who teach them a wide variety of skills. Both are connected with sovereign goddesses: in Lugh's case his foster mother, Tailtiu; in Llew's case his mother, Arianrhod, who names and arms him; and Llew's bride, Blodeuwedd, who is the earth itself. (In Celtic lore, kingship is a gift of the sovereign goddess.) Both have an epic encounter with a supernatural opponent.

In both the Irish and Welsh accounts, there is no clearly demarcated line between the supernatural and the earthly realms; men and women, gods and goddesses pass easily between one another, yet there is a subtle difference between the two traditions. The Welsh stories place a stronger emphasis on a special technique or professional magic as being the necessary preparation before entering the enchanted realms. This is possibly because mainland Britain was the center of specialized druidic training, and the Welsh tales reflect this bias toward a professional caste of magicians.

RECONSTRUCTING LUGHNASA

July is called "the hungry month" in Ireland, because the harvest cannot begin until the first day of August. It is unlucky to gather fruits or dig potatoes until Lughnasa. In ancient times, they could not be picked until precautions were taken to protect the rest of the harvest still to come and reparation made to the Earth in the form of a sacrifice. From all the associated legends, this would seem to have been a bull, though in prehistoric times, it may well have been a human being.

Lugh was admitted to Tara because of something called "Lugh's enclosure." The Christian recorder seems to have taken this to mean a chess move, but the enclosure was, in fact, a sacred mound, like Macha's Enclosure where a gathering took place on her festival, August 1. Its entrance was in the west (the direction of the setting sun), which connects it with death and sacrifice. Crom Dubh's stone circle was on a hill and formed another enclosure. Human sacrifices took place there, later commuted to a bull offering. Such hills are harvest mounds or earth wombs, symbolizing the earth mounded up over the seed so that it might germinate. Perhaps the many "forts of Lugh" were, in fact, enclosures of this kind. In Celtic, a fort can be a mound or earthwork, as well as a fortified encampment. Classical writers recorded that gatherings took place at Lyon ("Fort of Lugh") on August 1. The various forts of Lugh may well be "mounds of the oath" or "mounds of the king."

The evidence is overwhelming that Lugh was connected with sacred kingship. Such kings were chosen to rule (probably by becoming the victor of the wake games held at Lughnasa) either for a fixed period or until they become "crooked" in some way, either physically, like Nuadha, or morally, like Bres. It has been suggested that the king was then haltered and lamed (made physically crooked) by being pierced in the foot (as Lugh and Llew were) before being sacrificed. The day of this sacrifice seems to have been August 1, when the spirit of the king was sent to the Underworld to appease the powers of blight and death in order to protect the harvest still standing in the fields.

Lugh may be cognate with lugal, the Mesopotamian term for the sacred king. Willow withies or lugos were used to bind or scourge the scapegoat, the sacred king or statues of the gods in ancient Greece. It seems likely that there is some common Indo-European root to the word "Lug." Lud or Lug appears so often in connection with kingship that it goes beyond the bounds of chance. Ronald Hutton (*Stations of the Sun*) speculated the word occurred so frequently that it must have had some other meaning for the Celts and could not always have been connected with the god. The word also appears on inscriptions in plural—Lugoves. This might refer to a triple aspect of the god or to a number of sacred kings. Macha offered her sexual favors to three different kings, but as each approached, she set on them and tied them up, forcing them to construct the enclosure for her. In other words, three sacred kings were married to the sovereign goddess, each in turn was taken to her enclosure, bound, and sacrificed. The enclosure is her womb, standing for the whole of the productive land, and the actions of the king were answerable for its fertility. Lugh similarly met his death on top of a hill, as did Balor.

One account says that Lugh's battle with Balor took place at Samhain (October 31), but this must be a misreading or "improvement" on the part of the myth recorder. This date has led to speculation that Lugh is the summer sun, opposing Balor, the winter sun (the baleful eye). But Lugh wins the battle, so this is plainly nonsense. The forces of winter and blight triumph at Samhain. It is also sometimes said that Lugh is the dawn sun, while Balor is the setting sun. Lugh is often said to be a sun god, but this claim is based on very little evidence and some erroneous etymology. Lugh is not derived from the Latin *lux* but from lugos or "oath," the oath of a king at his anointing. Caesar wrote that the Celts worshipped "Mercury" who was the god of all arts, travel, and commerce. He went on to say that next to him "they reverence Apollo, Mars, Jupiter and Minerva, about whom they have the same ideas as other nations — that Apollo averts illness, and Minerva teaches the principles of industries and handicrafts; that Jupiter is king of the gods, and Mars the lord of war."[23] He identifies the sun god as Apollo, separate from Lugh/Mercury who has no sun associations. The only thing in the legends of Lugh to associate him with the sun is the descriptions of him as having "a red color on him from sunset to sunrise" and as wearing a shirt of red-gold. The red color might be connected with the red clouds of sunset and sunrise, but Lugh is red at night; he does not shine during the day.

Red is associated with death in the Celtic world. Red food is described as the food of the dead and is taboo for humans. At the Hostel of Dá Derga ("the Red"), Conaire the doomed king saw three red-haired riders, accoutered with red armor, riding on three red horses.[24] Red horsemen convey the dead to the house of Donn, the god of the dead. Red is the color of completion and harvest. In Rome, red-haired puppies were sacrificed to influence the ripening of the corn, while in Egypt, red-haired men were buried alive as a sacrifice to the god of the corn and the dead, Osiris.[25] Lugh's red color was the mark of the sacred king, doomed to die.

When Nuadha became disqualified from kingship (became crooked) because of his lost arm, Bres took over. Then Bres became crooked in another way — he was a bad king who oppressed his people. Nuadha acquired a silver arm and became king once more, but when Lugh proved how skillful he was, stood down for thirteen days to allow Lugh to lead the battle against the Formorians, or forces of blight. This is further evidence that Lugh was not a sun god. He took over from Nuadha who had no associations with the sun at all; he was high king.

Another crooked king with a "lug" prefix is King Lugaid mac Con who ruled from Tara for seven years. When he gave a false judgement, the side of the house in which the decree had been given fell down the slope and became known as "the Crooked Mound of Tara." After that, Lugaid was king in Tara for a year and "no grass grew, no leaves, and there was no grain." After this he was dethroned by his people for he was a "alse prince."

The story of Lugh corresponds to the many tales of boys born crooked (illegitimate or lame) that are predestined to kill their fathers or grandfathers. The story survives in fairy tales as the boy who wants to marry the princess and is set a task by the old king, which is designed to kill the boy. The boy is the new sacred king who wants to marry the sovereign goddess, and the old king knows that once he has been chosen his own death is the inevitable result. The crooked birth foreshadows the boy's own end as lamed and crooked king. The king is not an individual but a King with a capital K, one incarnation of the divine ruler. When one quitted his mortal body in death, his soul passed into the next incumbent. The story of the king replaced by his grandson or son, who is really the king himself, is paralleled in the myths of the corn gods such as Osiris, whose son Horus is himself reborn as the next year's harvest.

In late July and early August, the Dog Star rose with the sun to threaten the crops with its baleful, withering eye, but at the end of that period, the same cosmic dog accompanied the soul of the sacrificed king to the realm of the gods. There is plenty of evidence that the divine king was associated with dogs. At the temple of

Nodens, several representations of dogs were discovered. Nudd is father of Gwyn ap Nudd, Lord of the Wild Hunt who rides out with a pack of dogs. Lugh is the father or grandfather of Cuchulain, "Hound of Chulain." The dog is associated with the underworld realm of the dead and often guides the soul to the Land of the Dead.

The date of Lugh's festival irrefutably connects him to the harvest. It is celebrated on hills and mounds and ancient enclosures. He is appointed for king for thirteen days only, a substitute for the maimed king, to protect the harvest for the period of the Dog Days.[26] At Old Lammas, August 12, the Dog Days end and he wins the secrets of the harvest from Bres; the harvest begins. Then he is lamed and meets a triple death — haltered and stabbed on top of the hill and drowned in the nearby river or well. After his death, Lugh rules in the Otherworld within the mounds as king of the dead, with the goddess of sovereignty as his wife. He is then known as *lugh-chromain*, "little stooping Lugh," and this is the origin of the leprechaun. Like Crom Dubh, he is a crooked one of the mounds.

Notes

1. Craft hymn to Lugh.
2. Peter Beresford Ellis, *Dictionary of Celtic Mythology* (London: Constable, 1992).
3. Ronald Hutton, *Stations of the Sun* (Oxford: Oxford University Press, 1996).
4. Julius Caesar, *The Conquest of Gaul*, trans. S. A. Handford (Penguin Classics, 1951).
5. Ellis, *Dictionary of Celtic Mythology*, 1992.
6. Ronald Hutton (*Stations of the Sun*) argues that it is possible that the word "lud" had another significance to the Celts, and that these cities were not named after the god at all. He contends that the worship of the god was probably not so widespread, and it was a variety of local gods that were associated with Mercury.
7. David Clarke, *A Guide to Britain's Pagan Heritage* (Hale, 1995).
8. Dáithí Ó hÓgáin, *The Sacred Isle* (Cork: The Collins Press, 1999). According to Dr. Ó hÓgáin, at the same time the god Nuada (or more correctly, Nuadhu) was also introduced from Britain, where he was known as Nodens, his principle shrine being at Lydney on the River Severn in Gloucestershire, where he is depicted as a sea god in the guise of the Roman Neptune, complete with trident. Nodens took over the role of Elcmhar as husband of Boinn and became the father of her son Aonghus, who was given the title Macán Óicc ("the young son"), paralleling the British Maponus or Mabon ("the young son" god).

9. Ibid.

10. Robert Graves, *The White Goddess*, 1961.

11. Ó hÓgáin, *Myth, Legend & Romance*, 1991.

12. Http://www.gatewaystobabylon.com.

13. This gives us a connection with Danu, or Dôn, the Celtic goddess described as mother of the gods. Her name is also reflected in the River Danube.

14. David Clarke, *A Guide to Britain's Pagan Heritage*, 1995.

15. In Irish lore, "Spain" may just mean anywhere outside the country and often refers to the Otherworld or Fairyland.

16. Identified as invading Celtic tribes.

17. This didn't mean good in a moral sense but in a practical one. The Dagdá was "good at everything" and had magical powers. The Egyptian pharoah was similarly called the "good god."

18. This was, according to one source, seven years later and took place at Samhain. The fact that he only had the throne for thirteen days seems to have been forgotten or overlooked by this particular recorder.

19. Charles Squire, *The Mythology of the British Isles*, 1905.

20. J. Fraser, *The First Battle of Moytura*, Eriu 8, 1915.

21. Ó hÓgáin, *Myth, Legend and Romance*, 1991.

22. "Thigh" is probably the myth recorder's polite rendering of "groin," since sacrificed gods are often described as being castrated.

23. Caesar, *The Conquest of Gaul*, 1951.

24. Anne Ross, *Pagan Celtic Britain*, 1974.

25. Eric Maple, Red, *Man Myth and Magic*, n.d.

26. Lugalbanda means "junior king" and suggests he served the same purpose.

Part 2

Celebrating Lughnasa

Chapter 4

Ancient Themes for Modern Pagans

Month of August — covered with foam is the beach;
Blithesome the bee, full the hive;
Better the work of the sickle than the bow.[1]

Lughnasa/Lammas is a harvest festival, marking the end of the period of summer growth and the beginning of the autumn harvest. Today's Pagans celebrate eight annual festivals, including Lughnasa. Gerald Gardner, the founder of modern Wicca, introduced this pattern based on the quarter and cross-quarter days of English law, but the festivals of the old witches were somewhat different.[2] Montague Summers pointed out that, historically, British witches were unique in celebrating Lammas/Lughnasa.[3]

Another popular misconception is that Lughnasa was a fire festival; it was not. It was associated with water and earth, but fire played no part, unless you count incidental fires to cook the feast. The practice of calling the four Celtic cross-quarter festivals "the fire festivals" is a modern one. Fire is just as closely associated with the solstices and equinoxes, for obvious reasons.

Pagans today honor the sacrifice of the God at Lammas. As the vegetation spirit, he dies so that we might live and eat. At the autumn equinox, he will enter into the womb of the Goddess, as the seed enters the earth. At Samhain he rules as king of the dead, and at Yule he is reborn with the sun, and the cycle of growth begins once more.

Some branches of traditional Witchcraft celebrate Lughnasa as the festival of the God and the male spirit. He is visualized as a king in his prime who will die with the turn of the year. The primary theme of Lughnasa is sacrifice, and this is a difficult one to come to terms with. In ancient days, people thought that the God's sacrifice had to be mirrored on earth with the sacrifice of animals or even human beings. Today we know that the God sacrifices himself annually, because that is the pattern of things. He does it willingly, and he does it with love to sustain all the creatures of the earth, not just humankind. The law of the Craft tells us that the God and Goddess do not demand sacrifice, because all creatures are their children and are cherished equally. Therefore, modern Pagans respect and revere all life; it is a creed of joy. The God dies, but he will return with the newborn sun at the winter solstice and Pagans will rejoice. So long as they strive to maintain the natural balance and harmony that is the pattern of life, they are promised blessings. It is this pattern Pagans honor at these festivals and seek to maintain in their daily lives.

FIRST FRUITS

Lughnasa celebrates the fruition of the year's work with the weaning of calves and lambs, the ripening of the grain, and the first apples, pears, bilberries, blackberries, and grapes. In Ireland, Lughnasa is sometimes called Bilberry Sunday. It was once believed that these fruits should not be gathered until Lughnasa or ill luck would result.

For your Lughnasa celebrations, gather a basket of assorted ripe fruit and place it on the altar, or decorate the ritual area with the fruit. They may be blessed during the course of the ritual and shared with others at the end of the evening for luck.

An old custom was to pick the first apples and make them into a drink called Lammas Wool (see chapter 8 for the recipe). For the ancient Celts, the apple was sacred. The felling of an apple tree was punishable by death. When it is cut across, the apple is marked in its center with a pentacle, the sign of the Goddess. The sign of the pentacle and the apple tree mark the entrance to her Otherworld realm, Avalon, the "apple land," where the God travels to after his annual "death."

Another tradition you might like to enact is the election of the Harvest Lord and Lady to oversee the Lammas feast. They can be chosen by lot or by merit and crowned with wreaths of wheat ears, cornflowers, and poppies. At the end of the feast, the crowns are buried in the earth as an offering to the earth goddess.

THE SACRIFICE OF THE CORN GOD

Foods have always played an important part in rituals and the worship of the gods. Without food we would not live at all, and its production was one of the central themes of ancient religions; mysteriously, a small seed planted beneath the dark earth would shoot and grow into something that would provide a sustaining meal. It was as though by placing it in the womb of mother earth she would nourish and sustain it, magically transforming it, just as a woman would nurture the seed in her womb to produce a child.

One of the most valuable of these foods was grain, which could be made into flour and then bread. It is one of the most important symbols of the nurturing Goddess. It was often seen as her son, a god in itself, given life by the spirit of the corn lord. He would awaken in the spring, grow to maturity in the summer and autumn, and then die with the harvest, shedding his seed, which would be planted in the cold earth. There it would lie and be nourished by the earth mother, ready to shoot again in the spring in a never-ending cycle of life, death, and rebirth. In the Craft we call this cycle the Eternal Return. Myths of such dying or sacrificed vegetation gods are common throughout the world.

The god sacrificed at Lammas is John Barleycorn, the corn spirit. The gods are thanked, and the ritual sacrifice of John Barleycorn is reenacted with the baking and eating of bread. Part of the first loaf is offered to the gods in thanks. Nowadays, it is not possible for everyone to harvest and mill their own flour, but most can manage to bake a loaf of bread for Lammas (see chapter 8 for recipes). If you cannot, then buy an attractive loaf and bless it. You might be lucky enough to find one made in one of the traditional plait or sheaf shapes. During the course of the celebration, the loaf should be divided up and the first portion placed on the altar or laid on the ground as an offering to the gods.

The dedication of the bread and wine is one of the central points of every Craft ritual. It is the partaking of the sacrificed god of the corn. The fact that Christians also do this points to the fact that Christ was originally a sacrificed fertility god — but that's another story. Christians believe that the bread and wine is the transubstantiated flesh and blood of God. Looking at it this way, we can understand that the cakes and wine are magically changed during the ritual of consecration and imbued with the power of the gods. The cup is the equivalent of the cauldron or grail, which contained wisdom and inspiration. During the consecration, the priest and priestess may perform the act together, or they may simply be blessed by one or the other, recalling that we owe our divine parents, the God and the Goddess, for our lives and sustenance.

When bread is consecrated, it becomes the food of the spirit. Eating a food is meant to impart something of its spirit to the consumer, and the ritual partaking of bread and wine constitutes absorbing the spirit of the God and Goddess. Eating bread and drinking wine was an important part of the rites of corn goddesses and vegetation gods. An ear of corn was the central mystery of Eleusis at the worship of Demeter, and bread was eaten at the rites of Artemis and Cybele and other earth and moon goddesses. It was often baked in circle shapes and marked with a cross, representing the four phases of the moon or the passage of the sun, marked by the two solstices and two equinoxes.

Sheaves of grain make excellent decorations for a Lammas gathering. Decorate them with flowers and ribbons. You might also make a traditional corn dolly (see chapter 5 for instructions).

THE BLOOD OF THE GOD

The grape harvest also begins at Lughnasa. Whereas bread is viewed as the body of the sacrificed god, wine is his blood. The ancients thought that the state induced by wine was a sacred one, a different level of consciousness and a communion with the mind of the God. All plants that had the ability to change consciousness were considered sacred, but wine is more palatable than most, and the vine grows in a spiral pattern — a very ancient symbol of immortality. Wine was thought not to feed the body but the spirit with the divine inspiration of the god, freeing the imbiber from mundane thoughts and conventions, awakening the powers of the primal self within.

The story of the wine god is seen most clearly in the myth of Dionysus (Bacchus). He was the son of Zeus and Semele, a mortal woman. Zeus knew that his jealous wife, Hera, would try to harm the child, and smuggled him away to be brought up by foster parents, who disguised the young demi-god as a girl. However, Hera was not fooled and drove the foster parents mad. Zeus then turned Dionysus into a goat kid and sent him to be cared for by the nymphs of Mount Nysa. The Titans enticed him away from his guardians, tore him into pieces, and boiled him in a cauldron. The goddess Athene saved his heart, while Zeus rescued his limbs, and Apollo buried them on the slopes of Mount Parnassus, where the goddess Rhea brought him back to life, making him another death-and-resurrection god, sometimes called "the Thrice Born."

Hera continued to pursue Dionysus and drove him insane. In this condition he wandered through many lands. Eventually, he was received into the cult of the goddess Cybele and joined in the mystical orgies and frenzies that were part of her worship. There he learned to use his madness. Dionysus continued to travel with his band of followers, the bacchantes and satyrs, and discovered the secret of making wine. His festivals were the Bacchantia, mainly celebrated by women who used alcohol to overcome inhibitions, allowing them to do and say things that social conventions would not normally permit. Dionysus was a god that defied the social order, broke taboos and customs, and gained knowledge through divine madness. As such he was the opposite of the god Apollo — logical, dignified, lord of the sun and daylight — while Dionysus was attracted to the night and dark places. They perhaps represent the two sides of human consciousness, both necessary to be in balance.

You might bear this in mind as you bless the wine at Lammas. You can also make your own wine (see chapter 8 for recipes).

THE END OF SUMMER

Despite the fact that August is often the hottest month, according to Celtic lore Lughnasa is the last day of summer and the start of autumn. The days of growth are over and the harvest begins. The Flower Maiden becomes the Harvest Mother who, at Samhain, becomes the Cailleach.

In some parts of Ireland, this was symbolically reenacted with the burial of the flowers. Each person would climb the Lughnasa hill wearing a flower, which would be thrown into a hole at the summit, then covered with earth. You might like to include this ceremony as part of your Lammas ritual.

HILLS AND HARVEST MOUNDS

It was the custom to hold Lughnasa celebrations at a hill or harvest mound. Sometimes such mounds were artificially constructed like the massive Silbury Hill (Wiltshire, England) built nearly 4,600 years ago. Turves were used to construct the inner part of the hill in the Stone Age, cut at the beginning of the harvest about the time of Lughnasa. Then over a period of about fifty years, blocks of chalk covered the turf. It is a harvest mound, representing the womb of the Goddess. Originally, a water-filled trench surrounded it. The full moon in late July or early August (Lughnasa) would be reflected in the waters, so that it appeared a child's head was emerging from the womb. As the moon moved up through the sky, it appeared reflected at the breast of the image, as though suckling. As the moon moved higher, the "milk" was released from the breast as the moat reflected the lunar light. With the cutting of the umbilical cord (when the moon appears to detach itself from the hill), the signal was given to begin the harvest. Festivities were held on Silbury Hill into the eighteenth century with horseraces and bull-baiting followed by the slaughter and consumption of the bull.

Throughout the ancient world, a mound of earth was symbolic of the regenerative powers of the Goddess and was sometimes magnified into a mountain associated with the gods or a man-made pyramid, as in ancient Egypt. The symbolism is the same. Possibly this is the idea reflected in the towers built in Britain and Ireland and the mountain pilgrimages undertaken at Lughnasa. If possible, take a trip up a hill at Lughnasa. Treat it as a pilgrimage as the ancient Celts did. Make the walk an act of meditation. Take off your shoes and feel the earth beneath your feet. With each step reflect on the gifts of the Goddess that spring from the earth. With each step you leave behind the mundane world and step nearer to the world of the gods. With each step you leave behind those things you wish to be rid of. Feel the wind at the summit blow them away. Take a picnic with you and feast in the open air.

THE GODDESS OF THE LAND

Every land knows the earth goddess; she has many names and attributes. She is honored at Lammas as the earth beneath our feet, the land in which we live. She may be the tutelary spirit or anima locus of a particular area or of the whole country, as Érin is the goddess of Ireland and Britannia of Britain. She may be the Goddess of the whole planet, as Mother Earth herself.

In Celtic lore, the sovereignty of the land, or kingship, is a gift offered by this goddess. He is her mystical husband. To confirm this, she offers him a symbolic drink. She often manifests as a powerful white mare, which is one reason why Lughnasa is associated with horses. Gardnerian Wicca specifies that riding poles should be used at Lammas in honor of the Goddess of Sovereignty. These are poles with horses' heads, like children's hobbyhorses. These often appear in folklore ceremonies at various times of the year or accompany English Morris dancing troupes. Similar hobbyhorses can be found in several places: Pamplona, Spain, among the Basques; Krakow, Poland; Athens, Greece; Belgium; Germany; and France.

Below are just a few of this goddess' aspects for you to choose from and name in your Lammas ritual. Others may be found in appendix 4.

Adamah (Hebrew): Her name means "earth," and she is the personification of the earth as a goddess.

Britannia (British): Her name is the personification of the Isle of Britain from the root word for British and "Anu," after the Celtic mother goddess. She appeared on Roman coins, depicted with shield, helmet, and trident. She appears on British money to this day.

Gaia (Greek): The name of this goddess means "earth," and she is the Greek earth mother, titled "deep breasted" for her nurturing qualities. She created the universe, the gods, and the first race of humans. She was offered the first of the fruit and grain every year.

Epona (Gaulish): She is the horse-totem goddess of the Gauls, a sovereign lady of the land. She is also a mother and fertility goddess.

Érin (Irish): Érin is the personification of the island of Ireland. She is one of the queens of Ireland and the daughter of the Dagda. She was the wife of MacGreine, "son of the sun."

Macha (Irish): A sovereign goddess with horse aspects. She has a triple form: Macha, consort of Nemed; Macha, wife of Crunnchu; and Macha the Red. She is also known as Macha of the golden hair, signifying the corn. Her festival is August 1 and marks the harvesting of the grain. She is sometimes mentioned as one of the Morrigan triad.

Rhiannon (Welsh): Her name means "great queen," signifying she is a goddess of sovereignty. She is the Welsh fertility and horse goddess and rides a white horse (the moon or waves of the sea). Her seven blackbirds (the Pleiades) guide the soul of the sacred king/sacrificed corn god to the Otherworld.

THE HARVEST GODDESS

At this point in the Wheel of the Year, the Goddess becomes the mother who gives birth to the fruits of the land. She is Mother Nature, from whom all life emerges and who sustains all life. She is the earth itself, which bears fruit. (She appears as a virgin maiden at Imbolc, meets the young god at Ostara, and marries him when the earth flowers at Beltane. As the flowers are fertilized at Midsummer, earth and sky mate, and the goddess becomes pregnant.) She gives birth at Lughnasa, also called Bron Trograin, which means "the earth sorrows under its fruits," because mother earth suffers the pangs of birth in producing the fruits of the harvest, and also mourns the death of the vegetation god, killed with the cutting of the grain. The seeds are returned to the sorrowing earth, his mother. She is also the goddess of death, who wields the sickle that ends his life.

Harvest goddesses that may be honored at this time include:

Anat (Canaanite): She is the goddess of fertility who mated with her brother Baal — she in the form of a cow, he in the form of a bull — to ensure the fertility of the land.

Astarte (Canaanite): She is a fertility goddess, cognate with Ishtar. Lover of Adonis, her role was transferred to Aphrodite in Greek myth. Her cult was widely spread, and she had temples in Roman Britain.

Blodeuwedd (Welsh): The flower bride of Llew, Blodeuwedd is the personification of the flowering earth in summer. She becomes the winter hag after the completion of the harvest.

Ceres (Roman): This is the Roman corn goddess, whose festival was celebrated on August 1. Though she was originally a distinctive goddess from Campania, her story became assimilated to Demeter.

Ceridwen (Welsh): She is the Welsh moon, mother, grain, and initiation goddess, and owner of a magic cauldron in which she brewed a potion containing the wisdom of the entire world.

Demeter (Greek): The harvest goddess Demeter had a daughter called Kore (or some say Persephone). One day this girl was picking poppies when the god Hades stole her away and imprisoned her in his Underworld realm. Demeter sought her beloved daughter all over the length and breadth of the world, but because she was too distracted to carry out her duties, the earth became barren and sterile. Winter ruled. Then at last, overcome with weariness, she sat down for nine days and nights, and the gods caused poppies to spring all around her feet. Breathing in the soporific perfume, she fell asleep and rested. The gods, fearing for the future of the earth, ruled that Persephone could return to her mother providing she had not eaten anything while in the Underworld. Unfortunately, she had eaten six seeds from a pomegranate and so would have to stay in the Underworld for six months of the year, and this is why we have winter.

The name Demeter means "earth mother." She and her daughter together symbolise the flower and the fruit, life and the life to come, the manifest and the potential. The horse is sacred to her, as is the bee, the poppy, the snake, and the torch. The smith god Hephaestos made her sickle. The willow is sacred to Persephone and forms the scourge or bindings of the sacred king.

Several rites of Demeter and Persephone were celebrated all over Greece during the course of the year. At the Lesser Eleusinia in February, the maiden Kore returned from the Underworld and vegetation returned to the earth. At the Greater Mysteries in September, initiates processed to the temple, purified themselves in the sea, sacrificed pigs (a symbol of fertility) to the goddess, and contemplated a single ear of wheat, revealed with the words "behold the mystery." This mystery, of course, is the very one that underlies Lughnasa. A similar contemplation might form part of your Lughnasa celebration.

Isis (Egyptian): She is the queen of heaven and wife of the corn god Osiris. It is the appearance of Isis every year as the Dog Star, Sothis, that heralds the inundation of the Nile and the annual rebirth of Osiris. Isis has been worshipped for 3,500 years, and many of her myths and titles were transferred to the Christian Virgin Mary. She was the mother goddess who understood loss and suffering, listening sympathetically to the prayers of humans. Isis, Osiris, and their son, Horus, formed the Holy Family.

Her original Egyptian name, Aset, means "throne," as does the name of her husband, Osiris (Asir), associating them with royalty and sovereignty. She was also the mistress of magic and discoverer of many healing drugs. Her worship spread as far east as the Black Sea and as far west as York in England.

Sif (Norse): The golden hair of Sif represents the grain, cut when Loki, in his Dog Star aspect, is in the sky. She is the wife of Thor, the thunder god, who provides the fertilizing rain.

BATTLES AND GAMES

The ripening crops have to be protected from the forces of blight that come with the autumn and from the floods and winds associated with Lughnasa. In Irish mythology, this is symbolized by the battle between Lugh, the sun god, and Balor, a fearful one-eyed giant and leader of the Formorians, gods of blight. There are other stories of Lughnasa heroes fighting giants and winning their treasure (the harvest) at Lughnasa, including Tom Hackathrift in England's East Anglia, and Tom the Giant Killer. The fairy Phouka ("goat-head") represents another god of blight and spoils the berries after Lughnasa. Traces of this conflict are seen in the various battle customs associated with this time, such as the Battle of the Flowers in the Channel Isles, faction-fighting, and the competitive games of Lughnasa.

It is possible that the Lughnasa assemblies and fairs were wakes, mourning for the death of summer, or the death of the corn god, similar to the mourning for Tammuz/Adonis in the Mediterranean and Near East. The seasonal Lammas fairs in England were called wakes.

This old type of mourning ritual is still practiced in Ireland. A traditional Irish wake extends from the death of the person to the period when the body is taken to the church for burial. It is attended by friends and family and accompanied by food, tobacco, and, more importantly, alcohol. There is storytelling, singing, music, and dancing. It is thought that the wakes date back to Pagan Celtic days, and certainly, the church was always trying to put a stop to them, considering them unseemly and blasphemous. In the past the men often played raucous games.

The tradition of games at a funeral is an ancient one. It was the custom to mark the burial or cremation of a king or hero with competitions. The original Olympic Games were funeral games held every fourth year at Olympia in Elis in July.

In the more traditional branches of the Craft, Lammas is marked with games and contests. The victor of the games is declared king (or queen) and swears to protect the earth and his or her brothers and sisters of the Craft. The games can be great fun and may be arranged so that people of all levels of fitness and ability can compete. We have included some ideas for you in chapter 6.

WARRIOR MAGIC

In the Traditional Craft, Lughnasa is celebrated as the festival of the God before his decline and death with the reaping of the final sheaf of corn. It is the festival of man and "male" energies explored through competitions, battles, warrior magic, and hunting magic. It is the counterpoint to Imbolc, the festival of the Goddess, womankind, and "female" energies explored through spinning and weaving magic, crafts and skills, divination, poetry, and bardic inspiration.

We all have a male and female side to our personalities, and it is important to explore both of these. You can discover skills, qualities, and abilities that are hidden deep within.

We have written a whole chapter on warrior magic (chapter 7), but below are some warrior deities, both male and female, that you can call upon in your warrior quest.

Athene (Greek): Athene, or Athena, is a warrior goddess, depicted with helmet and shield. She was born fully formed and clad in armor, springing from the head of Zeus. One of her sacred tools is the sickle. She is patroness of Athens, architects, sculptors, spinners, and weavers. She invented the plow and the flute.

Bellona (Roman): This Roman battle goddess was the sister of Mars, the god of war. She had a temple in Rome near the gate of Carmenta in which there was a "war column." This had to be struck with a javelin when war was declared.

Cuchulain (Irish): The son or grandson of Lugh, Cuchulain ("Hound of Chulain") was the greatest warrior of Irish fable. He trained at Scathach's school for warriors where he learned the salmon's leap and mastered the art of throwing the *gaebolg*. He died the death of a sacred king, bound to a pillar and pierced by arrows while his blood fertilized the earth.

Heimdall (Norse): This Norse god was the champion of Freya and guardian of the Rainbow Bridge that led to Asgard, the home of the gods. When Loki stole Freya's necklace, she called on Heimdall's help. He chased Loki while they both shapeshifted into many forms, until finally he cornered Loki while both were in the form of seals. After a great battle, he retrieved the necklace.

Herakles/ Hercules (Greek): The son of Zeus and a mortal woman, Herakles had the strength of many men and was a remarkable warrior. He performed twelve great labors and, when he died, took his place among the gods on Olympus.

Scathach, Warrior Queen (British): One of the most fascinating characters in Celtic myth is Scathach nUanaind, the warrior woman, though, she is also described as a witch and a prophetess. Her name means "shadow," and she dwelt on Scathach's Island, the Land of Shadows, thought to be the Isle of Skye. She was titled the Amazon Witch Queen, and legend has it that she originated in Scythia, but chose to make her home in the Land of the Shadows, teaching her craft to the young warriors of Britain and Ireland. She knew every art of war and every weapon, every trick and every strategy. She was also a druidess and mistress of the arts of magic, prophecy, and shapeshifting.

Warriors often call upon the strength and powers of animals to help them, and this will be explored in chapter 7.

HUNTING MAGIC

Old Style Lughnasa is also the start of the hunting season, another kind of crop, and another reason for the sorrowing of Mother Earth. It is known as "the glorious twelfth," corresponding to Lughnasa Old Style. For Pagans, it was and is associated with gods of hunting and culling, such as Herne, with the stag god Cernunnos, and with Ker, the deer goddess.

In ancient times, hunting and killing was a mystical as well as a practical experience. Life, in necessity, preys on life, and this is a mystery in itself; venerated in a sacred manner; life would be reverenced as it was taken.

Arthur's knights would take part in a yearly hunt of the white stag, and its head would be presented to the fairest lady in the land. This is probably a seasonal tale of the battle between summer and winter. It was once thought that the "King Stag," leader of the herd, should be ritually hunted and killed every year to ensure the return of summer.

The Horned God is both Lord of the Animals and Herne the Hunter. The Lord of the Animals was associated with the annual cull of the herds, a process of purification to clear away the old growth in order to make way for the new. He is a sacrificial god, giving up the life of the stag for the good of the many, representing growth through sacrifice.

The Wiccan hunter does not seek to hunt and kill living animals but practices a different kind of hunting magic. He hunts for knowledge for his own soul. He is aided by the skills of the hunter: unwavering concentration on the object in hand, attention to detail, single-mindedness, a quest for the truth, the courage to pursue his quarry, and knowing what his quarry is.

The Wiccan hunter may practice with the bow to hone his concentration. He may study the habits of animals in order to learn from them and increase his respect for nature, spending time in the field and forests. He may work with animal powers in the form of totems and familiars as the warrior does. (See chapter 7.)

Hunting played a significant part in the training of warriors from early times onward to the chivalric mediaeval period. The hunter must blend into the background, utilize camouflaging skills, be aware of all the habits of the animals, and be in harmony with the environment.

Below are some deities of the hunt that you may call upon to help you with your quest.

Artemis (Greek): This virgin goddess of the moon and hunt was depicted as a tall slim girl driving a chariot drawn by silver stags. She carried a silver bow and strode through the forests, accompanied by her dogs. She was the patroness of the Amazons, or warrior maidens.

Britomartis (Cretan): She is a virgin huntress, daughter of Zeus. She escaped the attentions of King Minos by jumping off a cliff, being rescued from the sea in the nets of fishermen.

Cernunnos (Gaul): It is likely that this Celtic horned god was a fertility and hunting deity of the ordinary people, rather than the priesthood, as his names and legends do not come down to us. He is generally called Cernunnos from a single inscription on a carving in Gaul, probably a Latin version of a Celtic name. From the depiction of the Horned God, he is clearly the Lord of the Animals, always shown in the company of various beasts. He is sometimes shown holding a serpent and a torc (a Celtic horseshoe-shaped necklace), showing that he is a god of winter and summer, sky and Underworld, death and resurrection.

Devana (Slavonic): She is the Slavonic goddess of the hunt; a maiden goddess who hunts the forest accompanied by a pack of hounds. She is a form of the goddess Artemis/Diana.

Diana (Roman): Diana is the Roman goddess of the moon and hunt. At her sanctuary in Nemi, the priest was an escaped slave who had to fight and kill his predecessor. She is said to be a virgin, but this probably indicates the original meaning of the word "virgin." The Farrars speculate that she was a sacrificial-mating goddess.[4]

Herne (British): In Britain, the Horned God was called Kern or Herne. Herne the Hunter is said to still haunt Windsor Great Park and ride out with the Wild Hunt in winter. He is described as a mighty, bearded figure with a huge pair of stag horns on his head. He wears chains, carries a hunting horn, and rides on a black horse with a pack of ferocious hunting hounds. His name may have been discerned from the call that the hind makes to the stag in the mating season, "Hh-ern."

HOLY WELLS

The ancient powers of the Goddess can also be seen in the sacred nature of wells at Lughnasa. These are still honored with pilgrimages and well dressing in parts of England and Ireland. Wells and other openings were seen as entrances into the womb of the Goddess or, perhaps, birth canals. Many wells are said to have sprung from the hoof-strike of a white horse — the sovereign goddess herself — including St. Anne's Well at Carshalton in Surrey, and the one below the Uffington White Horse.[5]

These powers were activated at Lughnasa when people would seek the waters for healing or honor them by dressing the wells with flowers and decorative pictures made from blossoms. There is a meteor shower from the foot of the constellation of the white horse at Lughnasa, and this may be why wells are considered empowered and are dressed at this time.[6]

Though the wells were originally sacred to various Pagan goddesses, the Christian Church renamed them in honor of Christian saints, often thinly disguised goddesses.

A FINAL THOUGHT

In an age when crops can be imported all year round, we tend to forget just how important this time was to our ancestors; the failure of the harvest meant starvation and death. This is just as true today in many parts of the globe, as disturbing televised pictures of hungry children in the Third World show us. Let us remember them as we thank the gods for their bounty, and offer a prayer for the less fortunate and some practical aid in the form of a charitable donation.

Notes

1. An anonymous Welsh poem.
2. The three chief festivals being May Eve, Midsummer, and Halloween.
3. Montague Summers (1880-1948), *The History of Witchcraft & Demonology*, n/d.
4. Janet Farrar and Stewart Farrar, *The Witches' Goddess*, 1987.
5. Michael Bayley, *Caer Sidhe*, 1997.
6. Ibid. The constellation is Pegasus, but the Celts may have viewed it as Epona in horse form.

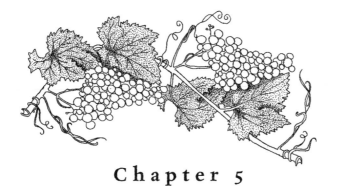

Chapter 5

Lughnasa Magic

O Lady, your breast is the field. Inanna, your breast is your field.
Your broad field pours out plants, your broad field pours out grain.
Water flows from on high for your servant.
Bread flows from on high for your servant.
Pour it out for me, Inanna. I will drink all you offer.[1]

OSIRIS HEALING SPELL

The ancient Egyptians would bury an Osiris doll covered in seeds, and when it sprouted in the growing season, they would know that the god had been reborn. You can use this ancient power of regeneration in a healing spell.

Take an oblong piece of cloth and cover it with quick-germinating seeds, edible ones such as aduki beans or mustard cress. Tie off the "head" and the "body" to make a vaguely human shape, saying:

As Osiris shoots and grows, so all things are reborn. As these seeds grow, let me grow in strength and health.

Water it, keeping it damp but not wet. In a few days the Osiris doll will be covered in fresh leaves and shoots. Eat these and visualize taking the strength and healing of Osiris within.

CORN DOLLIES

It was once believed that the spirit of the corn had to be preserved from one harvest to the next to ensure the success of the crops. The cutting of the final sheaf was particularly dangerous, because it contained the life spirit of the corn, which had retreated and retreated into the final stook (bound sheaf of grain). Sometimes the harvesters would approach it reverently with the call, "The neck," or sometimes, "The mare," and cut in a single stroke with the cry, "I have the neck." This was then carefully woven into a corn dolly, or kern-baby, which would preserve the corn spirit safely until the next year. It would be kept in a place of honor until the spring, when at Imbolc ears of corn would be taken from the doll and plowed into the fields to bring them life.

The earliest recorded instances of corn dollies date from the eighteenth dynasty of the ancient Egyptians (1570–1320 B.C.E.) and represented Osiris. The last sheaf was often plaited into a vaguely human shape or a more abstract and symbolic representation of the corn spirit. The British Celts called them *sanct ffraid ys ydd*, or "holy bride of the corn." In Welsh, the word for religion is *crefydd*, from *crefu*, "to implore for," and *ydd*, "corn."[2] Each locality developed its own variations on the basic theme of the plaited sheaf. There are dozens of different traditional designs, such as the Durham chandelier, the Northamptonshire horns, and the Suffolk horseshoe. The ribbons that bind it are significant for their colors: yellow for the sun, red for sacrifice, blue for love, green for wisdom, and white for strength.

Over the years, the ritual significance of the corn dolly decreased and making corn dollies became a widespread rural craft and folk art, with the designs becoming increasingly elaborate and varied. Corn dolly-making is still a popular hobby, and, nowadays, there are hundreds of different types of varying levels of complexity. Enthusiasts often spend many years collecting and learning new designs. Corn dollies are woven into representations of a wide variety of traditional symbols: bells, cornucopia, crosses, horns, horses, horseshoes, human figures, spirals, stars, and sun wheels.

The modern Pagan can relive something of the spirit of the harvest by making one of these ancient symbols each year. It can be placed on the altar at Lammas and at the autumn equinox Harvest Home festival. Afterward you can hang it in the kitchen until next spring, when it may be buried in the garden or just kept to remind you that what is sown will be harvested. This applies to all areas of life, not just farming.

The best wheat straw for making corn dollies should be taken from the field when it is almost ripe but not completely dry. Ideally, the lower part should still be slightly green. Hang it up in bunches for a day, and then remove the leaves, and cut off the head of the wheat just below the first joint. Sort the straw into bundles of similar length.

Just before beginning to plait the corn, it needs to be moistened by placing it in a container of lukewarm water for 20 to 30 minutes. Wrap it in a damp towel so that it remains moist. Only dampen the materials you need for each session, as the unused corn will otherwise become mildewed.

Depending on where you live, suitable straw may be difficult to obtain. Contact your local craft shop for raffia, as used in basket weaving. Raffia is available in a wide range of colors, and although not the traditional material, it can be fun to produce corn dollies and plaits using a selection of different colors.

Following are instructions for three dollies you can make, starting with the easiest. Study the diagrams before starting, and you should get a good idea of how they are constructed. All three designs really are simple.

Small Corn Dolly

This is a method of making the simplest corn dolly, and it is an ideal project for younger children.

5   8-inch (20 centimeters) hollow straws
4   4-inch (10 centimeters) hollow straws
Raffia

Take the five 8-inch straws and tie them in the middle. Fold the bunch in half and tie again to make the head. Take the four 4-inch straws and tie them together a short distance from the ends. These will form the arms of the figure. Slide this into the straws that form the body. Tie the ends of the longer straws to make the legs. This should give you a figure about 3 inches tall (7.5 centimeters). (See Figure 1.)

Mare or Cripple Goat

This design is traditional in several counties in the English West Midlands and Welsh borders. On the Isle of Skye, Scotland, this dolly was known as the Goabbir Bhacage, or Cripple Goat. It is one of the oldest English corn dollies and is easy to make.

1   small bunch of straw (with ears of grain)
1   large bunch of straw (twice the diameter of the small bunch)
Raffia

The ears on the larger bunch of straw should be spread out to give an impression of a horse's head and neck, with all the ears (seeds) of grain falling to one side to represent the mane. The ends of the stalks will form the hind legs. The smaller bunch will form the tail and the front legs. (See Figure 2.)

Divide the straws of the larger bunch into two parts and insert the smaller bunch, facing in the opposite direction. Both sets of stalks should protrude farther than the ears.

Tie the bunches together with raffia in-between each bunch of ears, to make a body about 4 inches long (10 centimeters). Bend the stalks downward at either end and divide these in two to make the legs. Bind the legs together with raffia. When finished, your mare should stand about 8 inches tall (20 centimeters).

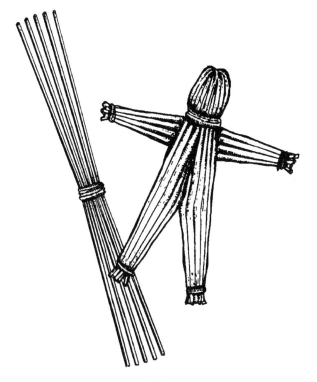

Figure 1

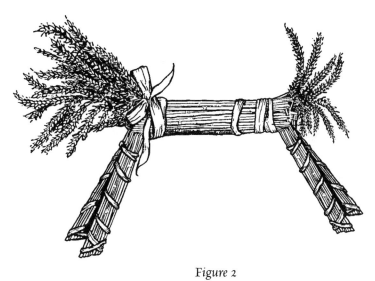

Figure 2

Corn Maiden

This one is a little more complicated and produces a typical corn dolly.

> 1 bunch of wheat straw, 12 inches long, 4 inches in diameter
>   at the top, and 7 inches in diameter at the base
>   (30 cm / 10 / 18 centimeters)
> 1 small bunch of wheat straw (for the arms)
>   wheat straw with seeds (for the face and head, shoulders,
>   and waist)
>   String, dampened
> 1 piece of elastic (such as a rubber band)

Take the 12-inch bunch of the straw and tie it together at the three lower portions as shown in Figure 3. This will form the head and neck of the maiden. Trim the top to a point and trim the bottom so that it is even.

Take a smaller bunch of straw and make sure that it is even in thickness. Tie this bundle in the middle and around each end. Poke it through the maiden's body to form the arms. (See Figure 3.) Tie it in place around the neck. Now you have the basic structure and you can begin to elaborate.

To represent the face and head, arrange a bunch of grain with the seeds (ears) still on, and tie it just below the seeds. (See Figure 4.) If you wish, you could use a variety of different types of grain (such as barley, wheat, oats and rye), which will give you a different effect.

Set this bunch firmly on the head of your maiden and arrange it into the most effective shape. Tie it onto the figure both above and below the arms. (See Figure 4.) Be careful not to give the maiden too long of a neck.

Loop a bunch of straw over each arm to form the shoulders. Tie this at the shoulders and waist. (See Figure 4.)

Tie a piece of elastic around the waist of the maiden. Take some even-sized wheat straws with the ears still attached and arrange these around the base of the maiden, holding them in place with the elastic. This forms the skirt. (See Figure 5, page 92.) When all the straws are in position, tie them off just above the seeds and at the maiden's waist.

Figure 3

Figure 4

Figure 5

Figure 6

Tie the arms to make elbows and wrists; if necessary, shorten them so that they are in proportion with the body.

The basic corn dolly is now complete. It can now be decorated with flowers and ribbons as desired.

To finish it off, why not make a "Rose of England" hair plait (see Figure 6). You can use either straw or raffia for this.

Take a thin bunch of straw and tie it to a door handle, divide into three, and plait it as you would braid hair, left strand over the center strand, then right over center, then left over center again, etc. (Practice with three strands of string if you are unsure how to plait).

As you come to the ends, introduce replacements, inserting the new straw on top. When your plait is about 4-feet long (120-centimeters), tie off the ends and trim them. Place it on a damp towel and roll it well with a bottle or rolling pin, so that it becomes more flexible.

While it is still damp, loop it as shown in Figure 6. (Practice the loop using string before you try it with the straw.)

Attach to the back of the maiden's head with a needle and thread. Arrange the ends of the plaits to hang down in front of the maiden's shoulders. (See Figure 5.)

If you wish, you can make shorter plaits to stitch in place around the waist of the doll and above the ears of grain on the skirt, or use colored raffia. (See Figure 5.)

Lammas Gloves

It was once a custom to give a pair of gloves as a present at Lammas. Farmers gave gloves or glove-silver (money) to the harvesters. A glove was often raised on a pole at the Lammas fairs as a sign that the event was in progress.

Gloves feature widely in custom and folklore, often as a symbol of authority or intent. For example, putting on your gloves is a sign that you are leaving somewhere. If you forget to take your gloves when you leave a house and have to go back for them, you must sit down before putting on the gloves, or you will never return to that place again.[3] During the Middle Ages, a glove might be thrown down as a challenge to honor; to pick it up was to accept the challenge. In later ages, to be struck with a glove meant a challenge to a duel. If a friend has been dragged into a fairy ring, toss one of your gloves inside, and the revelers will disperse.

You could revive the old custom and give someone whose friendship or work you respect a pair a gloves. In the mediaeval period, it was the custom to scent fine gloves. You can use the opportunity to work a little magic into them.

2   small rounds of white cloth, about 4 inches in diameter
        (10 centimeters)
    Red ribbon (for friendship)
    Orris root powder (to fix the sachets)
    Rose petals (for love and friendship)
    Drop of orange oil (for energy)
    Sandalwood chips (for harmony)
    Cloves (for bonding)

Mix the ingredients together with your hand, saying:

> *Hear my words and see my actions,*
> *Ancient Goddess*
> *I invoke you in your shrine*
> *Stretching from earth to the heavens*
> *I beg blessing of you, friendship and love*
> *Hear my prayer on this Lammas Day*
> *Bless these talismans that I prepare*
> *In love.*

Place the mixture in two roughly equal parts on the two rounds of cloth. Tie up the cloths with ribbon and slip one inside each glove.

Lughnasa Bracelets

This is based on an Irish tradition from Croc na Béaltaine in County Donegal, where the young men would gather bilberries and thread them through the stalks to make bracelets for their girlfriends by way of a love spell.

Ideally you should use firm berry fruits with their stalks attached. Take a needle and strong cotton or nylon thread to make the bracelet. Seeds, grains, nuts, corn, or ears of wheat can also be used. Or try a mixture and see who can produce the most decorative. To add to the fun, make a necklace of fruit and eat it while your partner is wearing it.

Traditional Ash Charms

The ash is the tree totem of Lughnasa, sacred to Lugh as the alder tree is sacred to Balor. At Lughnasa we have the ash and alder in oppositions, reminiscent of the holly and oak at Yule and Midsummer, which is probably more familiar to Pagans. There are a variety of traditional spells and charms associated with the ash.

Ash Dream Divination

In Lancashire (northern England), triple leaves plucked from the common ash were used by girls to cause prophetic dreams of future lovers. The spell worked better if the ash had an even number of branches on each side of the tree — count them! Put an ash leaf beneath your pillow, saying:

> *Even-ash, even-ash, I pluck thee,*
> *This night my own true love to see,*
> *Neither in his bed nor in the bare,*
> *But in the clothes he does every day wear.*

Pin Healing Spell

The ash was a tree of healing, a tradition preserved in folklore. The ash tree reputedly had the ability to cure disease by taking it from the sufferer. The following is a very old healing spell for the cure of warts, pimples, boils, and other skin problems.

Wear a pin for three days, then go to an ash tree and say:

> *Ashen tree, ashen tree, pray buy this sickness of me.*

Insert the pin into the tree. The disease will appear as knobs on the tree and you will then be free of it.

Ash Leaf Charm

A Cornish (southern England) tradition is that a leaf from an even ash (one that has the same number of branches on each side) is a particularly lucky charm, as are leaves with an even number of leaflets. Pick the leaf, saying:

Even ash, I do thee pluck,
Hoping thus to meet good luck.
If no good luck I get from thee,
I shall wish thee on the tree.

Keep the leaf in your purse or wallet.

ASH STAFF

The wood of the ash is used to make staffs. It is no coincidence that wizards and shamans everywhere are depicted with a staff, though its purpose is rarely understood. It is not a fancy walking stick or an accessory to make the magician look more imposing. The staff is a portable world tree, or *axis mundi*, which connects the magician to the three magical realms of the heavens, middle earth, and the Underworld. The world tree grows with its roots in the Underworld, its trunk in middle earth, and its branches in the heavens, connecting all three. A staff is a symbolic pole with the same purpose.

A staff should be a wooden pole the same height as you are and wide enough for your hand to curl comfortably around it. Strip the bark from it, and polish with a cloth. If you wish, it might be carved with your personal symbols, but it should not have any crystals incorporated into it.

Consecrating a Staff

A staff may be consecrated with Consecration Incense (see page 113) and with the following words:

God and Goddess, deign to bless this staff which I would consecrate and set
aside. Let it obtain the necessary virtues to link all the realms of the Lord and
Lady, the Heavens, Middle Earth and the Underworld. I consecrate this staff in

*the names of the Lord and Lady. God and Goddess, I call upon you to bless this
staff which I have prepared in your honor.*

Plant the end in the ground and say, "Let blessing be." Use the new staff as soon
as possible.

Making a Stang

A variation on the staff is the stang, a forked staff or stave, favored by some witches.
You will need to find a long, straight ash branch that ends in an even two-pronged
fork. The straight part should stand shoulder height, then cut the forks to a length
of 6 or 9 inches (9 or 24 centimeters) to form the horns of the stang. Peel off the
bark and allow the staff to season before polishing. Do not varnish it, or you will seal
off some of its power. Do not add crystals, but you can add feathers, shells, ribbons,
etc. if you really want to, though it is traditional to keep it plain.

The stang represents the Horned God. It may be used in the circle, when it is
planted in the ground and decorated with seasonal greenery. At Yule, it stands in the
north of the circle, at Imbolc northeast, at Ostara east, Beltane southeast, Midsummer south, Lughnasa southwest, autumn equinox west, and Samhain northwest.

VERVAIN

Vervain (*Verbena officinalis*) must be picked in the morning at the rising of the Dog
Star to be magically effective. It was one of the most sacred herbs of the druids, who
used it in lustral water to cleanse their altars and sacred spaces.

Vervain Lustral Water

| ½ c | ½ oz. | 12 g | dried or fresh vervain |
| 2 c. | 12 fl. oz. | 400 m | boiling water |

Infuse for 15 minutes and strain. Use the water for cleansing your temple and
magical tools. (Note: The measurements given are in US, imperial, and metric,
respectively.)

SPELLS

Hilltop Rainbow Spell

7   ribbons, 12 inches long (30 centimeters), one in each of the
following colors: white, violet, blue, green, yellow, orange, red

The seven ribbons represent the seven chakras, or energy centers, of your body. Red is the root chakra, which governs physical energy in your body. Orange is the spleen chakra, which relates to sexuality and levels of vitality. Yellow is the solar plexus chakra, which relates to the mental aspect of your emotional life. Green is for the heart chakra, which is concerned with how you give and receive love. Blue is for the throat chakra, which is concerned with communication. Violet is for the third eye chakra concerned with psychic ability. White is the crown chakra; it relates to your spirituality and unites the actions of all the other chakras.

Take the seven ribbons, go to the top of a hill, and holding the ribbons tightly in one hand, let the wind blow through them. Feel its power as it rushes past you, chasing through the trees and grass. Feel the power of the hill itself, raised above the surrounding countryside. Let its power enter you through the soles of your bare feet and rise up through you. Say:

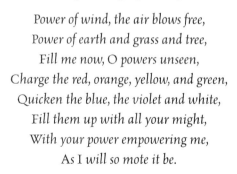

Power of wind, the air blows free,
Power of earth and grass and tree,
Fill me now, O powers unseen,
Charge the red, orange, yellow, and green,
Quicken the blue, the violet and white,
Fill them up with all your might,
With your power empowering me,
As I will so mote it be.

Release the power into your fluttering ribbons. Take the ribbons home and tie a knot in one end. Hang them above your bed, or place them on your altar so that you can draw on the power of the spell when you need it.

Lammas Bread Wish Spell

Make a loaf of bread at Lammas, and before you put the loaf into the oven, dip a paintbrush in milk and write on the crust what you most desire. Bake the bread, and then eat it while it's still warm.

Lammas Bread Protection Spell

A book of Anglo-Saxon charms advised the crumbling of the Lammas loaf into four pieces and the burying of them in the four corners of the barn to make it safe for all the grain that would be stored there.[4] You can use this old spellcraft in a protection spell for your home.

Bake a Lammas loaf, and when it is cool, break it into four pieces—don't cut it with a knife. Take one to each corner of your property, saying the words:

I call on the spirits
Of north and south, east and west
Protect this place
Now, at the time of the Blessing.

Leave the bread for the birds to eat or bury the pieces.

Rowan Cross Protection Spell

Lammas is one of the times when farmers and cottagers would renew protection on their homes, byres, and barns by putting a rowan cross above the door. Two twigs of rowan are tied with red thread and hung up with the words:

Red thread and rowan wood
Out evil, in good.

Spell to Gain Courage

If you find that your life is constrained by your timidity, or perhaps if you are facing a difficult and frightening situation, try the following spell that calls on the strength of the bull and boar to help you. You will need:

6-inch (15-centimeter) square of orange cloth
Red thread or ribbon
Pinch of dried thyme
Pinch of fried basil
A few black peppercorns
A few drops of orange oil

Lay out the cloth and sprinkle the thyme, basil, peppercorns, and orange oil onto it, saying:

> *The strength of bull, the daring of boar*
> *Grant me courage, now and more*
> *Grant me bravery in my life each day*
> *To follow my path and have my say.*

Tie up the sachet with the red thread or ribbon and keep it near you. Keep it in your bag or pocket, and place it beneath your pillow when you sleep. Every full moon, replace the herbs and oil. When the sachet has served its purpose, untie the knot and bury it.

BIRD AUSPICES

If you are on top of a hill at Lammas, this is a good time to practice the ancient art of bird augury, though it can be performed anywhere in the open air. In ancient Rome, special augers were employed to interpret the future from the behavior of birds: their appearance in unexpected places, their flight, and their calls.

Generally speaking, birds flying straight toward you indicate good luck, while birds flying in from the left indicate delays or bad luck, but it may depend on the type of bird. Here are some examples.

Blackbird: This bird indicates a message from the higher powers. Note the direction of the bird's flight: from the left and you are being warned to behave better, from the right and you will receive a blessing.

Corncrake: As the fields are cleared at the harvest, the corncrake is flushed out, and its screech a cry of omen. If it makes a frequent rasping note, rain is due. If it is heard calling in a nearby field, it heralds bad fortune.

Crane: In Ireland, the unexpected appearance of a crane was thought to herald the cessation of hostilities in a war. If you suddenly see a crane, it means a disagreement will be resolved. A flight of cranes in a triangular formation means that business matters will be profitably handled.

Crow: A cawing crow flying about a house indicates a death. A flock of crows flying from the woods indicates bad times ahead. In some parts of England, the rhymes relating to the magpie (one for sorrow, two for joy, etc.) are applied to the crow, and to see a single crow is very unlucky.

Curlew: Sailors used to think that the cry of the curlew was a warning from a drowned comrade, and that when a curlew flies overhead calling, a storm is brewing at sea and it is unwise to sail. It is a sinister omen for anyone who hears it calling at night.

Dove: If a dove appears from the right, this indicates luck in love and, perhaps, a marriage. In mediaeval times, the dove was a good omen or friendly warning. Miners would not go down a pit if a dove was seen near it. Doves were thought to be death omens if they circled someone's head.

Duck: It is lucky to see one before embarking on a journey. A duck and drake seen together announce the union of lovers and mutual happiness.

Gull: If a gull touches you as it flies by, it is a bad omen for someone close to you.

Hawk: If the hawk appears from the left, beware of the activities of your enemies.

Hen: A crowing hen heralds evil, since she is expropriating the function of the rooster. If one crows near the house or roosts at an unusual time, it presages very bad luck. In the English Midlands, it was thought that hens could foretell the death of the farmer; on the day of his demise, they will roost at midday instead of the usual time. Hens also predict the weather; if they gather on a mound and preen their feathers, rain is on the way.

Kingfisher: If it appears from the left, scandal threatens; from the right, a magical experience.

Magpie: Magpies are considered to be important birds of omen, hence, the old fortunetelling rhyme:

One for sorrow
Two for joy
Three for a girl
Four for a boy
Five for silver
Six for gold
Seven for a secret, never to be told
Eight's a wish
And nine's a kiss!

It is unlucky to see a magpie when setting off on a journey. The bad luck presaged by the appearance of a single magpie may be averted by greeting it with the cry "Good day lord magpie!"

Owl: If an owl hoots three times near you, this is an omen of bad luck or illness. If one appears during the daylight, disaster looms.

Nightjar: In parts of England, the nightjar is known as the "Corpse Fowl" and is regarded as a bird of misfortune. To hear its cry at night is a bad omen.

Raven: If ravens are seen flying toward each other, it is an omen of quarrels. In Wales, it is thought that if a raven perches on the roof, it means prosperity for the family. If a girl sees a raven at Lammas, she can tell the direction of her future husband's home from its flight; it will come from his point of the compass. In Ireland, ravens with white feathers were believed to be birds of good omen. It was especially favorable to see a raven with white on its wings, flying on one's right hand and croaking simultaneously. If you hear a raven before setting out on a journey, you will achieve all you want from the trip.

Robin: It is an omen of death if a robin flies into a house through a window. If one should tap on the windowpane of an ill person, they get worse. If you see one sheltering in a tree or hedge, rain is on the way. If it sits on an open branch chirping, good weather is coming.

Rook: It means good luck if rooks settle on your land. They are said to be able to predict the future; they know when the tree in which they are nesting is about to fall and will move. If rooks leave an area where they have been settled, it is a bad omen for the landowners—it means that no heir will be born. If they build high, the summer will be fine; if low, the weather will be wet and cold. If they perch together, facing the wind, a storm is on the way.

Rooster: You might not be able to see a rooster from the top of your hill, but there is a wealth of lore surrounding the calls of roosters. A crowing rooster as you go off to work signals a good day. If a rooster crows early in the evening, it means bad weather. If it crows late at night, it means a death in the family. If a rooster crows facing the door of a house, a stranger will arrive. If it stays on its perch, rain is imminent.

Stork: Its German name *adebar* means "luck bringer," and a stork perching on your house indicates very good fortune.

Sparrow: If two sparrows appear from the right, this is good luck for lovers.

Swallow: They generally mean good fortune. If a swallow flies into a house, it brings joy with it. It is bad luck if the swallow deserts its nest. If a swallow is disturbed, it means a bad harvest. To see swallows fighting is a bad portent.

Wagtail: It is good luck when it approaches from the right.

CRYSTAL HOME PROTECTION

Lammas is an ideal time for protection spells and rituals. This spell uses crystals to protect, calm, or energize the various rooms of your home.

When you have chosen your crystals (based on the recommendations that follow), wash them in running water to rid them of any vibrations they may have picked up before you obtained them.

Place them in a prominent place in the selected room. The windowsill is ideal, as the light of the sun and moon will keep your crystals charged with energy. The gem you use for the bedroom might be placed on the bedside table or even under your pillow.

Place each stone in position, saying: "Protect this space and all the people that enter it."

Once a month, preferably at the waning moon, repeat the cleansing process so that any negative energies stored are washed away, and your living space is left clear and harmonious.

Bedroom: There are several stones that are useful in the bedroom. The lovely purple amethyst will help you fall asleep and bring good dreams. It will help calm you down and "de-stress" you after the rigors of the day. On the other hand, the blood-red ruby excites sexuality and strengthens the relationship between a couple. Turquoise (a blue-green stone) helps to bring together a man and wife who have quarreled.

Child's bedroom: The delicate pink-rose quartz gently calms a fractious child and brings peaceful sleep. The dark blue sodalite will be calming and cooling for a feverish child or will simply help a child to sleep on a hot summer night. Jasper, an opaque green form of quartz, will prevent nightmares.

Family room: Place blue lace agate in the family room. It promotes harmony and smoothes quarrels. Sardonyx is a reddish-brown stone, surmounted by a layer of white chalcedony, which can help make a cantankerous person more tractable. Avoid smoky quartz in the home — it can cause arguments and stress.

Dining room: Placed in the dining room, raspberry quartz will aid food digestion. Green jade also aids digestion and promotes good health and good fellowship.

Another green stone, malachite, will help prevent digestion troubles, such as indigestion, colic, and intestinal cramps.

Kitchen: The kitchen is often the hub of the home where everyone gathers. Keep a tiger's-eye stone on the windowsill to foster close bonds between members of the family, stimulate individual responsibility, and to help everyone recognize their faults. It helps dispel negativity. Tiger's-eye protects the family's possessions and wealth. Be sure to keep some unikite nearby as this pink and green feldspar awakens love in the heart chakra and heals emotional hurts. It helps to balance the emotions.

Home office: If you work at home, then certain crystals may help improve your concentration, creativity, and attract business. Jacinth, a red-orange gem, will keep you alert and help attract money and success. Green aventurine is useful for creative people such as writers and artists. The green of the stone has the added benefit of attracting money.

SUN CATCHERS

Lammas is also a good time to hang crystals, faceted glass, and sun catchers in the windows of your house. These deflect negative energy and shed cheerful rainbows throughout your rooms.

DIVINATION FROM ASHES

If a bonfire or barbecue forms part of your Lughnasa celebration, you can rake out the fine ashes and use them for divination. Take a handful and shake them at random onto a piece of cleared ground or white paper. Look carefully and read from the shapes the ashes have made. Try to figure out the shapes before looking them up to avoid being influenced.

Acorn: Good fortune in all areas.

Anchor: Travel.

Ants: A variety of small problems.

Anvil: Hard work needed to succeed.

Apple: Choices in love.

Arrow: Sacrifice.

Axe: Danger ahead.

Baby: New beginnings.

Ball: Restiveness.

Basket: Gifts and favors.

Bat: Bad luck ahead.

Bees: Busy times.

Bell: Happy marriage or engagement.

Birds: Good news.

Book: Study, new knowledge.

Boot: A house move.

Bottle: Ill health.

Branch: New friendships.

Bridge: Disagreements resolved.

Broom: New start.

Butterfly: Fleeting happiness.

Button: New friend.

Cage: Frustrated desires.

Castle: Secret desires fulfilled.

Cat: Independence.

Clouds: Dilemmas.

Clover: Good luck.

Coffin: Failure or death.

Comet: Unforeseen events, visitors.

Cow: Nurture, prosperity.

Cradle: A new baby.

Crocodile: A false friend.

Cross: Suffering.

Crown: Inheritance.

Dagger: Danger, malicious gossip.

Dog: Loyal friends.

Dots: Money.

Dragonfly: Help from unexpected quarters.

Drum: Quarrels.

Eggs: Affluence, fruitfulness, and accomplishment.

Elephant: Wisdom.

Eye: Watch out!

Feather: Impermanence, instability.

Fence: Limits and restrictions.

Fire: Anger.

Fish: A very lucky omen.

Flowers: Wishes granted.

Fly: Domestic worries.

Forked line: Decisions to be made.

Fox: Cunning will be needed.

Frog: Recovery from illness.

Garter: Marriage.

Glove: Authority.

Goblet: Gift.

Gun: Attacks.

Hammer: Ruthlessness.

Harp: Happiness at home.

Hat: New job.

Horn: Guardianship.

Horse: Travel with a loved one.

Horseshoe: Protection.

House: Security.

Kettle: Domestic tranquility.

Key: New opportunities.

Knots: Restriction.

Ladder: Progress.

Leaf: Growth.

Lion: Influential friends.

Moon: Love.

Mouse: Poverty.

Moustache: Untrustworthy man.

Nail: Injustice.

Rabbit: Timidity.

Razor: The end of a friendship.

Ring: Marriage, happiness, and completion.

Scissors: Endings, disappointments.

Sickle: You reap what you have sown.

Skull: Endings.

Snake: Good luck.

Spade: Hard work.

Spider: Money.

Spoon: A surprise.

Squirrel: Messages.

Star: Hopes and wishes.

Swan: Stormy times ahead.

Table: Setting up house.

Telephone: Communication.

Tobacco pipe: Unfaithful lover.

Umbrella: Help from an authority figure.

Walking stick: Fortunate journey.

ANNA'S LUGHNASA INCENSES

Incense consists of herbs, woods, and resins burned to release perfumed smoke as offerings to the gods. Different perfumes also affect the senses of the magician, inducing the mood required and concentrating the mind on the ritual. On a more esoteric level is the effect of the vibration of the perfume. When something vibrates at a given frequency, any object near it will begin to vibrate with the same frequency, a principle used in both healing and in magic. Each plant, like every crystal or stone, has a particular vibration. When we use an incense or oil, it is for the purpose of changing the vibration of the atmosphere to the level needed for a specific magical operation, not because it has a "nice smell."

There are several types of incenses, including the familiar joss sticks and incense cones. Loose incense is probably the easiest type of incense to make and the most useful kind for magical ritual. The recipes in this book are all for loose incense.

Making the Incense

First of all, assemble your ingredients and tools: your pestle and mortar, mixing spoons, and jars (glass) and labels.

All the measurements in these recipes are by volume, not weight. I use a spoon to measure out small quantities when I am making a single jar of incense, and a cup for large quantities and big batches. Therefore, if the recipe says:

> 3   parts frankincense
> ½   part thyme
> 1   part myrrh

This means 3 spoons of frankincense, ½ spoon of thyme, and 1 spoon of myrrh. When using resins and essential oils, these should be combined first, stirring lightly with the pestle, and left to go a little sticky before you add any woods, barks, and crushed berries. Next, add any herbs and powders and, lastly, any flowers.

Charging the Incense

As you blend the incense, concentrate on the purpose for which the incense will be used, and "project" this into the blend. If you like, you can make a whole ritual of the event, perhaps even picking and drying your own herbs, then laying out the tools and ingredients on the altar, lighting a candle, and asking the God and Goddess for help:

> *God and Goddess, deign to bless this incense which I would consecrate in your names.*
> *Let it obtain the necessary virtues for acts of love and beauty in your honor.*
> *Let Blessing Be.*

The incenses should then be stored in screw-topped glass jars.

Burning Incenses

Loose incense is burned on individual self-igniting charcoal blocks or thrown directly onto the bonfire. To use your incenses, take a self-igniting charcoal block (available from occult and church suppliers) and apply a match to it. It will begin to spark across its surface and eventually glow red. Place it on a flameproof dish with a mat or pad underneath (it will get very hot). When the charcoal block is glowing, sprinkle a pinch of the incense on top—a little goes a long way.

Lughnasa Incense

- 1   part benzoin resin
- 1   part myrrh resin
- 1   part oak wood
- ½   part heather flowers
- ¼   part basil
- ½   part borage flowers
- 2   parts frankincense
  A few drops pine oil

Lammas Incense

- 1   part oak bark
- ½   part pine resin
  A few drops oak moss oil
- 2   parts red sandalwood
- 1   part cedar wood
  A few drops cedar oil
- 3   parts frankincense
- ½   part sunflower petals

Lugh Incense

3   parts frankincense
1   part oak bark
1   part ash wood
¼   part poppy seeds
1   part heather flowers
    A few drops red wine
1   part barley grains, crushed

Llew Llaw Gyffes Incense
(Welsh, son of Arianrhod)

½   part borage flowers and leaves
1   part hazel wood
½   part holly wood
1   part crushed rowan berries
1   part oak bark
4   parts frankincense
    A few drops oak moss oil
    A few drops cedar oil

Horned God Incense

1 part cedar wood
1 part benzoin
1 part pine resin
1 part frankincense
2 parts crushed juniper berries
   A few drops oak moss oil

Courage Incense

3 parts frankincense
½ part borage leaves and flowers
   Pinch of dragon's blood powder
¼ part thyme
   A few drops orange oil

Warrior Incense

4 parts frankincense
½ part borage
¼ part basil leaves
¼ part fennel seeds
½ part sunflower petals
½ part nasturtium petals
1 part ash wood
   A few drops of juniper oil

Consecration Incense

3 parts frankincense
1 part myrrh
1 part sandalwood
   A few drops cedar oil

Adonis Incense
(Greek Vegetation God)

½ part fir needles

1 part myrrh

½ part anemone flowers

2 parts frankincense

1 part acacia resin

A few drops bay oil

½ part narcissus flowers

Aphrodite Incense
(Greek Goddess of Love)

½ part cypress needles

A few drops cypress oil

3 parts benzoin

½ part red rose petals

1 part apple wood

½ part cinnamon sticks

¼ part daisy flowers

A few drops geranium oil

¼ part violet flowers

Arianrhod Incense
(Welsh Goddess of the Moon, Initiation, and Rebirth)

½ part ivy leaves and stems

2 parts oak bark

½ part flax flowers

2 parts frankincense

2 parts myrrh

A few drops rose oil (optional)

Astarte Incense
(Canaanite Fertility Goddess)

3 parts acacia resin
1 part myrtle blossoms
1 part pine wood
½ part pine resin
½ part rose petals
 A few drops rose oil

Attis Incense
(Anatolian Vegetation God)

1 part pine resin
2 parts myrrh
3 parts pine wood
¼ part almond blossoms
¼ part narcissus flowers
½ part fir needles
¼ part heather flowers
 A few drops myrrh oil

Blodeuwedd Incense
(Welsh Flower Goddess)

1 part broom flowers
1 part bean flowers
1 part horse chestnut flowers
1 part oak flowers
1 part meadowsweet flowers
1 part flowering nettle
1 part primrose flowers
1 part hawthorn flowers
1 part flowering burdock
1 part blackthorn flowers
1 part corncockle flowers

Ceres Incense
(Roman Corn Goddess)

½ part bay laurel leaves

½ part wheat grains

½ part poppy seeds

3 parts willow wood

1 part chaste tree leaves

½ part narcissus flowers

2 parts frankincense

2 parts myrrh

Crom Dubh Incense
(Irish God of Corn and Underworld)

3 parts myrrh

1 part wheat grains

1 part oak bark

1 part crushed dried bilberries or rowan berries

½ part fern

  A few drops cypress oil

Demeter Incense
(Greek Corn Goddess)

½ part grains of wheat

½ part rose petals

2 parts frankincense

2 parts myrrh

½ part pennyroyal herb

½ part bean flowers (optional)

½ part red poppy petals or seeds

½ part cypress needles

  A few drops rose oil (optional)

  A few drops cypress oil

Dionysus Incense
(Thracian/Greek God of Vegetation/Wine/Fertility)

- 1 part apple blossom
- ½ part ivy leaves
- 1 part pine resin
  A few drops pine oil
- ½ part fir needles
- ½ part fennel leaves
- ½ part vine leaves
- 2 parts myrrh
  A very few drops of red wine

Inanna Incense
(Sumerian Queen of Heaven)

- 2 parts mixed cereal grains
- 1 part date palm leaves
- 1 part vine leaves
- 1 part flax flowers
- 4 parts myrrh
  A few drops juniper oil
- 3 parts crushed juniper berries
  Pinch of cinnamon powder

Ishtar Incense
(Semitic Queen of Heaven)

- 2 parts acacia resin
- 1 part mixed cereal grains
- ½ part date palm leaves
- ½ part vine leaves
- 1 part frankincense
  A few drops frankincense oil (optional)

Isis Incense
(Egyptian Queen of Heaven)

½ part heather

5 parts myrrh

½ part rose petals

¼ part vervain

¼ part wormwood

¼ part orris root powder

½ part ivy leaves

A few drops geranium oil

¼ part horehound

¼ part olive leaves

½ part white willow bark

2 parts cedar wood

A few drops cedar oil

½ part cypress needles

¼ part poppy seeds or petals

Pinch of dragon's blood powder

Odin Incense
(Scandinavian Chief God)

3 parts frankincense

2 parts ash wood

½ part mistletoe

1 part oak wood

½ part amaranth (optional)

½ part storax

1 part elm wood

Osiris Incense
(Egyptian Vegetation God)

3 parts frankincense
2 parts acacia resin
1 part pine resin
½ part storax
½ part ivy leaves
1 part willow wood
2 parts cedar wood
½ part horehound
¼ part nettle
½ part dittany of Crete
½ part heather flowers
   A few drops marjoram oil

Persephone/Proserpina Incense
(Greek/Roman Goddess of the Underworld)

4 parts myrrh
2 parts willow wood
½ part red poppy flowers or seeds
¼ part cypress needles
   A few drops cypress oil
½ part dried pomegranate rind
¼ part parsley
½ part forget-me-not flowers (optional)
   A few drops myrrh oil

Venus Incense
(Roman Goddess of Love)

1   part benzoin
1   part pine resin
4   parts frankincense
4   parts red sandalwood
     Pinch of cinnamon powder
1   part red rose petals
¼   part myrtle blossom (optional)
¼   part violet flowers
¼   part white lily flowers (optional)
¼   part daisy flowers
     A few drops geranium oil
     A few drops rose oil (optional)

Vulcan Incense
(Roman Smith God)

½   part wood aloe
1   part red poppy seeds or petals
½   part nettle leaves
4   parts frankincense
¼   part mustard seeds
1   part cedar wood
     Pinch of dragon's blood powder

Wake Incense

4   parts myrrh
¼   part forget-me-not flowers (optional)
¼   part rue
¼   part rosemary
¼   part parsley
     A few drops cypress oil

PAUL'S NATURAL DYES

This is the traditional time of the year for gathering natural materials for dyemaking. Before the invention of synthetic dyes, plants were the major source of colorings for clothing, paints, and stains. Ever since the cave paintings of prehistoric times, humans have produced pigments from naturally occurring materials for both decorative and ritualistic purposes. One of the best-known examples of these plant dyes is the woad of the ancient Celts. Other users of herbal pigments for coloring fabrics and for bodily decoration were the Native Americans.

Dyeing was a magical process to the ancient Celts. It was a woman's craft, and there were strict taboos on dyeing fabric in the presence of men. There were additional rules on the proper days on which to dye fabric. Dyeing was closely associated with herbalism and healing, many of the plants used also had healing or psychotropic properties. The old Irish Gaelic word for dyestuffs was *ruaman*, from *ruam* meaning "red," probably originating with the Celts' love of vivid colors.

Not all colors were available to ancient cultures. There are a wide range of substances that will produce various shades of brown, fawn, and tan. There are fewer natural pigments that give reds and yellows, and fewer still that produce blues and greens. Tyrian purple, extracted from a small gland in a species of Mediterranean shellfish, was the rarest of all — 8,500 shellfish being needed to produce 1 gram of dye.

You can use your dyes to color magical robes, cords, and altar cloths.

Herbal Dyes

Many plants contain coloring materials. As children we must all have stained our hands with juice from berries. The first dyes probably originated from food stains in exactly this manner. The simplest way of extracting these dyes is by boiling the plant material in water. The problem with this method is that the color produced is not permanent and will soon wash out or fade. Our ancestors may have overcome this difficulty by the lengthy process of repeatedly dyeing and drying the fabric over a period of weeks. Some dyes, woad for example, were fixed by being fermented in stale urine — not a pleasant process to our modern sensibilities.

Dyes can now be made more colorfast by the use of a mordant. This is the term for a chemical, often a metallic compound, which fixes a dye. These substances produce another problem, that of their environmentally safe disposal. Think very carefully before using mordants; if ancient cultures could manage without them, then so should we.

Fortunately, simple household substances such as vinegar, baking soda, cream of tartar, and wood ash can provide a practical and "greener" alternative. They will not produce a completely permanent dye, but will greatly reduce fading.

Take into consideration what the dye is going to be used for. If it is for magical purposes or to dye robes, then it highly desirable for the dye to be as natural as possible.

Mordants

Alum (aluminum potassium chloride): This is probably the most popular mordant and works with a wide variety of dyestuffs. It was mined in ancient times and was considered to be a vitally important mineral resource. A tribe that controlled the supply of alum would have considerable political power. It is often combined with tartaric acid to produce brighter, clearer colors. Use 1 ounce for every pound of dry fabric weight.

Iron (ferrous sulfate): This is known as a "saddening agent," as it dulls and deepens the color. It should be used after treating the fabric with alum. Use $\frac{1}{8}$ ounce for every pound of dry fabric weight.

Copper (copper sulfate): This is used to give a blue-green tint to a color. Use $\frac{1}{2}$ ounce with $\frac{1}{2}$ pint of vinegar for every pound of dry fabric weight. **Poisonous!** Handle with care.

Tin: Tin will brighten colors. Use $\frac{1}{2}$ ounce for every pound of dry fabric weight. **Poisonous!** Handle with care.

Dyeing the Fabric

Natural dyes work best on natural materials such as cotton, silk, and wool. Although a natural fabric, linen takes dye less readily than other materials. Rayon is the only synthetic fabric with which natural dyes can be used successfully.

The fabric should be thoroughly washed and soaked overnight, if necessary, to remove any greasy residues. Give it a final rinse in warm water to which a tablespoon of vinegar has been added. If you are using a mordant, it should be added at this stage. The mordant should be dissolved in a small quantity of hot water, and an additional 4 gallons of water gradually added. Totally immerse the fabric in the liquid, and gradually bring to the boil, simmering for an hour.

An alternative method is to soak the cloth in the mordant mixture for twenty-four hours. Remove the fabric from the solution and dye it immediately.

Use approximately 2 ounces of the plant material for every ounce of fabric. The plant should be chopped or crushed and tied in a muslin bag or the foot of an old pair of pantyhose and covered with a gallon of water. If you are using the juice of berries, add this directly to the water. Add the fabric and bring to a boil. Simmer gently, stirring the fabric occasionally to ensure even dye penetration. Remove from heat when the required depth of color has been achieved.

Rinse several times, gradually decreasing the temperature of the rinsing water. Hang up the fabric to dry naturally. You can repeat this process two or three times to increase the color density of the fabric and improve its resistance to fading.

Plants To Use

Most plants will produce some kind of dye, but *tinctorum*, or *tinctoria*, in their Latin name, indicates a plant that is long established as a dyestuff. As a general rule, herbaceous perennials are the best plants for dyes, but there are exceptions, such as woad, a biennial.

Various parts of the plant can be used: bark, berries, flowers, juice, leaves, shoots, or roots, depending on the particular plant.

The following plants are associated with the festival of Lammas and can be used to produce dyes.

Alder: (*Alnus glutinosa*) The alder is a tree symbolizing death and resurrection, representative of the preserved life spirit of the corn lord. It produces three dyes: brown from the twigs, green from the flowers, and red from its bark. Fairies are said to dye their clothes green using alder flowers. The plant has a strong association with the Celtic god Bran, whose story enacts the cycle of the sacred king.

Bilberry, blackberry, blueberry, and elderberry: Each of these berries can be crushed to produce pink-purple stains to dye fabric. Blackberries are the best to use, as the berries are the easiest to collect in the required quantity. The young shoots can also be used, with alum as a mordant, to produce a light gray dye for wool. The blackberry was a sacred plant of the ancient Celts. Its berries, which change in color from green to red to black as they ripen, are said to represent the three aspects of the Goddess. Bilberries produce a blue dye, called *Fraochán* in Gaelic, when used with an iron mordant, and a purple color when alum is used. Elderberries require alum as a mordant. The young shoots of elder can also be used and will give a green coloring.

Lichen: There are around 20,000 different species of lichen, and many of these have been used for medicinal purposes and the production of dyes since ancient times. They are extremely slow-growing organisms and may take several hundred years to develop a thriving colony. Take care when collecting them; leave enough remaining so that the lichen can regrow. Many cultures have used lichen-based dyes; the beautiful blankets woven by the Native American Navajo people were often dyed using lichen to produce their rich earthy colors. "Ground lichen" (*Xanthoparmelia chlorochroa*) is a good source of brown colorings.

Lichen dyes do not usually require a mordant, as they are very permanent. The Celts usually collected lichen in late July and early August, around the time of Lughnasa. The lichen was left to dry in the sun and would then be fermented in stale urine over a low heat, sometimes for two or three weeks. A more acceptable modern alternative is to use an ammonia solution. A whole range of colors, from yellows and browns to reds and purples, can be produced from lichen, depending on the variety.

Lily of the valley: (*Convalleria magalis*) Lily of the valley is sacred to Maia, the mother of Mercury. The ancient Romans identified Lugh with the god Mercury. In Christian lore, the lily of the valley symbolizes the tears shed by the Virgin Mary at the crucifixion. The leaves will produce a green dye if picked in spring and a golden yellow dye if picked during autumn. The chopped leaves should be mixed with lime water, and alum can be used as a mordant. The green dye is excellent for coloring Beltane robes.

Oak: In Britain, many old oak trees are called "bull oaks," the sacred bull being the animal kingdom's counterpart in strength and virility to the oak tree. Oak bark or acorns can be used to produce a variety of dyes, depending on which mordant is used. Iron gives a black suitable for dyeing robes used in the waning half of the year. Alum produces a brown color, ideal for autumn equinox, while tin or zinc mordants give a yellow dye that can be used for Midsummer robes.

Pine: Among the northern Celts, the pine tree was associated with heroes and warriors. It was also a sacred tree to Native Americans, who planted pine trees to commemorate their tribal gatherings. Pine cones produce a reddish-yellow dye.

Sunflower: (*Helianthus annus*) The sunflower represents the warrior virtues of strength, courage, and action. The seeds are readily obtained, and the plant is easy to grow. The petals are used to make a yellow dye, suitable for coloring the robes and ritual clothing used at Midsummer.

Woad: (*Isatis tinctoria*) Woad has been cultivated since ancient times for its blue dye, used by the Celts to stain their bodies. It was also used extensively by the Romans and the Saxons. It was mixed with a substance called dyer's weld to produce the famous "Lincoln Green" worn by the legendary Robin Hood and his band of outlaws.

To produce a woad dye, fill a large plastic, sealable container with leaves. Add 2 tablespoons of washing soda (sodium carbonate), cover with warm water, and stir the mixture thoroughly. Put the lid on the container and leave in a warm place for 24 hours. Strain out the leaves, and squeeze out any moisture back into the container before discarding them.

Add 2 cups of bran to the mixture, and soak the wool or fabric in it. Seal the container and keep it in a warm place for 24 hours. Remove the fabric, and air it out for 10 or 15 minutes before returning it to the container. Repeat this process until you have achieved the required depth of color. Remove the cloth, rinse, and dry.

Notes

1. Ancient hymn to Inanna.
2. Michael Bayley, *Caer Sidhe*, 1997.
3. Phillipa Waring, A *Dictionary of Omens and Superstitions*, 1978.
4. T. O. Cockayne, ed., *Leechdoms, Wortcunning and Starcraft of Early England*, 1866.

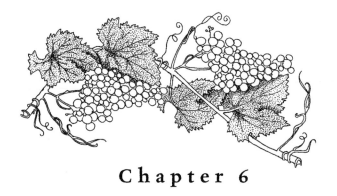

Chapter 6

Lughnasa Games

Immortal fame shall be thy meed
Due to every glorious deed;
Which latest annals shall record
Beloved and victorious lord! [1]

Lughnasa was celebrated with games and contests. Warriors were able to demonstrate their skills and compete for prizes. This custom is continued in the Traditional Craft. The God is honored as a male in his prime, just before his sacrifice and death with the harvesting of the corn. All of the coveners celebrate the male side of themselves, exploring the themes of warrior magic, hunting magic, and competing for the honor of becoming Champion of the Goddess. [2]

Our own coven's games include wrestling and staff-fighting matches and culminate in fire-walking, but these should only be practiced by experts and under expert supervision. We suggest that you try some of the games listed here. We also play these, and they are great fun and are not dangerous. They are all traditional games that were popular at Lammas and other rural festivities. Similar games were often played at Irish wakes.

Be warned! Lammas games tended to be very rough and boisterous, harking back to the warrior games of antiquity. Several of these are fun and would give a traditional atmosphere to your Lammas celebrations, but the more violent activities are also included out of interest and are best avoided.

PRISON BARS

This traditional Lammastide game originates in Shropshire, England. Two teams face one another with their arms linked. The object of the game is to reach the opposite side of the playing area. When a player attempts to run to the opposite end of the pitch, one (but only one) of his opponents gives chase and attempts to stop him. With several players from each team running in different directions, the game can get somewhat chaotic. A point is scored for each successful run or for stopping an opponent. In its original form, the game can be fairly rough, but a tamer version can be played by turning it into a game of "tag." The game can be made more difficult if a player can only stop an opposing player by touching a specific part of their body, such as a shoulder, rather than being able to grab any limb. If the length of the playing area is extended (say, from half the length of a soccer field to the full length of the field) then the game becomes more demanding.

LAMMAS

There is an old Scottish schoolyard game called Lammas, which originated with the custom of cowherds at hiring fairs putting straws in their mouths to show their occupation. To play the game, each contestant must grip a straw between his or her chin and bottom lip. The winner is the one who can recite the following rhyme the most times without dropping the straw:

I bought a beard at Lammas Fair,
It's a' awa' but ae hair—wag, beardie, wag!

LIFTING STICKS

This was a game played at Irish wakes, which were often jolly affairs with laughter and celebration to send the dead off on their journey.

To play, two people should sit on the floor, facing each other, with their legs outstretched and the soles of their shoes touching. A broom handle is placed over the shoes and gripped at either end by the competitors. By pulling on the broom handle, they then try to lift each other off the floor a few inches without bending their legs. The soles of the shoes should remain in contact the whole time. The aim is to try to stay sitting on the floor. As soon as one of the player's buttocks leave the floor, the other player wins.

LIFTING THE HORSESHOE

This game is played indoors against a wall. The horseshoe is placed 3 inches from the wall (8 centimeters), and the contestant stands 3 feet from the wall (1 meter). The object is to pick up the horseshoe without bending the knees or placing the hands against the wall or floor. It was often played at Irish wakes.

HORSERACING

Horseracing was traditional at Lughnasa. You may not be able to race your own horses, but you could arrange a coven outing to the racetrack.

HORSESHOE PITCHING

Horseshoe pitching is an appropriate activity for Lammas/Lughnasa, given the festival's association with the goddess Epona and equine sports and folklore. Horseshoes of various types were first used by the nomadic tribesmen of the Eurasian steppes during the second century B.C.E. The U-shaped metal type are thought to have been invented by the Romans a century later. The earliest record of horseshoe pitching dates from Roman army camps during the early part of the second century.

The game has long been popular in the United States, but had no set rules until 1914, when the game's popularity increased after a group of men made up rules for play and equipment. A few years later, the National Horseshoe Pitchers' Association of America was incorporated from this group.

The game is played by throwing horseshoes at a stake. Two, three, or four persons can play. Points are scored by getting the shoes closest to or around the stake.

To play: Horseshoes can obviously vary, but to keep the game fair, you should collect ones that are similar in size, weight, and shape. As a guide, the official regulations require shoes to be 7¼ inches wide (18.4 centimeters) and 7⅝ inches long (19.4 centimeters) and not to weigh over 2 pounds, 10 ounces (1.2 kilograms). They also must not have more than 3½ inches (8.9 centimeters) of space between the open ends. The stake should stand about 15 inches high (40 centimeters) and tilt slightly toward the thrower.

The pitching area should be about 6 feet wide (1.8 meters) and about 50 feet long (15 meters). Two steel or iron stakes 1 inch in diameter (2.5 centimeters) are driven or anchored into the ground 40 feet apart (12 meters). Each stake stands 15 inches high (38 centimeters) in an area of clay, soil, or sand that is 6 feet square (1.8 meters), where the horseshoes land.

Two or three people play by competing individually. If four play, two people make up a team. Players take turns throwing the horseshoes. Each player throws two shoes, taking turns. Men pitch the shoes over a distance of 40 feet from the stake. Women and players under the age of seventeen throw from a distance of 30 feet (9 meters). Players pitch the shoes underhanded. Players control the shoes with their fingertips to flip them so the open end lands facing the stake.

Scoring: A ringer scores three points and consists of a shoe that encircles the stake in such a way that a straight edge can touch both tips of the shoe without touching the stake. If a shoe comes to rest within 6 inches (15 centimeters) of the stake, one point is scored. A shoe that leans against the stake, called a "leaner," is also worth one point.

Two main systems of scoring are used: cancellation and count-all. In cancellation, a game usually consists of forty points. If opposing players throw ringers or shoes that land equally close to the stake, the shoes cancel each other. Points are scored by counting the ringer or shoe closest to the stake that is not tied by the opposing player. A count-all game normally consists of twenty-five turns; that is, fifty shoes are thrown by each player. All ringers and horseshoes within 6 inches (15 centimeters) of the stake are scored according to their point values in a count-all game.

RHIBO

Rhibo is a traditional Welsh game that was often played at Lammas. Three pairs of players face one another and hold hands. The rest of the participants take turns to lie across the clasped hands and be tossed in the air, representing the manner in which grain is winnowed.

ARM WRESTLING

This is one of the "warrior games" we often play at Lughnasa, and you are probably already familiar with it. Two people face each other across a narrow table. They place their right elbows on the table and grip the hand of their opponent and try to force it down onto the table. The elbow must not be lifted off the table.

STICK JUMPING

This is another Irish wake game. Competitors take a short stick, about 4 feet in length (120 centimeters), and holding both ends, try to jump over it without letting go of either end. It is more difficult than you think!

ARCHERY

Competitions of warrior skills were a feature of the ancient Lughnasa games that were retained at the English wake fairs for many centuries. Since all men were required to practice their archery skills on a regular basis, archery often formed one of the competitions. One such contest is described in the famous tale of Robin Hood defeating the king's archer at Nottingham Castle.

If you have the equipment and expertise, you could hold your own archery contest, or a modern substitute might be a darts match.

SHIN-KICKING

This rural "sport" was a widespread form of fighting, especially popular with carters as a means of settling arguments. (A carter is a person who drives a cart; carters typically have a reputation for being boisterous and unruly.) Opponents held one another by the lapels of their coats and kicked at each other's shins with iron-tipped boots. The loser was the first to fall to the ground or give in and had to pay for the day's drinking. The sport died out in the late nineteenth century. We most definitely do NOT recommend that you try it!

HOODMAN BLIND

This game is similar to the modern Blindman's Bluff and can be played indoors or outdoors. In mediaeval times, when everyone wore detachable hoods with shoulder capes, the person to be "hoodman blind" wore the hood drawn tight about the face and tied at the neck so that he could not see. The other participants would beat him with their own hoods until he caught one of them and named them. This person would then have to take his place.

SLAP HANDS

To play this mediaeval game, one player kneels down with his or her hands behind their back, and the other players tap the hands of the kneeling player. If the kneeling player can guess the striker, then that person will have to take his or her place.

KAYLES

This mediaeval game is similar to the modern one of skittles, or ten-pin bowling. However, the kayles were wooden cone shapes knocked down by a thrown stick, rather than a rolled ball. Conical kayles may be constructed from stiff cardboard. We suggest that you make eight of them about 6 inches high (15 centimeters). Set them up within a chalked circle and throw the stick at them from a distance of 10 to 15 feet (3 to 5 meters). Everyone should take three turns, and whoever knocks over the most wins.

ROBIN'S ALIGHT

In Scotland and Cornwall, a game called "robin's alight" was played. It involved passing a burning brand from hand to hand. The person holding it when the flames went out had to pay a forfeit. This may once have been a method to select a human sacrifice.

You might play a similar game with a lighted candle, but make sure that that it is in a safe container, and that the participants will not be burned or splashed with hot wax. Pass the candle around very quickly, so that the air passes over it and may or may not blow out the flame. The person holding the candle when the flame goes out has to pay a forfeit, which should be decided on beforehand.

ORANGES AND LEMONS

This old children's game may once have been a method of choosing a sacrifice. Two players are chosen to be the "choppers" and hold their linked arms in an arch for the other players to pass under. The verse (below) is chanted by all, and the person caught by the choppers at the last "chop, chop, chop!" must pay a forfeit, which should be decided on beforehand. This version of the rhyme dates from 1858.

Oranges and lemons
Say the bells of St. Clement's

You owe me five farthings,
Say the bells of St. Martin's.

When will you pay me
Say the bells of Old Bailey

When I grow rich
Say the bells of Shoreditch.

When will that be
Say the bells of Stepney

I'm sure I don't know
Says the great bell at Bow.

Here comes a candle to light you to bed,
Here comes a chopper to chop off your head
Chop! Chop! Chop!

TUG-O-WAR

The name "tug-o-war" comes from the old German *toga werra*, which translates as "a contest of pulling." Tug-o-war contests have probably existed as long as rope. The earliest evidence of the sport originates from southeast Asia, where rope-pulling contests formed part of religious ceremonies. In Korea, for example, tug-o-war contests were closely associated with the harvest. In a similar manner to Irish faction-fighting, competitions were held between neighboring villages to foretell whether the crops would be successful.

Later on, tug-o-war became a purely physical contest. A wall carving on a tomb at Sakkara in Egypt, dating from 2000 B.C., depicts such a sporting competition. The earliest recorded history of tug-of-war in western Europe comes from the Scandinavian and Germanic heroic sagas of around 1000 C.E. In fifteenth-century France and Britain, tug-o-war contests were a popular feature of tournaments.

Since then the sport has long been a favorite activity at rural sports and festivals. It was originally part of the modern Olympic games, but was deleted from the program in 1920.

To play: There is an international federation that sets out the rules of the sport. The following is a much simplified version of these, which you can vary according to circumstances. The game consists of two teams pulling against one another on a rope. In the official version of the sport, each team consists of eight contestants, and co-ed teams are not allowed.

The rope should be about 35 feet long (33 meters) and 4 or 5 inches in circumference (10 to 12.5 centimeters). The rope should be free from knots and marked with cloth or colored tape in five places (use electrical insulating tape, for example). A brightly colored tape should mark the center of the rope, with white tape at 12 feet (4 meters) from either side of it, and blue tape at 15 feet (5 meters) from the center. The ground should be flat and grass covered with a center line marked on it.

A coin is tossed to decide which position the teams take. The rope should be held taut and gripped normally with both palms facing up. Any other grip is not allowed and can be dangerous. The feet of the contestants must be placed ahead of their knees. The contestants grip the rope behind the blue markers. The end man or woman of each team is known as the anchor. The rope should pass under one of his or her armpits and diagonally across his or her back and over the shoulder, from back to front. To prevent it tangling under the feet of the anchor, the trailing end of the rope is tossed to one side.

To start a contest, the judge shouts, "Pick up the rope." The next command is "Take the strain." When the rope is taut with the center line steady over the ground marking, the judge shouts, "Steady." To start the contest, the judge gives the command "Pull." A pull is won when one of the white markers on the rope is pulled over the mark on the ground. The outcome is decided by the best of three pulls. The teams rest for 5 or 6 minutes between pulls and then switch sides.

There are various infringements that are not allowed: sitting, locking the arms around the rope, unorthodox grips, touching the ground with any part of the body other than the feet, or making footholds in the ground before the command "Take the strain" is given. If a contestant accidentally falls over, he or she must get up immediately, or the team is disqualified.

WELLY WANGING

In Britain, "welly" is a colloquial term for a wellington boot. Wellington boots are a type of leather riding boot named after the Duke of Wellington. In the United States, the term has retained its original meaning, but in Britain it has come to mean a rubber boot worn about the farm or in wet weather. A very silly game that involves throwing, or "wanging," wellies is popular at school sports and local fairs. Contestants take turns throwing a welly, and the one who throws it the greatest distance is the winner.

Throwing competitions, such as the *roth-clea* (wheel throwing), formed an important feature of the ancient Tailtean Games. Welly wanging is a safe and easily organized means of including a throwing event in your own Lughnasa games. The boots used need not necessarily be rubber; any knee-high boot with a slightly flexible upper and a relatively heavy sole are suitable. Or you could just throw a ball.

WIFE CARRYING

This type of contest is a feature of several traditional gatherings. Basically it consists of a race in which each contestant runs with his wife thrown over his shoulder, holding her around the legs with her head facing backward. Of all the different variations of racing while carrying a weight, this is probably the easiest to include in your Lammas games. The pairs of contestants need not necessarily be of the opposite sex, but try and make sure they are reasonably matched so that the race is fair. A hundred yards or meters is a practical distance for a wife-carrying race.

Notes

1. Gruffudd Llwyd, *Ode to Glyndwr*, 1400.
2. In the Traditional Craft, Lughnasa is a counterpoint to the festival of Imbolc. Imbolc celebrates the Maiden Goddess and her gifts. The coveners explore the female/goddess parts of their personalities.

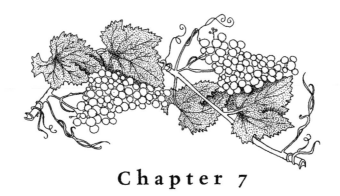

Chapter 7

Warrior Magic

Heaven, Earth, Sun, Moon and Sea,
Fruit of Earth and Sea-stuff,
Mouths, ears, eyes, possessions,
Feet, hands, warriors' tongues.[1]

The Traditional Craft celebrates Lughnasa as a festival of warrior magic and male energies. The warrior here is a psychic warrior; his weapons are his body, mind, and spirit. These must be trained to work in harmony. The warrior faces his own fears; he develops his spiritual courage and hones his will.

The warrior may subject himself to physical extremes to force his will and consciousness beyond the ordinary. We are all subject to many fears, and it is the warrior's purpose to seek them out and defeat them. It must be recognized that the body has its own fears: fear of injury, fear of physical danger. These are natural and proper. Without these fears we would put our hands in the fire, crash our cars, or jump off cliffs. The body has an innate mechanism of self-preservation. It clings to life — that's its job. The warrior may decide to face many of his physical fears to develop his will and courage. Fear facilitates a change in consciousness; to conquer a fear facilitates the development of the will. To do something so dangerous that it may result in injury or death, however, is no part of the warrior's path; it is a self-indulgence.

BODY PAINTING

The ancient Pictish warriors of the Celts painted their bodies with woad to present a threatening appearance to their enemies. Woad was also used for dying garments, including those worn by contestants during the Lughnasa games. After the sacred king had been chosen at Lughnasa, it was traditional to paint spiral patterns on his body using woad before he underwent the symbolic marriage with the land. Woad is a yellow flowered plant containing the same blue dye, although in a far lower concentration as indigo, which eventually replaced it and is used nowadays to dye jeans. Woad was used for dyeing police and naval uniforms until the middle of the last century; a lingering reminder of its associations with the ancient Celtic warriors.

The dye is complicated to prepare as a body paint, and an easier alternative is to use henna, which gives a brown coloring. Known as *mehndi*, henna body painting originated in the villages of northern India and the deserts of North Africa, and dates back over 3,000 years. The hands and feet of the bride and groom are still ritually decorated with henna at many Hindu and Islamic weddings. In Morocco, the Berber women use mehndi designs to ward off evil spirits.

Mehndi has become a fashionable and less-permanent alternative to piercing and tattooing. Kits containing everything needed are readily obtainable, or you can make your own using henna and a couple of other simple ingredients. Make sure to do a patch test to make sure the skin is not sensitive to the ingredients. Mehndi designs are not a suitable decoration for children to apply to themselves (it stains too easily), but they enjoy wearing them. Indian children have worn them for centuries.

You will need the following materials:

Stencils (or stencil acetate or paper to make your own)
Scalpel or craft knife
Henna
Eucalyptus oil
Lemon juice
Stiff brush or small spatula
Soft brush
Masking tape or low-tack adhesive

Making Stencils

Trace Celtic knotwork, spirals, sun wheels, or stylized totem animals onto the stencil acetate, remembering to leave "bridges" of material so that the design does not fall to pieces when cut out. Use a scalpel or sharp craft knife to cut out the design.

The included illustrations can be enlarged and should give you some ideas to start off with: Celtic knotwork (Figures 7 and 8, page 140), sun wheels (Figures 9 and 10, page 140), the Eye of Horus (Figure 11, page 140), Epona (Figure 12, page 140), and the Uffington horse (Figure 13, page 140).

There are also many sourcebooks of Celtic artwork available. Dover Publications produces several books of suitable copyright-free artwork that can easily be photo-copied to the right size and adapted to stencils.

Experiment and apply them wherever you wish: repeated patterns encircling the arms and legs, spirals or sun discs around the navel or chest (avoiding the more sensitive areas), or a large, stylized plant or animal pattern across the back or chest. Hold the stencils in place by coating the back with a low-tack adhesive, such as Spraymount, or affix them with masking tape. (The stencils can also be used in face painting and to add borders and images to totem shields.)

Figure 7

Figure 8

Figure 9

Figure 10

Figure 11

Figure 12

Figure 13

Application

Wash the area where you wish to apply the design and pat it dry. Mix the henna powder with water to the consistency of a pancake batter, and let it stand for about 30 minutes. Rub a small amount of eucalyptus oil into the skin. Put your stencil in place, holding it taut and in position using masking tape or adhesive. Spread or dab the henna mixture over the stencil and leave in place for 10 minutes until the mixture is dry to the touch. Remove the stencil. Gently brush lemon juice over the design. This acts as a sealant and fixative. Wait for another 30 minutes and apply more lemon juice.

As an alternative to using a stencil, you can paint on patterns freehand, gradually building up the henna with several applications.

As it dries, the henna will harden on the skin. The darkness and permanence of the design will depend on your skin type and color and how long the henna mixture is left in place. (If you have very dark skin coloring, the effect will hardly be noticeable.) Leave in place for 3 to 24 hours (this may feel itchy; see safety note below). Keep the painted skin area out of direct sunlight. Remove the hardened henna with water. As a rough guide, mehndi designs can last anywhere from a couple of days to several weeks.

Safety note: Mehndi is usually trouble-free but should not be applied to damaged skin, the face (especially near the eyes), or other sensitive areas. Although it is safe and has been used for thousands of years, it is best to take care when applying it to children. If you have allergies or sensitive skin, test the procedure on a small area before applying a large design. Avoid getting the henna on your hands, clothes, furnishings, or anywhere else where you don't want it to stain. If this does happen, wash it off immediately.

FACE PAINTING

Different cultures from around the world have practiced face painting for thousands of years for a variety of reasons: as part of religious rituals, to frighten their enemies, for dramatic performances, or just for fun. Faces were blackened, whitened, smeared with dirt or blood. These face-painting traditions have survived in European folklore rituals. The Peterborough Plough Monday performers had faces blackened with soot and red ochre. English Morris men can be found with faces painted in various colors including red, yellow, black, and green. Such traditions are constantly being reinvented. Supporters at international soccer matches often paint their faces in the style of their national flags.

As with body painting, the techniques described here offer an easier and more convenient method than using the traditional woad of the ancient Celts.

For your Lammas celebrations, you can paint on tribal marks and Celtic patterns, or make up yourself and your friends to represent the totem animals associated with the festival. We've shown a couple of examples to get you started. Don't worry if you feel you have little skill or artistic ability; simple patterns using symbolically important colors can be surprisingly effective. Children find face painting great fun, and it is perfectly safe. Just remember to be careful when applying the make-up near the eyes.

You will need the following materials:

> Water-based make-up (various colors)
> Artist brushes (synthetic sable and bristle)
> Make-up sponges
> Glitter (optional)
> Natural materials such as leaves, feathers, and shells (optional)

Ideally you should use a water-based make-up of the type sold for children's face painting. Water-based make-up can be applied easily and dries quickly. It doesn't rub off and is easily removed from the face and clothes using soap and water. This can be bought as sets of colors on a palette or in individual pots. If you intend to do a lot of face painting, the individual pots will be cheaper.

You can use theatrical grease-based make-up if nothing else is available locally, but we would advise you to avoid this if possible. It feels uncomfortable, is difficult to remove, and, more importantly, fine lines and complex designs are virtually impossible to apply successfully.

You should start with a basic palette consisting of black, gray, white, red, orange, yellow, green, blue, purple, and brown. Later, you may want to add Day-Glo colors, glitter, and hair gel for more specialized effects. You can also apply make-up to the hair using a sponge, or apply one of the colored hair sprays, which are widely

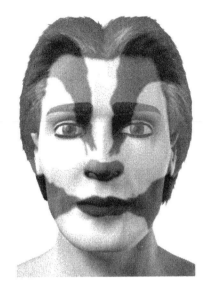

Figure 14

Figure 15

Figure 16

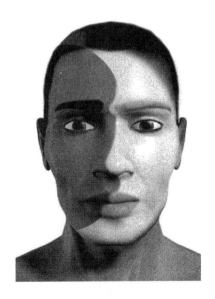

Figure 17

available. Make a collection of natural materials such as leaves, feathers, and shells that can be tied or pinned to the hair to add to the effect.

To apply the make-up, use a selection of bristle and synthetic sable artists' brushes. These need not be expensive; student quality will suffice, but avoid really cheap brushes. You will also need sponges; make-up sponges are the best to use. A cheaper alternative is to buy baby sponges (sponges used specifically for washing infants) and cut them into "cheese-shaped" wedges. This will give you both a fine edge and a broad surface to work with.

You should start with the basic background colors, then smooth in blended areas, and apply fine, sharply defined details to complete the design. The following illustrated examples should give you some ideas.

- The badger is closely associated with warriors in Celtic lore. You will need only black and white face paints. Comb a little talcum powder into the hair to continue the white stripes. (See Figure 14, page 143)

- The Eye of Horus is mainly in black and white but can look even more effective if combined with brightly colored or glitter eyeshadow. (See Figure 15, page 143.)

- For the sun wheels, use the stencils from the section on body painting. Reds and yellows are effective in this design. (See Figure 16, page 143.)

- The moon can be applied to all skin types, but is particularly effective against a dark skin tone. (See Figure 17, page 143.) Color the crescent in white or pale yellow. The shadow areas can be left natural on black skin, or use a dark blue or purple.

SACRED SYMBOLS

There have always been many concepts that are beyond words, and every civilization has consequently used symbols to represent ideas that are difficult to define or understand. This is the reason that all cultures have used images to represent their religious beliefs. Use these symbols on totem shields, masks, and in face and body painting. Select your colors carefully to reinforce or modify various aspects of their meaning.

Ankh: This ancient Egyptian symbol meant life and the zest for life; it was also used as the hieroglyph for reproduction and sexual union. The ankh combines the male and female sexual symbols: a female oval surmounting a male cross. It was also called the Key of the Nile, as it was said to represent the sacred marriage between the God and Goddess, which took place each year at the source of the Nile before the river flooded. Egyptians regarded the ankh as a universal life charm. In hieroglyphics, the ankh stood simply for the word "life." The goddess of life and death, Hathor, carried a staff in the form of an ankh with which she bestowed the breath of life. A similar symbol, but with the head filled in, was also used in pre-Columbian Mexico, leading some people to speculate that there were contacts between the ancient Mediterranean cultures and the New World.

Circle with a point: This is one of the most ancient symbols and would appear to have been used throughout history by every culture. Wherever it appears the meaning is always the same; it represented the sun or something closely associated with it. The Cabalistic mystics used this ideogram to represent Michael, the archangel who fought Lucifer. This is an appropriate symbol for Lughnasa, with its theme of a symbolic battle between the forces of light and darkness.

Cross: We are all familiar with the cross as a Christian symbol, but it was an important image for thousands of years before the birth of Christ. The cross was a fairly common symbol throughout Europe from before the Bronze Age period. It was used to represent the staff of Apollo in ancient Greece, and one of its arms was lengthened to form what we now call the Latin cross. Apollo was the sun god and the son of Zeus, and this association of the cross with the sun was common throughout many ancient cultures. In Babylon, the cross was attributed to Anu, god of the heavens. The cross has come to mean resurrection, rebirth, and eternal life.

Eye of Horus: The Eye of Horus was frequently made into an amulet, the *udjat*, which would protect the health and ensure the good fortune of the wearer. Horus was the son of Isis and Osiris, and in the form of a falcon he was the Lord of the Sky and closely identified with the sun. The Eye of Horus represents a human eye with the cheek markings of a falcon. Traditional Mediterranean fishing boats still have a version of this symbol painted on their prows to avert danger.

There is one Egyptian myth that has close parallels with the story of the battle between Lugh and Balor. Horus fought Set for the right to the throne, and Set tore his eye to pieces and threw it into the celestial ocean. Thoth then recovered and restored the eye. In addition, each part of the eye represented one of the senses: touch, taste, hearing, thought, sight, and smell. The line that curved down from the eye represented a sprouting stalk of wheat. This ancient symbol is well known for its inclusion on the Great Seal of the United States and on every dollar bill. The designers of the seal were influenced by Freemasonry, which had adopted a number of Egyptian religious symbols, including this one. Where the eye is shown within a pyramid it represented the god during his "dead" period, entombed in the Underworld while he was awaiting his rebirth. The open eye was a symbol that the god's soul was still alive and watchful. A somewhat similar image is the Eye in the Hand. This ideogram combines the all-seeing eye of Greece and Turkey with the downward-pointing open hand of the Middle East. It is frequently encountered as a protective talisman in India and the southern Mediterranean region.

Scarab: The Egyptian scarabaeus beetle represented Khepera, a solar deity. Khepera was said to roll the ball of the sun across the sky in a similar manner to the way in which beetles roll their balls of dung over the ground. The ancient Egyptians believed that these balls of dung contained the fertilized eggs from which the next generation of beetles would hatch; therefore they used the scarab to symbolize Khepera's self-regeneration.

Spiral and the shamrock: This triple spiral symbol is called the spiral of life and dates from Neolithic times. The most famous example of this design is carved into the entrance stone at the passage tomb of Newgrange, in the Boyne Valley, Ireland. The sign is drawn using a single line without a beginning or end, thus representing the eternal cycles of life. The triple spiral is similar in form to the Irish shamrock, a symbol of good luck that has been used to represent both the Christian holy trinity and the threefold aspect of the Goddess. The three-lobed trefoil symbol actually originated in the East, where the pre-Islamic Arabs called it *shamrakh*, the three-lobed lily or lotus flower of their ancient moon goddess, whose trinity consisted of Al-Lat, Kore (or Q're) the Virgin, and Al-Uzza, the Powerful One. This triple goddess was known as Manat, or the Threefold Moon. The shamrakh was a fertility symbol and signified an interaction of three *yonis* (female sexual parts) to these ancient people. It appeared on pottery, stone, and woodwork in Mesopotamia, Crete, and Egypt between 2300 and 1300 B.C.E., and it was also used by the ancient Indus Valley civilization. A similar symbol was closely associated with the ancient Celts. It is now used by *l'alliance des pays celtes*, a French separatist group — a modern demonstration of the power and fascination that ancient symbols still hold over us.

Sun wheel: This is an incredibly widespread symbol with a multitude of variations. At its most basic, it consists of a cross within a circle. It was a common symbol in Nordic countries, where it can still be seen in many churches. The well-known Celtic cross is a variation of this image. It was widespread throughout ancient cultures and represented the sun, divided into its year by the solstices and equinoxes. The variation that contains three crossed lines to divide the circle into six was one of the most popular symbols of the Gauls (Celts from ancient France). The Celts used this ideogram to represent Taranis, the god of thunder. It is frequently seen as a circle surrounded by rays. The swastika is a variant of the sun wheel surrounded by rays. Still widespread in Hindu culture, it is best avoided in the West. It is a very ancient sun symbol, originating in Indo-European culture. It has been used in various forms as a sun symbol by most civilizations. Although the counterclockwise version merely symbolizes "national rebirth," it has become tainted since its use by Hitler and his Nazi party.

COLOR MAGIC

We respond to color in many different ways. Some of our responses are innate, others are influenced by culture. Throughout history different civilizations have assigned meanings to specific colors. In Middle Eastern countries, for example, blue is seen as a very protective color. Such color symbolism can sometimes have similar meanings across different cultures. Native Americans of the southeastern United States also see blue as protective, painting their doors this color to ward off evil spirits. Colors can often have several, sometimes contradictory, meanings depending on their context, and different colors can sometimes have similar associations. Western countries associate black with mourning and death, but put into a different context, it can also suggest beauty and elegance. Red is the color of blood and can symbolize either violence or a warm, loving emotion.

Color has been proven to have pronounced psychological and physiological effects. Studies have shown that people will gamble more recklessly under red as opposed to blue lighting. Pink lighting was found to have a calming effect on violent prisoners. Where we live can influence our color preferences. People from sunny climates like bright, saturated colors, while those from temperate areas prefer cooler hues.

The following is intended as a basic guide to help you choose the most appropriate and meaningful colors for the projects in this section of the book. Choose your colors to emphasize the meanings of the symbols and totems that you use.

Red: Red light has the longest wavelength and is the most physically energizing color. Red is associated with blood and with the element of fire. It represents conflict, courage, energy, fertility, lust, and vitality and is the most arousing color. Astrologers believe that red is the color of Mars, the god of war, and has power over iron. In Western culture, it is the color of danger. To the Chinese, red is the color of joy and festive occasions; it is the traditional color for wedding dresses. When mixed with white to form pink, it symbolizes love, friendship, happiness, harmony, peace, and compassion. A deep magenta pink represents vision, creativity, and insight.

Orange: Orange is the color of ambition, courage, joy, optimism, success, and sexuality. It is a combination of the red of passion tempered by the yellow of wisdom. While red stimulates the body, orange is said to influence the emotions. In Ukrainian folklore, it symbolizes endurance, strength, and worthy ambition. When mixed with black to form brown, it represents earthiness, sexuality, practicality, environmental awareness, and the planet Earth.

Yellow: This is the color of the sun and signifies air. Yellow is associated with the mind and intellect and with the planet Mercury. Its negative aspect is that of caution and cowardice. The Buddha always dressed his priests in yellow. It is also the sacred color of the Hindu religion; the robes of holy men are dyed with saffron. In the Middle East, it represents happiness and prosperity.

Green: The color of the Green Man of Celtic myth, it represents freshness, health, and happiness. It is the color of fertility and the rebirth of nature during springtime. Green symbolizes life, growth, and the earth. It is associated with love, attraction, the emotions, and the planet Venus. Green is also closely allied to music and the arts. It is the color of change and balance, wealth and financial matters. In some tropical countries, it is the color of danger, probably from its association with venomous reptiles or insects. In China, it is the color of infidelity; a green hat means that a man's wife is fooling around.

Blue: Blue represents the element of water, healing, teaching, and the planet Jupiter. In both Middle Eastern and some Native American cultures, it is a popular color for front doors and porches and is believed to have the power to ward off ghosts and evil spirits. It is considered to be a lucky color. Blue has a calming influence. In China, it symbolizes power and strength, whereas in Japan, blue is the color of villainy. Blue tempered with green to form turquoise is associated with inventiveness, conception, and philosophy.

Purple/Violet: Purple is the color of the highest rank and has long been associated with nobility and royalty; it was the color of emperors and bishops. This association of purple with power, mastery, and status is partly economic. Before synthetic dyes were introduced during the nineteenth century, purple dyes were difficult and expensive to produce. It can also symbolize self-respect, spiritual development, and occult power. In eastern Europe it represents fasting, faith, patience, and trust.

Indigo: Indigo is the color of intuition, perceptiveness, and vision.

White: White symbolizes harmony, innocence, and purification. It also symbolizes psychic development, spirit, and tranquility. It is also a protective color and dispels negativity. While in the West white is the color of weddings, in many Eastern countries it is the traditional color of mourning; in Japan, white carnations signify death.

Black: Black is the color of the planet Saturn, the elderly, and the crone aspect of the Celtic triple goddess. It symbolizes anticipation, destruction, endings, mystery, and the possibility of release, reincarnation, and death. The rejection of the ego is represented by black. The ancient Egyptians painted statues of Osiris black to symbolize the seeds dormant within the earth.

Gray: Gray is associated with communication, divination, study, teaching, and the planet Mercury.

Silver: Silver is the color of the moon and represents enlightenment, intuition, psychic ability, and truth. It is also associated with agriculture, domestic matters, and medicine. For the ancient Incas, silver was formed by the "tears of the moon."

Gold: Gold is associated with service to others, friendship, healing energy, spiritual strength, and zest. To the Incas, gold was the "sweat of the sun."

WARRIOR TOTEM MAGIC

It is often said that various religious cultures have worshipped animals, particularly so-called primitive tribes. This is a misunderstanding of the complex relationship that exists in such cultures with the environment, its animals, and plants. Animal powers are never worshipped, but often represent certain forces or attributes seen as intrinsic to the balance of the environment and the cosmos. We know that in every tribal society, including ones that still exist today, that animals were considered as having particular virtues and abilities.

Celtic art is rich with depictions of animals. Celtic tribal names were derived from animal totems such as the Epidii (horse), the Lugi (raven), and the Tochrad (boar). Mythological characters were described as having their destinies bound with the fate of certain animals. Celtic gods and goddesses were said to turn into animals, to have animal companions, and to gain knowledge from talking to animals. Druids were credited with similar abilities, while animal herdsmen were often also magicians. Celtic gods were described as being nearly always accompanied by their cult animal or appearing as an animal: stag, horse, dog, etc. The Lord of the Animals (sometimes called Cernunnos) is a horned figure surrounded by animals.

In ancient times, warriors would identify themselves with animals in order to partake of that animal's strength and courage. Later, animals were relegated to a symbolic role, depicted on heraldic shields.

Totem Shields

The Lughnasa games were a time for different tribes to assemble and for their warriors to engage in sporting competitions. Shields representing totem animals and tribal emblems can be used as decorations and to mark the start and finish lines during your own games.

Suitable designs can be found in books on Celtic art or heraldry. Choose totem animals or symbols associated with Lughnasa.

Cardboard
Craft knife
Steel ruler
Spray paint
Hobby or household paint
Masking tape
Pencil
Colored paper
Spray adhesive
Small nails or a staple gun
1-inch by 1-inch piece of wood
Tenon saw (handsaw)
Spray or brush-on varnish

Mark out a piece of card in a shield shape, between 18 inches and 2 feet high (45 centimeters and 60 centimeters), and 12 inches to 16 inches wide (30 centimeters to 40 centimeters). Carefully cut the shape out using a ruler and craft knife. Use this shape as a template for making additional shields. To add a little variety to the shields, produce some in a circular shape.

Lay the shields on old newspaper and spray the backs with gray, black, or silver paint, and allow to dry.

Turn the shields over, and spray each one with its main background colors. Mask off the different areas with tape and scrap paper. You can make very effective shields just by using simple shapes, but a better idea is to enlarge traditional Celtic or medieval heraldic designs onto colored paper using a photocopier or computer and laser printer. Cut out the designs and paste them onto the shields. To finish them off, you can give them a coat or two of clear varnish. (If you use an inkjet printer for the designs, the ink will smudge with brush-on varnish, so use a spray variety).

Attach loops of string to display the finished shields on your walls, or attach them to wooden stakes for outdoor use. Trim the timber to 7 or 8 inches in length, and saw one end into a point. Attach the shields using nails or a heavy-duty staple gun.

Safety Note: Be careful using the craft knife when cutting the thick cardboard. It is safest to use a sharp blade, as it is less likely to slip out of control. Only use spray paints or adhesives outdoors or in a well-ventilated environment.

MASKS

Early theater was a religious performance dedicated to a god; in Scandinavia, for example, to Frey, and in Greece to Dionysus. Actors wore character masks to play the parts, donning the personality of the part with the mask. In England, mummers and guisers wore masks at their seasonal plays and parades. During a ritual, people might be masked and disguised by natural objects, such as the burrs of the Burryman, and the various leaf-covered Green Men and the Straw Men of mumming plays. In Austria, the *zapfenmanndl* was covered in fir cones and the *verschmanndl* covered in lichen.

A person in a mask is no longer themselves; they take on the persona of the mask. Their own face is hidden, and the consequent freedom of this was exploited during masked balls and carnivals when people could behave as they normally would not. Go to a fancy dress ball and you will see people beginning to adopt some aspects of the personality portrayed by their costume.

Masks have been used for ritual purposes for thousands of years. There are ancient cave paintings depicting humans wearing animal masks and horns. When a priest or performer dons a mask of the god, he becomes the god. When a shaman or warrior dons the mask of an animal, he becomes that animal. Lughnasa is the perfect time to experiment with the magic of masks.

Papier-mâché Masks

Papier-mâché ("mashed paper") is cheap and easy to work with. It is light yet strong and durable, so much so that it was used to manufacture furniture during the nineteenth century. One disadvantage is that it can take a while to dry out; any papier-mâché project needs to be spread over a number of working sessions as a result. It is safe and simple enough (if rather messy) for children to use yet with skill and imagination it can produce stunningly effective masks.

> Old newspapers
> Cellulose wallpaper paste (or flour-and-water paste)
> Balloons
> Masking tape
> Craft knife
> Scraps of cardboard
> Paints (PVA poster paints are ideal)
> Selection of brushes
> Spray paint (optional)
> Varnish
> Hole reinforcers
> Cloth tape

As the papier-mâché takes a while to dry, it is probably a good idea to work on several masks at once. Inflate a balloon for each mask. The balloons are used to form a face-shaped temporary foundation on which to build the masks. Mix the wallpaper paste in a large bowl, tear off strips of newspaper, and soak them in the paste. Pastes vary so it's best to experiment with a small quantity at first, until you can gain an idea of how thick to make the mixture.

Spread the pasted strips of paper in alternate directions over one side of each balloon. Continue on, building up criss-crossed layers of paper, until about ⅛-inch thick (3 millimeters). Leave to dry for at least 24 hours in a warm place. (See Figure 18, page 155.)

Deflate and remove the balloons, carefully trimming the edges of each mask with a craft knife, if necessary. Mark the position and shape of the eye, nose, and mouth openings, and cut out using the knife. (See Figure 19.) You should now have a number of blank forms on which to build up the features.

This type of mask lends itself to the representation of almost any creature you can imagine. Cut odd scraps of cardboard into shapes to produce noses, beaks, ears, etc. Attache these in place with masking tape (see Figure 20), and then cover with layers of the papier-mâché (newspaper soaked in paste) to build up and elaborate the features.

Papier-mâché can be kneaded into shape to add detail and texture. (See Figure 21.) You can use this method to build up a ridge over the eyes, for example. Animal snouts can be constructed over a base consisting of a polystyrene cup taped to the mask. Horns can be created by using cones formed out of thin cardboard. Table-tennis balls cut in half make excellent protruding eyeballs. With a little bit of practice with papier-mâché, if you can think it, you can make it.

Now you can paint and decorate your masks. Most paints are suitable, but PVA poster paint is ideal. It dries quickly, and it is inexpensive and water-soluble. Paint your mask all over with the basic colors, and then fill in the details with finer brushes. Spray paints can be used to good effect to add soft highlights, or use metallic, Day-Glo, or glow-in-the-dark finishes. Parts of the mask can be painted with PVA adhesive and sprinkled with glitter.

Finish off your masks with a couple of coats of varnish. It can be very effective to finish some parts with a matte varnish, and others, such as eyes and mouths, with a gloss finish.

Think carefully about your choice of colors. Study the artifacts of different cultures to understand their characteristic use of color. For example, many African cultures were restricted to the locally occurring pigments, so why not try a restricted and subdued palette of ochre yellow, rust red, off-white, and black for a more tribal and African feel.

In addition to painting, you can also include natural materials in your masks. Experiment with shells, feathers, leaves, twigs, and large seeds and grains to add color and texture.

Figure 18

Figure 19

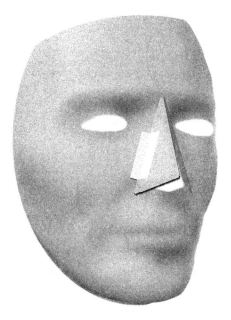

Figure 20

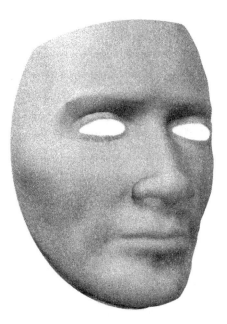

Figure 21

Finally, punch a hole at each side of the mask, strengthen these with hole reinforcers (available from office supply stores), and thread with thin cloth tape, so that you can tie it in place.

WORKING WITH ANIMAL SPIRITS

Warriors often had animal totems or called upon animal powers to help them in battle, invoking the strength of the bull, the courage of the boar, and so on. Stories of Norse beserkers are well-known. To be a beserker meant to go into battle wearing no armor or protection — only a bearskin shirt. These warriors were feared, because they knew how to draw on the power and strength of the bear and fought in a kind of tranced frenzy, without fear or hesitation. They received the power of the bear at their initiation and were also believed to be able to shapeshift. Akin to the beserkers were the *ulfhamir,* or "wolf shirts," who fought clad only in wolf skins. Certain ancient Celtic warriors were said to be able to turn themselves into wolves to tear and rend their enemies.

Animals were depicted on helmets and other pieces of armor. Perhaps in early times warriors wore animal masks in battle or during their initiations.

Worldwide, magicians and shamans work with animal powers. The qualities of the animal are called upon to help the magician in his or her work. The horse may be called upon for its swiftness, the fox for its cunning, the hawk for its sight, and so on. These are spirit animals, and a single creature may stand for the whole species, not a boar, but Boar; not a swan, but Swan. Because the animal is a spirit, it is also a guide to the Otherworld.

There are various kinds of relationships with animal spirits:

Totem: A representational totem animal may be adopted by a person or a clan. They then have kinship with the animal and may not kill the species or marry someone with an inimical totem.

Tonal: This term, used by South American shamans, denotes the animal that embodies the inner person or soul, rather like the animals of the Chinese zodiac signs.

Nagual: This South American term refers to the animal guardian, servant, alter ego, or even the animal form of a shaman or witch.

Familiar: This English term is similar in meaning to nagual. It refers to a spirit helper in animal form.

Power animal: This is a loose term that may be used to describe one or all of the above.

Animal ally: This is a spirit helper in animal form that helps the shaman or witch perform tasks that he or she would not otherwise be capable of. While some types of animal spirits choose their own time to make themselves known, an animal ally may be actively sought, summoned, and invoked.

It is usually necessary to make a deliberate effort to obtain the help of a spirit animal. Though some people say that a particular animal is with you for life, which is true of the tonal creature, other helpers come and go as we develop.

Finding Your Animal

Animal guides may appear to you in pathworkings, meditations, and visions. You may already have a feeling about your animal helper. Perhaps you feel drawn to a certain animal or feel a connection to a particular creature. Maybe your family already has a totem animal. The following pathworking is designed to help you discover your animal helper.

There are many varieties of meditations. Perhaps the easiest to come to terms with is pathworking. The best way to experience a pathworking is under the guidance of a narrator, who will help you relax and then ask you to imagine a scene in your mind's eye. Another way is to try to memorize the narrative, or you could ask a friend to read it to you, or perhaps record the pathworking on audio tape. Remember to speak very slowly and leave plenty of pauses.

At first you may find pathworking difficult to enter into. Many people have problems with visualization at first. Make sure your body is completely relaxed and allow yourself to drift into it. Don't try too hard; this is counterproductive. After a few attempts, you will find it becomes easy and pleasant.

Discovering Your Totem Pathworking

Find a comfortable, warm space where you will be undisturbed. Take the telephone off the hook. You might like to lie down on the floor with a cushion under your head, lie on your bed, or sit in a comfortable chair.

Lie or sit comfortably, arms and legs uncrossed, and allow all your muscles to relax.

Concentrate on your breathing. With each breath you become more and more relaxed. With each outward breath you let go of tensions, you let go of the events of the day, you let go of problems.

Center your attention on your toes. Be fully aware of them, and let them relax.

Move your attention to the soles of your feet. Be fully aware of them, and let them relax. Feel the tension drain away.

Continue moving in the same way up through the tops of your feet, your ankles, your shins and calves, your knees, your thighs, your buttocks, your stomach, your spine (feel each vertebrae separate and relax), your chest (be aware that your breathing has become slow and rhythmical), your shoulders, your arms and elbows, your hands and fingers, your neck, your scalp, your face, feel the muscles of your forehead relax, the muscles around your eyes, your nose, mouth, cheeks, and jaw.

Concentrate again on your breathing. With each breath you become more and more relaxed. With each breath you go deeper and deeper into a warm, pleasant state of relaxation.

Imagine that you are walking in a beautiful forest. The sun glances through the branches, forming dappled light on the forest floor. It is peaceful and silent but for the rustle of the leaves and the occasional bird song. You are following a faint but clear path through the trees.

(Pause.)

Eventually you come to a clearing. Seated beneath the tree you recognize Cernunnos, the stag-horned god who is Lord of the Animals. He is surrounded by animals, large and small, all gathered peacefully around him. Though cats rub shoulders with mice, and lions with deer, they are all calm and content under his influence. You gaze in wonder at the beasts.

(Pause.)

Cernunnos beckons you forward, and as you move toward him, the animals scatter and retreat into the trees. Soon they are all out of sight.

(Pause.)

You may be disappointed, but Cernunnos smiles. He alone is Lord of the Animals with the power to still them all. He knows that you have come to discover your own totem animal and he nods. He will help you.

(Pause.)

He lifts up his arms and utters a piercing whistle. The forest falls silent.

(Pause.)

Then from the trees an animal emerges. It is your animal helper. You may be surprised, it may not be the animal you were expecting, but you must accept it.

(Pause.)

The animal moves toward you, and you touch it, make friends with it.

(Pause.)

When you are ready, you thank Cernunnos, and accompanied by your animal, make your way back down the forest path.

(Pause.)

Let the scene fade around you, and return yourself to waking consciousness.

THE LESSONS OF THE ANIMALS

Every animal has its own lessons. You may choose to explore these by studying the real animal, by imitating its movements in dance, perhaps while wearing an animal mask. You could explore its lessons in a pathworking or a meditation on its qualities. You could call upon its power in a spell or ritual.

Below are some animals that were well-known to Celtic warriors who painted them on their shields, tattooed them on their bodies, or invoked them in battle.

Bear: *Regeneration and strength.* The bear cult is probably the oldest one in existence and has survived through many changes. The bear is one of the most revered animals in the world and was thought to have enormous powers.

There were two Celtic bear Goddesses: Andarta ("Powerful Bear") and Artio. The Celtic word for bear was *arthe* (Artos in Latin). It can be found in place-names and gives rise to the name of "Arthur." Bears are associated with hunter gods and goddesses and are often depicted with the stag and the boar. They were sacred to Artemis/Diana, and during the rites of Artemis-Callisto (the moon/bear goddess) at her temple at Brauron near Athens, young girls, dressed in yellow, performed a dance and were called "bears."

Among Finns, Lapps, Estonians, and Lithuanians, the priest or shaman identified with the bear god and took on his spirit when he wore his bear robes. The north European warriors would invoke tribal and personal totems before going into battle and might dress in bearskins and go "berserk," summoning the spirit and courage of the animal to aid them and possess them. In Native American teachings, the bear is associated with the Dream Lodge.

The bear is a symbol of the sun. He hibernates in the winter, as the sun seems to decline and "hibernate," the hours of daylight getting shorter each day. Just as the bear emerges "reborn" from his hibernation, the sun is reborn at the winter solstice, renewed and getting stronger each day. The bear hibernates, entering the womb of the Earth Mother, the place where questions are answered and solutions found.

The lesson of Bear is that strength comes from within — not from what you own, or what you say, or what other people say about you. Bear does not waste energy; he moves slowly and deliberately, with purpose. Call on his strength, and enter the silence within to find your answers.

Boar: *Courage.* In Scandinavian myth, the boar was sacred to Frey, Freya, and Odin. At Yule, the god Frey rode the golden-bristled boar Gulliburstin, whose bristles formed the sun's rays. Scandinavian warriors wore boar masks and boar tusks on their helmets or placed representations of boars on shields and war equipment to put them under the protection of Frey. Oaths were sworn "by the golden boar" as a symbol of honor and truthfulness.

The boar was also a symbol of the fertility of the earth. In Germany, when the corn waved, it was said "the boar is rushing through the corn." The last sheaf of the harvest was often called the "sow" and was saved and baked into a loaf in the shape of a boar at midwinter, which was placed on the festive table until the end of the Yuletide season. It was then put away and kept until the spring sowing, when one part was eaten and one part mixed with the corn.

The boar is instrumental is the death of vegetation and corn gods, who are killed and often dismembered only to be resurrected later on. In Egyptian myth, the god Set as a boar killed the vegetation god Osiris. In Greek myth, Apollo as a boar killed the vegetation god Adonis/Tammuz, lover of the goddess Aphrodite. In Irish myth, Finn Mac Cool as a boar killed Diarmuid, lover of Grainne. An unknown god as a boar killed King Ancaeus, devotee of the goddess Artemis, in his vineyard. Attis was slain by a boar. The ancient Cretans said that Zeus was ripped apart by a boar and buried in their midst.

Boar hunting was very dangerous and a favorite sport of warriors to prove their skill and courage. Boars were considered the fiercest of all prey. Boars often feature in the heraldry of warriors. The Norse boar-warriors fought together in a tight formation called the *svinfylking*, which resembled a boar's head.[2]

The Celts venerated the boar as a sacred animal connected with prophecy, magical powers, and with the protection of warriors.

Bull: *Power.* The bull symbolizes the masculine, generative forces of the sky gods who bring the fertilizing power of the sun to earth. In myth, the boar is often ridden by such gods, by solar heroes, and by storm and thunder gods. As the representative of such gods, the divine king also adopted the symbolism of the bull, perhaps wearing horned headdresses or a curly beard. Several thunder gods were associated with the bull, such as Zeus/Jupiter. The bull's bellow sounds like the roar of thunder. Many old oak trees are known as bull oaks. Lightening strikes the oak more than any other tree and were particularly associated with the thunder god.

For the Druids the bull represented the fertilizing power of the heavens while the cow represented the productive abundance of the earth. The Egyptian goddess Amaunet took a cow form to couple with Amun, the sun god, after he hatched from the cosmic egg. The Canaanite goddess Anat took the form of a cow to mate with her brother Baal, who was in the form of a bull.

In Celtic countries, a druid would choose the High King by undertaking the ceremony of Tarbhfhess, or "Bull Feast." A white bull was sacrificed, and the druid would eat his fill of the flesh of a bull, drink its blood and broth, and sleep on its flayed hide, while a spell of truth was chanted over him — a vision quest to dream of the rightful king. He would dream of the man and also what that man was engaged in doing at that moment.

In Egyptian myth, Osiris was associated with the bull. His cult absorbed that of the Apis bull, sacred to Ra, the sun god. The worship of Apis was spread by Narmer-Menes, the king who united Upper and Lower Egypt sometime before 3000 B.C.E. Apis became Serapis in Graeco-Egyptian myth, a lord of the Underworld, like Osiris.

The sacrifice of a bull played a part in the ancient Lughnasa rites, and several harvest customs are associated with bulls. If a farmer in Rosenheim (Germany) was late getting in his harvest, then his neighbors set up a "straw-bull" on his land. This was large figure of a bull made of stubble on a framework of wood, decorated with flowers and leaves. Comic verses ridiculing the farmer would be attached to the "bull."

Cat: *Independence.* Cats love curling up by the hearth fire, and they protect the house by destroying the mice and rats that eat out the pantry and spread disease. Cats were thought, therefore, to be protective animals.

To the ancients, the cat seemed to be an animal of the moon, its changing eyes reflecting its waxing and waning. Because of this and their nocturnal hunting habits, the cat is associated with moon goddesses. Pliny said that a she-cat would bear a total of twenty-eight kittens during her lifetime — the same number as the days of a lunar cycle. They are associated with fertility as they can produce several litters a year, and also because they prey on the rodents and even snakes that can devastate grain stores, and, therefore, protect the harvest.

In some places, the cat was a representative of the corn spirit. If children trampled cornfields, they were warned the phantom cat would get them. In France, it was traditional to deck out a cat with ribbons, flowers, and ears of corn at the start of the harvest. A harvester cut by a scythe should get a cat to lick the wound or the harvest would be in danger. In other parts of France, the unfortunate animal was placed under the last bundle of corn and flailed to death. In France, the last sheaf of corn to be harvested was called "the cat's tail." In Germany, the reaper was called "catcher of the cat."

The cat is connected with Osiris, one statuette showing his missing genitalia replaced by a cat. He was the father of Bast who played a large part in the rite of passage through death and the afterlife. Vegetation gods are slain and some-times dismembered and conveyed to the Underworld, an analogy for the seed being sown in the underground womb of the earth goddess. Goddesses associated with cats, such as Isis, Freya, etc., have to seek and rescue their partners from the Underworld. A representation of Tutankhamun shows him travelling to the Underworld on the back of a cat. The Teutonic goddess of the Underworld and death, Hel, had a cat totem.

Cat is an independent being, aloof and self-contained. Cat knows what she wants and quietly waits for the opportunity to get it, then moves like lightning.

Cow: *Nurture.* The cow is the symbol of plenty, nourishment, and nurture. Nomadic and pastoral peoples regarded the cow as a symbol of life and fertility. They depended on it for food, milk, and prosperity. The cow is associated with the Great Mother in her many forms. In Hinduism, the humped zebu cow is the symbol of Prithive, the earth, the all-embracing goddess. The Egyptians regarded the cow and the earth as the image of Isis and Hathor. The Greek sun and sky god, Zeus, is said to have been nursed by a cow. His wife Hera is described as cow-eyed (*boopis*) by Homer. In Celtic lore, Madron, the Great Mother, was also associated with the cow and is often depicted as a matronly woman holding a cornucopia (horn) filled with fruit and grains. In Ireland, the cow was associated with the goddess Boanne and was also one of the sacred animals of Brighid. In Norse myth, the primal cow Audumla sprang from the ice at the beginning of time with Ymir, the frost giant. He fed on the four rivers of milk that flowed from her teats.

The horns of the cow place it under the dominion of the moon goddess. In Greek myth, when Io was turned into a cow, her color changed from white to red to black and back again — the colors of the three phases of the moon waxing, full, and waning. They are also the three faces of the moon goddess: white for the virgin, red for the mother, and black for the crone.

In parts of Germany, the man who gave the last stroke at threshing was called the "Barley-cow," "Oats-cow," and other names, depending on the crop. He was covered in straw with two sticks tied to his head to represent horns. He was led by ropes and had to "moo" like a cow.

Crane: *Knowledge.* The Irish sea god Manannan owned a magical bag made from crane skin. It contained six treasures: the shears of the king of Scotland, the helmet of the king of Lochlainn, the bones from Assails' swine, the hook of the smith god Goibne, a shirt, and a strip from the back of the great whale. These were the vowels of the Irish ogham alphabet, and the strip of the whale represented the horizon (the sea was called "the whale road"), the stave on which ogham was written.

Cranes are associated with writing, because during flight their long legs resemble the letters of ancient alphabets. Many early alphabets were angular in appearance since they had to be carved into stone or scratched onto bark. It was said that the Greek god Hermes invented the alphabet after watching the cranes in flight, while the Egyptian god Thoth invented hieroglyphs after watching the flight of the ibis. The Celtic god Ogma is said to have invented ogham after seeing the flight of cranes. The Druids kept their ogham lots in a crane bag.

In ancient Greece, the mating dance of cranes was once thought to be a magical ritual, and the movements were imitated by human dancers to mark the start of the New Year and the death of the old, around Lammas. The climax of an ancient Chinese crane dance, with a similar purpose, was the burying of the dancers alive.

Crane keeps the secrets of magical writing. In ancient times, to write a character was to connect with the thing that the character represented and to call it into being.

Dog: *Loyalty and guidance.* The dog became a companion to humankind early on. Dogs are loyal friends and brave guardians of property and people.

As well as being mundane guardians, dogs are mythological guardians of the Underworld realm of the dead. In Greek myth, Cerberus, the three-headed dog, guards the entrance to the Underworld. In Egyptian myth, Anubis, the jackal or dog-headed god, is the guide to the Underworld and oversees the mummification process. In Norse myth, the dog Garm guarded the road to the Underworld. In Celtic myth, the Underworld pack of dogs are called the Cwn Annwn ("hounds of the Underworld") and ride out on stormy nights to hunt the souls of humans. The supernatural dog is a psychopomp who conveys the soul of the dead to the Underworld. The Dog Star, Sirius, rises at Lammas to convey the soul of the sacrificed sacred king to the Otherworld.

The dog is connected with Lugh's son, the Ulster hero, Cuchulain. He was originally called Setanta and, with his uncle, Conchobar, was invited to a feast by the smith Chulainn, who owned a fearsome dog. Arriving late, Setanta was attacked by the dog but succeeded in killing it. The smith was devastated by the death of his faithful hound, and in recompense, Setanta offered to raise the hound's pup until it was old enough to take the place of its parent. In the meantime, he would perform its guard duties himself. After this he was known as Cuchulain ("hound of Chulainn"). He was thence under a *geas* ("taboo") that he should never eat dog flesh, but also under a geas that he should never refuse hospitality. Three crones offered him a meal of roasted dog flesh, and he had to agree. His strength and skills deserted him, and he was overcome in battle.

Eagle: *Authority.* The power and strength of the eagle associate it with authority and royalty. It was the ensign of the kings of Babylon and Persia, the Ptolemies and Seleucides. It was a symbol of the empires in France, Austria, Prussia, and Russia. Scottish chieftains wore three eagle feathers in their bonnets, while the Romans used the eagle as a standard of imperial power. For the Egyptians, the eagle was a chief representative of the sun, Ra, and was said to descend in a shaft of light over the head of a pharaoh during his coronation.

The sacred king's soul was said to leave the king's body in the form of an eagle, while the souls of lesser men might leave in the form of butterflies. A Roman knight claimed to have seen the Emperor Augustus' soul rise from his body in the form of an eagle, proclaiming his deity, and was rewarded by his widow, Livia. Ganymede rose to heaven in the form of an eagle, or in another version, was carried off by an eagle to become Zeus' cup bearer. Llew's soul escaped in the form of an eagle and perched on an oak tree.

The eagle is often a representative of the sky powers at war with the powers of the Underworld in the form of a serpent. The Aztecs saw the rising sun as an eagle, devouring the powers of darkness. In Norse myth, an eagle sits at the top of Yggdrasil, the World Tree, warring with the serpent at the tree's roots. The Hindu god Vishnu rides an eagle when he is at war with the Nagas, or serpent spirits. In Hittite myth, the eagle with the serpent in its talons symbolized the strife between the weather god and the serpent Illuyankas. The warring of the eagle and serpent symbolizes the tension between the sky and the Underworld, between summer and winter, or between light and darkness.

Fox: *Cunning.* The fox is regarded as the archetypal trickster, having great slyness, craftiness, humor, and charm. It is meant to hunt well away from its own lair to lay the blame on other foxes. It is famous for its *kunning*, or hound wisdom. With its wily speech it is known to enrapture an audience of geese, later to carry one off. The fox is sometimes known as Reynard, and this derives from a fourteenth-century Gothic epic in which the fox is called *raginohart*, meaning "cunning in counsel."

The fox was a sacred beast in many ancient cultures, associated with knowledge and power from the Underworld, since it lives in burrows. Because of this, the Christians associated it with the devil. Its reputation was so evil that its bite was thought to be fatal; any person bitten would die seven years later. It was a favorite shape-changing form of witches.

Goat: *Fertility.* Because the new winter solstice sun is born in the sign of Capricorn and was seen as being nourished by the Capricorn goat, goats' milk had powerful mythological significance. Zeus' nurse was a goat nymph. In Norse myth, the she-goat Heidrun ("Sky") yielded enough milk to sustain Valhalla. It used to be the custom to bathe young goat kids in goat milk to help them survive.

In the fifth century B.C.E., Herodotus reported that the people of Mendes in the Nile Delta venerated all goats, particularly male ones. For the Greeks and Romans, the goat represented virility. Goats are fertile and reputedly lusty, so they have a prominent significance in nature-based religions. The Greek god of the wild, Pan, was the son of Amalthea ("Goat"). Pan and his satyrs had the legs, horns, and beards of goats.

In Ireland, "goat-heads" were evil spirits associated with leprechauns and the Formorians, suggesting there may have been a pre-Danann goat cult in Ireland. Goats were sacred to various Celtic deities and fairies like Bucca and Puck or Phooka. In Ireland, the Puck Fair is held July/August, when a goat decked in royal purple is hoisted into the air in an enclosure with foliage to eat.

In Jewish tradition, the scapegoat was imbued with the sins of the tribe and cast out into the wilderness. Christ as the scapegoat took on the sins of the world. In parts of Europe and America, goats are lured into grounds to eat grass near the house and when driven away will take sickness from the house with it.

A good harvest was foretold when the wind tossed the corn in Germany, as the "goats were browsing there." In another part of Germany, two horns were set up on the last sheaf, which was then referred to as the "horned goat." In Switzerland, a live goat was decorated with flowers and ribbons and let loose in the fields. It was caught, beheaded, and eaten at the harvest supper. The skin was made into a cloak, which the farmer had to wear if rain or bad weather threatened the harvest. In parts of Bavaria, it was thought that the Oats-goat was in the last sheaf. He was represented by a rake with an old pot for a head. The local children were then encouraged to "kill the Oats-goat."

Hare: *Fecundity.* The hare is associated with lusty sexuality and fertility. The hare is quick, a prolific breeder even, as observed by Herodotus, conceiving while already pregnant. It was sacred to the Greek goddess of love, Aphrodite, and her son Eros (and the Roman equivalents, Venus and Cupid). Philostratus said the most suitable sacrifice to Aphrodite was the hare, as it possesses her gift of fertility in a superlative degree.

Celtic hunt and moon deities were associated with the hare and were often depicted holding them in their hands. Killing and eating the hare was taboo and was thought to result in being struck with cowardice. The Celts lifted the restriction on hunting the hare at Beltane and made a ritual hunt and consumption. The Anglo-Saxons also venerated the hare, and a ritual hare hunt was a feature of the spring festival of the goddess Eostre, who is often depicted as hare-headed. Her hare laid the egg of new life to herald the rebirth of the year. Even now the Easter bunny is said to distribute eggs in springtime.

The hare is associated with the rising sun, the east, and resurrection. In Native American lore, the Great Hare is the Savior and Hero of the Dawn. In Egypt, the hare is depicted as greeting the dawn. The risen Osiris is linked to the hare, as is the risen Christ, Hermes, Mercury, and Thoth.

In Europe, the hare is also associated with the corn spirit. In Anglo-Saxon poetry, the hare is addressed as "the stag of the stubble, long-eared," "the stag with leathery horns," "the cat of the wood," "the cat that lurks in the broom," and "the furze cat." Hares hide in cornfields until the last reaping, and the last sheaf is often called "the hare." Its cutting is called "killing the hare," "cutting the hare," or "cutting the hare's tail off." In Galloway (Scotland), the last sheaf standing was called the Hare. It was divided into three and plaited, with the ears tied into a knot. The reapers then threw their sickles at it until one of them cut it down. In Norway, the man who "kills the hare" must give "hare's blood," in the form of brandy, to his fellow workers.

The hare is touched by a divine madness, the anarchy that overturns dogmatic tradition and restrictions and brings new ideas and inspirations.

Horse: *Virility, strength, and swiftness.* Horse cults existed in Britain and Ireland long before the coming of the Celts, and horses were favorite tribal totems of the Iron and Bronze Ages. They represent virility, fertility, strength, and swiftness.

A horse, as evidenced by the ceremony used to invest an Irish king, often represented the sovereign goddess. The ritual is obviously a very ancient one, but survived into the twelfth century C.E. and the Christian period. Giraldus Cambrensis recorded that the rite began with the king crawling naked to a white mare. He would mate with her (perhaps symbolically), and then she would be killed, cut up and boiled in a cauldron. When the brew had cooled the king would get into it, drink some of the broth and eat some of the meat- the body and blood of the goddess. He would then stand on a stone, holding a white wand, and turn three times sunwise and three times anti-sunwise in honor of 'the Trinity' or rather the Triple Goddess. In Sanskrit and Norse sources, the association of the sacrifice of a horse with the investiture of a king is also found. The land is symbolized by the powerful female animal.[3] In Greece, she was the mare-headed Demeter, and in Crete, Leucippe the White Mare. Certainly by the Roman era the cult of the Gaulish horse goddess, Epona ("Divine Horse"), was widespread and became merged with that of the Welsh Rhiannon and the Irish Macha. Epona is always depicted with a horse, sitting on a horse, or with two foals. Her name gives us the word "pony."

The Irish horse goddess was Macha who, heavily pregnant, entered a footrace against a horse at the midwinter solstice. She won but died giving birth at the finish line, cursing the king of Ulster who had forced her into the race.

The curse said that in times of battle, the warriors of Ulster would become as weak as women in childbirth.

There used to be a custom in Hertfordhire (England) known as "Crying the Mare," which reflects the connection of the horse goddess with the land. The last corn standing was tied together, and the reapers would throw their sickles at it. After one of their number had succeeded in cutting it, the reapers would cry, "I have her! I have her! I have her!" Others would reply, "A mare! A mare! A mare! Whose is she?" "Whither will you send her?" was asked next. The sheaf would then be given to a neighboring farmer whose corn was still standing. In this way, the corn spirit was passed on to take refuge in the neighbor's fields.

The Celts believed that souls traveled to the land of the dead on horseback. Shamans may visualize traveling to the Otherworld on the back of a spirit horse, and the drum that provides the trance-inducing beat may be called the shaman's steed. Gods and shaman tether their horses to the World Tree, via which journeys to all the realms are possible. The Norse World Tree is Askr Yggr-drasill, which means "the ash tree that is the horse of Yggr" (Yggr is one of the titles of Odin).

Lion: *Leadership.* Though the lion is not a native beast, it has become important in British and Irish symbolism and lore. It represents courage and sovereignty and is a heraldic beast of England and Scotland. The lion's size, shape, strength, and magnificence associate it with divinity and royalty. It is still described as the King of the Beasts. At the Congo and Zambesi rivers, the souls of dead chiefs were believed to pass into lions.

Big cats were significant to the Celts associated with Lugh (Lugos, Llew), whose totem was *lug*, the mountain lion. In heraldry, the ordinary lion is substituted and remains an emblem of Albion. The golden lion was an early symbol of English kingship, with the red lion representing Scotland and silver lions representing Wales. Some think that the Celtic words for a mountain lion—llew, lleu, leo, lug—may be derived directly from an Indo-European root, not Latin as is usually supposed.[4]

The lion is associated with several goddesses. Sekhmet was the lion-headed goddess of ancient Egypt, described as "Time" or the "Devourer of Time," consort of Ptah, the Bull of Memphis. At Syracuse in Sicily, a lion led the procession in honor of the huntress goddess Artemis.

It is a solar symbol, sometimes seen in combat with the lunar unicorn, or it represents summer, while the unicorn represents spring. When the Scottish King James took over the English throne as James I, he included them both in the coat of arms: the unicorn to symbolize his kingship of Scotland, and the lion to symbolize his kingship of England.

Women in African tribes give a piece of lion's heart to their baby sons to make them grow strong and brave. Lions often become the companions of warriors in myth. Androcles in Aesop's fables removed a thorn from a lion's paw and was later rescued by the lion. In Arthurian legend, Owain rescues a lion beset by serpents. Sir Bevis of Hamtun was befriended by two lions in the Holy Land. The lions rescued him from danger.

Otter: *Fluidity.* In Irish tradition, the otter was sacred to the sea god Manannan, lord of deep magic. It was much prized for its skin. Fishermen used to hunt otters with a three-pronged spear (symbol of the water god) for its waterproof pelt. The skin made the traditional bag for the Celtic harp and was used as a lucky lining for shields. Powerful North American Indian medicine women have otter skin medicine bags, as the otter is considered an animal of strong feminine healing magic.

The otter was a popular beast for shapeshifters and was one of the forms taken by Ceridwen in her battle with Taliesin. In Scotland, the kelpies transformed into horses or otters to lure mortals into the sea. In Norse myth, Odin, Loki, and Honir came across an otter sleeping by a pool with a freshly killed salmon. Loki killed the otter with a stone, but the otter turned out to be the son of the magician Hreidmar, who demanded compensation. Loki had to fill a bag made from the otter skin with red gold.

Otter catches the salmon of wisdom by being fluid and swift, not serious and ponderous.

Owl: *Magic.* The wise old owl is often the familiar of the witch in European lore. Witches shapeshifted into owls in many tales. In ancient Greece, the owl was one of the familiar animal companions of the witch goddess Hecate. The owl is associated with the witching time of dusk; the death of the day whose eerie light is called "owl light." Witches use the dusk as a time to slip through into the Otherworld.

Owl totems are called upon to learn the secrets of magic, and such magic is that of the crone goddess; it is knowledge of the night, darkness, winter, the Underworld, decline, and death. An old kenning reminds us that all life germinates in the dark, whether it be seed, animal, or human. Light emerges from the darkness and order from chaos. In Athens, the little owl was associated with Athene, goddess of wisdom. It was the emblem of the city and appeared on its coins. It is also the companion of other goddesses of wisdom, such as the Roman Minerva and Celtic Sulis. In the Welsh story of Olwen, the owl is named as one of the five oldest beasts on earth (with the blackbird, stag, eagle, and salmon). As such it has ancient knowledge.

Owls are associated with the death time of the year. They are very vocal in November and then fall silent until February. Their cries accompany the hag goddess in her death and winter aspect. In Scotland, the owl is known as Cailleach, which means "hag" and Cailleach Oidhche Gheal ("Hag of the Night Moon"). In the *Mabinogion* story of Llew, he marries a bride made from flowers, Blodeuwedd ("Flower Face"). She is unfaithful to him and plots to kill him. She is unsuccessful and is turned into an owl. Blodeuwedd is a Welsh name for the owl. After her transformation, she was called Twyll Huan, or "deceiver of Huan," Huan being one of the titles of Llew. The Welsh for "owl" is *tylluan*. The meaning is plain; the flowering goddess of summer becomes the hag of winter.

Ram and sheep: *Inner strength and purity.* The god as shepherd is a very ancient image and occurs in Sumerian, Iranian, Orphic, Hermetic, Pythagorean, and Tibetan traditions. Ra was "the Shepherd of All Men." Tammuz was a shepherd and protector of flocks. The Iranian Yima was titled "the Good Shepherd." The Hindu gods Shiva and Krishna were both herdsmen, while the Tibetan Chenerzig, "the All-merciful Good Shepherd," is incarnated in the Dalai Lama. In Greek myth, Orpheus Boukolos is a herdsman who carries a lamb on his shoulder. Pan is also a herdsman, and Hermes (Mercury) is a shepherd of souls. Christ was also said to be "the Good Shepherd."

The sheep is sometimes seen as a savior and transporter of souls and has associations with the god of the dead. Both the shepherd and the Underworld god carry a crook and a staff as their emblems. Some shepherds were buried with a tuft of wool in their coffins so that they might be excused attendance at the last judgment, as no shepherd would leave his flocks.

The lamb represents innocence and purity, and Christ was called "the lamb without blemish," the suitable sacrifice. As sacrificial lamb, Christ was crucified for the sins of the world. The fleece of a lamb has special associations, since it is equated with the fat of the animal, regarded as its life force and sustenance. In the well-known Greek myth of the Argonauts, Jason ("Healer") and his crew journey to recover a sacred ram's fleece, guarded by a dragon, described as "golden," a metaphor for the sun rescued from the dragon of darkness. The horned god Cernunnos is depicted as holding a ram-headed serpent. The serpent is the waning year and the Underworld powers, while the ram is the waxing year solar power. At the vernal equinox, the sun enters the constellation of Aries the Ram, making the ram a symbol of the regeneration of the year.

In Egypt, at the inundation of the Nile during the Dog Days, the pharaoh traveled from Memphis to the temple of Amun, the ram-headed god, at Karnak, to renew his right to rule as the divine son of the god on earth.

Raven: *Hidden knowledge.* Raven is the teacher and protector of seers and clairvoyants. It was thought to be the most prophetic of birds, having knowledge of public and private events. People are still spoken of as having "the foresight of a raven."[5] The raven was the messenger of the gods and warned the Irish god Lugh of the invasion of the Formorians.

The raven is associated with the Celtic god Bran (from the Slavic *branu*, "raven"). Bran's head was taken to the White Mount in London, where it continued to prophesy and protect Britain from invasion. King Arthur removed the head as a sign that he was now responsible for protecting Britain. The Tower of London now stands on the site, and Bran's ravens still live there. According to legend, if they ever leave the tower, Britain will fall to invaders. The Gaulish city of Lyon had the white raven Lugos as its totem bird.

Ravens feed on carrion and were once a common sight feeding on gibbet corpses. They were regarded as omens of death and war, associated with the battle goddesses Morrigan, Badbh, and Nemain, who could all take raven form. The Morrigan was invited to battles by war horns, which imitated the croaking of ravens.

Robin: *Sacrifice.* Robin presides over rituals connected with fire and with initiations through fire. He speaks of the persistence of spirit and of light in darkness. Robin speaks of the necessity of sacrificing one thing to gain another. The sparrow in the famous nursery rhyme kills the robin with his bow and arrow (see appendix 5 for the rhyme's full text). This may relate to its symbolic death or sacrifice at the end of its six-month rule over half of the year. The robin is also the husband of the wren who rules the other six months.

The robin is said to have burned its breast, making it red, by throwing itself onto the wren to stifle the flames that were burning it when it was bringing fire to humankind. The Welsh for robin, *bronrhuddyn*, means "scorched breast." Others say that the robin was part of a relay of birds that brought fire from the sun for humankind. The robin held the brand too close to the flames and burned its breast. In Scotland and Cornwall, the game "robin's alight" was played (see chapter 6). It involved passing a burning brand from hand to hand. The person holding it when the flames went out had to pay a forfeit. This may once have been a method to select a human sacrifice.

Rooster: *Healing.* The cry of the rooster at sunrise indicates the end of the darkness and the start of the day. The Greeks believed that the rooster was sacred to Apollo, the sun god, his son Asclepius, the healer god, through its association with the sun and its life-giving powers. A corn dolly was often made into the shape of a rooster and placed on top of the hayricks to protect them. Because of its power of driving out evil and darkness, the rooster was credited with healing powers. In many areas, medicine taken at the crow of the rooster was believed to be more effective.

Austrian children are warned that the corn-rooster will peck their eyes out if they stray in the fields. In parts of Germany, it was traditional for the farmer to release a live rooster or hide it under the last sheaf. The bird belonged to whoever caught it. This "rooster-catching" was a highlight of the harvest festival, and specially brewed "rooster-beer" was served to the reapers.

Rooster is an animal of the newly risen sun; a guide that leads the way from the dark realms out into the light.

Salmon: *Wisdom.* In Irish myth, Conla's Well was the source of poetic and literary style. In it lived several large salmon, which fed on the hazelnuts that dropped into it. Each nut increased their wisdom and caused a red spot to appear on the salmons' back. If a person were to catch and eat one of these salmon, the wisdom would be transferred to them. Fish are still referred to as "brain food." The salmon was regarded as a store of ancient knowledge and wisdom by the Celts and was one of the five oldest animals. Particular salmon were considered to be the guardians of the wells or pools where they lived.

The early Christian fathers were called *pisciuli*, and fish were equated with the converted. Christ was depicted as a fish, ICHTHUS — I*esous* CH*ristos* TH*eou* HU*ios* S*oter* (Jesus Christ, son of god, savior). Three intertwined fishes were borrowed from earlier religions to denote the Trinity, and bishops wore fish-head headdresses called miters. This lore was borrowed from the Sumero-Semitic Ea-Oannes, Lord of the Deeps, who was served by a priesthood in fish-head headdresses. Fish was the eucharistic meal of Atargatis; her son, Ichthys, was the sacred fish. Fish was eaten at the feasts of the Mother Goddess on her day, Friday. It was a sacramental meal of the mystery religions associated with the ritual worship of moon goddesses of the waters and gods of the Underworld. As a fertility symbol, the fish was also phallic.

The salmon can live in salt and fresh water and has perseverance and stamina in returning to its spawning grounds. Its pure willpower enables it to overcome many obstacles. However, salmon is very wise and, instead of battling against the prevailing current, uses a reverse current to swim upstream. The Irish hero Cuchulainn was said to be capable of the "salmon leap," which enabled him to jump large obstacles and walls. Sometimes it is necessary to take an almighty leap into the unknown to gain knowledge.

Snake: *Transformation.* In ancient times, far from being the symbol of evil that it became among Christian cultures, the snake was a creature that represented both the Goddess and the God, the fertility of both bringing life to the earth. It was a beast of prophecy and divination, protection and guardianship, and a link between the three realms.

The snake usually lives within the earth, within the body of the Mother. Originally, the snake was the symbol of the virgin goddess, who gave birth to the cosmos unaided by any male principle. The coiled serpent represented her vagina.

The snake was a symbol of water. Its movements are sinuous and wavelike, like the course of a river or stream. Snakes were linked with water cults and were often seen as the resident guardians of a well, particularly in the Celtic culture where they are depicted with gods and goddesses of sacred wells and healing, such as Brighid.

Because of its phallic shape and its reputed fertility, the snake is also a symbol of the male principle. Lightning is known as the sky-serpent or lightning-snake. The thunderstorm was believed to be the mating of the Sky Father and the Earth Mother, bringing the fertilizing rain.

Worship of the serpent goddess was widespread in predynastic northern Egypt. The uraeus headdress, worn by the pharaohs, symbolically gave the wearer the power of the third eye. All Egyptian queens were given the title of "Serpent of the Nile."

Because the snake sheds its skin each year and appears renewed, it was thought to be immortal. The ancient Chinese saw the process of rejuvenation as a person splitting his or her old skin and emerging once more as a youth. The Melanesians said that to slough one's skin meant eternal life. Snakes were identified with the patron god of healers, Asclepios, who was said to have appeared as a snake to heal Romans during a plague. The caduceus, still a symbol of medicine and healing, shows two intertwining snakes.

Sow: *Luck.* The sow, with its large litters, has long been a fertility symbol, hence lucky pigs and piggy banks. In Ireland, pigs are considered lucky, and small carvings of pigs are used as good luck charms, but only if some part is broken, like a leg or ear. In Egypt, pigs were slain at grand weddings because of their reputation for fecundity. Pigs were sacrificed to deities of agriculture as they "taught men to turn up the earth," or plow; the foraging pig turns up the earth with its snout.

They are sacred to the moon goddess. Their colors vary from white and red to black — the colors of the three phases of the moon. Menstruation means "moon-change," and women's cycles are related to the moon. The white waxing phase is the virgin, the red full moon phase is the menstruating fertile woman, and the black waning phase is woman past the age of childbirth; maiden, mother, and crone — the three phases of the goddess. Pigs feed on corpse flesh, are prolific breeders, and sometimes eat their own young, symbolizing the waning goddess of dissolution and destruction. Their tusks are crescent-shaped, echoing the crescent moon.

Stag: *Power and sacrifice.* The stag was one of the most sacred animals of the Celts and has played an important part in folklore in many areas of the world. The earliest representations of the stag god, or of a shaman dressed in stag horns, date from around 12,000 B.C.E. Horned beasts were generally considered sacred, the horns a symbol of fertility. Antlers were among the earliest tools used to till the soil, and powdered stag antlers are among the best fertilizers known to human kind.

The stag is most closely associated with the Gaulish god Cernunnos, who wears stag horns. He is usually portrayed as a seated figure with antlers growing from his head. He holds a snake in one hand and a torc in the other, showing that he is a god of winter and summer, sky and Underworld, death and resurrection. He is surrounded by the animals of the forest as Lord of the Animals.

Stags clean their new antlers around Lammas, rubbing off the velvety coating on the branches of trees, and the rutting season begins from then on. This may be another reason why battles are associated with Lughnasa.

In Arthurian legend, the knights would take part in a yearly hunt of the white stag, and its head would be presented to the fairest lady in the land. It was once thought that the "king stag," the leader of the herd, should be ritually hunted and killed every year to ensure the return of summer. The stag was identified with the sacred king, whose sacrifice was necessary. It is the fate of the antlered king to be hunted and betrayed; it is this that gives the cuckold his horns.[6] Llew saw a stag baited to death and was soon afterward murdered by his wife Blodeuwedd's lover, Gronw.

In Welsh and Irish poetry, a wave of the sea is a "sea stag," and in myth, both of the solar heroes Cuchulain and Fionn fought the waves with spears and swords, perhaps a symbolic slaying of the king stag to ensure the turning of the year.

Swan: *Poetry.* It was believed that the mute swan sings only once, just before it dies, hence the phrase "swan song," referring to a person's final work. The song of the swan is associated with Apollo, Greek god of music. His lyre had a swan's neck, head, feet, and feathers carved upon it. His soul once became a swan. The bard Orpheus is also said to have become a swan after his death. Swan skin and feathers were used to make the cloak of a Celtic poet. In some stories, the song of a swan held magical properties that could make mortals sleep. Thus the swan became the bird of poets; Shakespeare is sometimes titled "the Swan of Avon." In this respect, the swan also stands for the necessity of solitude and retreat in order to create.

Swans are associated with prophecy (knowing its own death) and knowledge of the Otherworld. In story, heroes, maidens, fairies, and princes are often transformed into swans, recognizable by the golden chains around their necks. The Norse valkyries, who took the souls of slain warriors to Valhalla, were swan maidens. Swans also pull the bark of the sun across the Underworld sea at night. Swans pulled Apollo's chariot when he journeyed to the land of the Hyperboreans, the people who lived behind the north wind, the country of his birth, identified with Britain.

Wolf: *Teaching and warriorship.* Wolves were thought to be very wise and able to share their knowledge with humans. The druid Bobaran met the white wolf Emhain Abhlac and threw three rowan berries into the air, three at the wolf, and three into his own mouth to receive the insight of the wolf. In Native American teaching, the wolf totem is represented by the Dog Star, Sirius, said to be the home of teachers in ancient times. The Wolf People are the clan of teachers.

Wolves are sometimes described as being well disposed to humankind, suckling and caring for legendary heroes and kings. The Romans instituted the festival of the Lupercalia (March 15) in honor of the she-wolf, Lupa, who cared for Romulus and Remus, the legendary founders of Rome. Wolves suckled King Cormac of Ireland, and wolves accompanied him all his life. There are other stories of humans, saints, magicians, goddesses, and gods having wolves as close companions. Merlin retired into the woodlands for several years and took as his companion a very old wolf. Saint Francis of Assisi was said to have tamed the ferocious wolf of Gubbio. Cernunnos is depicted with a wolf on the Gundestrup cauldron. In Scandinavian lore, Odin is accompanied by two wolves, Freki and Geri. A wolf was said to faithfully guard the head of King Edmund, the Martyr.

On the other hand, wolves were known to be savage hunters and killers. Many Saxon and Danish kings used "wolf" as part of their name and title to denote ferocity. Some Scottish clans are associated with the wolf, for example, Mac Lennan ("son of the wolf") and Mac Millan ("son of the wolf servant"). The Romans connected the wolf with the god of war, Mars, as it was said that whoever lost the war, the wolf always won, feeding on the bodies of the dead. In Norse myth, the Valkyries rode wolves to collect the souls of dead warriors from the battlefield and take them to eternal feasting in the halls of Valhalla.

The wolf is associated with the corn spirit. When the wind waves the corn in a wavelike motion, European peasants would say, "The wolf is going through the corn," or "The mad dog is in the corn." Children were told not to play in the crops or "the Rye-wolf will come and eat you up." The Roggenwolf ("rye-wolf") of German folklore haunts the grainfields and ambushes peasants, strangling them. Its mother is Kornmutter ("corn mother"). According to Alby Stone, the fungus ergot is associated with the rye and is sometimes called "wolf" or *wolfszahn* ("wolf tooth").[7] Poisoning by ergot was once fairly common, causing tremors, writhing, convulsions, rolling eyes, dizziness, hallucinations, extreme thirst, heat, cold, itching, and blistering. Stone points out that these symptoms are similar to rabies, and an observation of these signs could convey that lycanthropy is conveyed by the bite of a werewolf. Beowulf means "Barley Wolf" and hints at the same theme — the warrior who can turn into a beserker or beast. In Rügen, the woman who binds the last sheaf was called Wolf. She had to bite the lady of the house and then was given a large piece of meat.

Notes

1. The Lammas Assembly, ancient Irish Pagan charge, quoted from Nigel Pennick's *The God Year*.
2. Nigel Pennick, *Crossing the Borderlines*, 1998.
3. Giraldus Cambrensis, *The Historical Works*, Thomas Wright (ed.), Bohn, 1863.
4. Kaledon Naddair, *Keltic Folk and Fairy Tales*, 1987.
5. Macaulay, *History of St. Kilda*, n/d.
6. Robert Graves, *The White Goddess*, 1961.
7. Alby Stone, *At the Edge*, http:/www.gmtnet.co.uk/indigo/edge/soma.html.

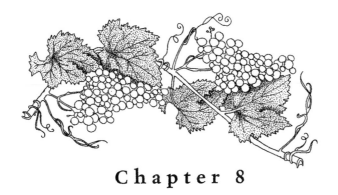

Chapter 8

The Lammas Kitchen

Lughnasa, make known its dues,
In each distant year:
Tasting every famous fruit,
Food of herbs at Lammas Day.[1]

Lammas is a time of abundance, with a plentiful supply of ripe summer produce. It is the start of the grain and grape harvests. Some of these recipes might seem "rich" or expensive, but they are what people would eat on special occasions. In addition there are some foods that are expensive nowadays but which used to be considered part of the staple diet. Apprentices in London used to complain if they were fed oysters or salmon too often.

Certain foods and herbs have an important ritual significance at Lammas — apples, basil, borage, chicory, fenugreek, fennel, grapes, honeysuckle, nasturtium flowers, poppy seeds, and vine leaves. Bread, beer, and wine are also meaningful.

The quantities of ingredients are listed in three types of measurement:

American (US)   Imperial   Metric

In some cases they have been rounded up or down, so make sure you stick with one set of measurements for each recipe. We haven't given precise quantities for some of the ingredients, as in the case of salt, pepper, herbs, etc., because these are a matter of personal taste and dietary requirements. Please note that in the ingredients lists, baking soda refers to bicarbonate of soda, while baking powder refers to sodium bicarbonate.

BREADS

Lammas celebrates the beginning of the grain harvest, so it seems fitting to start with a few bread recipes.

Soda Bread

This traditional Irish recipe produces a wonderful loaf, but it does need to be eaten quickly. Soda bread tends to go dry and crumbly very rapidly. As it is so delicious, this is usually not a problem.

US	Imperial	Metric	
2 c.	8 oz.	225 g	whole meal flour
2 c.	8 oz.	225 g	all-purpose white flour
1 tsp.	1 tsp.	1 tsp.	salt
3 tsp.	3 tsp.	3 tsp.	baking powder
1 tsp.	1 tsp.	1 tsp.	baking soda
1	1	1	egg
⅞ pt.	14 fl. oz.	400 ml.	buttermilk
			(or a mixture of ⅔ live yogurt and ⅓ water, if buttermilk is unavailable)

Mix all the dry ingredients in a large mixing bowl. Beat the egg and buttermilk (or yogurt and water) into the dry mixture. Turn out onto a lightly floured board, and knead thoroughly until the mixture is smooth. Shape the dough into a couple of round shapes and place on a lightly oiled baking tray or lightly oiled loaf tins. The round shape is more traditional, but be sure to incise a deep cross into the dough to represent the four main festivals of the Celtic calendar (it also helps the loaf to rise evenly).

Bake at 375 degrees F (190 degrees C/gas mark 5) for between 40 to 45 minutes. For a softer crust, wrap the loaf in a clean towel after it has cooled.

Plaited Bread

This is a basic white bread formed into a twisted plait to represent the corn lord and the spirit of the grain.

3 tsp.	3 tsp.	3 tsp.	Yeast
1 tsp.	1 tsp.	1 tsp.	sugar
¼ pt.	3½ oz.	150 ml	warm milk
6 c.	1½ lb.	675 g	all-purpose white flour
2 tsp.	2 tsp.	2 tsp.	salt
2 tbsp.	1 oz.	25 g	butter
¼ pt.	3½ oz.	150 ml	warm water
1	1	1	egg, beaten
			Sesame seeds

Prepare the yeast, either fresh or dried, by mixing with the sugar and warm milk. Leave it in a warm place until it is frothy; this should take between 10 to 20 minutes. Sift the flour and salt together in a bowl and rub in the butter with your fingers until the mixture resembles fine bread-crumbs. Add the yeast mixture and gradually add ¼ pint warm water to make a smooth and elastic dough. Turn out onto a lightly floured surface and thoroughly knead. Place in an oiled bowl, cover with a clean cloth, and leave in a warm place for an hour or two so the dough can rise.

Turn the dough back out onto a floured surface and knead for 5 minutes. Roll and shape the dough into a long, thin cylinder. Fold in half and overlap the two strands to form a plait. Place on a lightly oiled baking tray, brush with the beaten egg, and sprinkle with sesame seeds. Let rest for 1 hour in a warm place. Bake for 30 to 40 minutes in an oven at 375 degrees F (190 degrees C/gas mark 5).

St. Oswald's Gingerbread Squares

In the village of Grasmere (in the English Lake District), gingerbread is traditionally eaten on the Saturday nearest to St. Oswald's Day (August 5). The village children are given pieces of gingerbread stamped with the saint's name and a shiny new coin. St. Oswald's Gingerbread is popular with visitors to Grasmere; such well-known stars as Tom Cruise and Nicole Kidman have visited the village bakery to try it. The local recipe is a closely guarded secret, but the variation given below is probably even better.

6 c.	1½ lb.	675 g	all-purpose white flour
½ c.	1⅕ oz.	40 g	ground ginger
1 tsp.	1 tsp.	1 tsp.	ground cinnamon
1 tsp.	1 tsp.	1 tsp.	baking powder
1½ c.	8 oz.	225 g	brown sugar
3 tbsp.	1½ oz.	40 g	crystallized ginger
1 c.	8 oz.	225 g	butter
1¼ c.	1 lb.	450 g	treacle
¼ pt.	5 fl. oz.	150 ml	brandy or dark rum
1	1	1	egg, beaten
			Mixture of milk and egg yoke (to glaze)

In a bowl sift the flour, spices, and baking soda together. Add the crystallized ginger and mix in. Melt the butter with the treacle in a pan. Remove from the heat and stir in the brandy or rum. Add the beaten egg to make the dough smooth.

Grease a large baking tray and line with parchment paper (greaseproof paper). Spoon on the mixture and bake 70 to 80 minutes at 350 degrees F (180 degrees C/ gas mark 4). Remove from the oven and brush with the milk and egg glaze. Return to the oven for another 10 minutes.

Allow to cool for 10 to 15 minutes, then tip out onto a wire rack. Cut the gingerbread into squares and store in an airtight tin.

BANNOCKS

Bannocks, *aran corca* in Gaelic, are a traditional Scottish oatmeal cookie. At Marymass the Scots would dedicate the first bannock made with the new grain, the Moilean Moire, to the Virgin Mary. They can be sweet or savory and are eaten with fish, cheese, honey, or anything that needs an edible base.

Bannocks were originally cooked on a griddle, one of the oldest cooking utensils developed from the hot stones used for baking, known as *greadeal* to the ancient Gaels. They were introduced into Canada and the United States by Irish and Scottish settlers, and several Native American tribes produced varieties of bannock as a result.

Oatmeal Bannock

This is a very traditional type of bannock and can be cooked on a pan or griddle over a fire or barbecue grill.

1⅓ c.	4 oz.	125 g	medium oatmeal
			Pinch of salt
			Pinch of baking powder
2 tbsp.	1 oz.	30 g	melted butter
¼ c.	2 fl. oz.	50 ml	warm water

Mix the oatmeal, salt, and baking soda in a bowl and stir in the melted butter. Add enough of the water to make a stiff paste. Roll into a ball and knead on a breadboard lightly dusted with oatmeal. Roll the dough out to ¼-inch thickness (7 centimeters) and trim to a circle shape using a plate. Sprinkle with a little oatmeal and cut into quarters. Cook on a warm, lightly oiled griddle until the edges begin to curl. Flip the bannocks over and cook the other side. Bannocks can be served hot or cold.

Selkirk Bannock

There are hundreds of recipes for bannocks. This variety is a flat, round, yeasted loaf containing dried fruit. They were first made in 1859 by Robbie Douglas in his bakery at Selkirk (Scotland) and were a favorite of Queen Victoria on her visits to the Scottish Highlands.

½ c.	4 oz.	80 g	butter
½ c.	4 oz.	80 g	lard
1 c.	8 fl. oz.	200 ml	warm milk
1 tsp.	1 tsp	1 tsp	yeast
1 tsp.	1 tsp	1 tsp	sugar (for the yeast)
7 c.	2 lbs.	900 g	all-purpose flour
1 c.	6 oz.	180 g	sugar
3½ c.	1 lb.	450 g	sultanas or seedless raisins
			Warm milk and sugar (for glazing)

Melt the butter and lard until soft (but not oily). Then add the warm milk. Mix the yeast with the teaspoon of sugar and add to the mixture. Sift the flour into a bowl, make a depression in the middle, and pour in the liquid. Mix and cover the bowl with a cloth and leave for about an hour, or until the mixture has doubled in size.

Knead on a floured board until the dough feels smooth and elastic. Add the cup of sugar and the sultanas or raisins. Knead again for 5 to 10 minutes and shape the dough into a flat round, about 9 inches in diameter (23 centimeters). Place on a buttered baking tray and let rise for about 45 minutes. Bake at 350 degrees F (180 degrees C/gas mark 5) for about 45 minutes. Remove from the oven and brush with a little warm milk and sugar. Return to the oven and bake until golden, about another 20 to 30 minutes. When properly cooked, the loaf should sound hollow when tapped on the bottom.

POTATOES

The potato replaced wheat as the staple of the Irish peasant farmers when other produce was exported to pay rent to often absentee landlords. The potato harvest was crucial to their survival, and a successful crop was essential to avoid starvation.

Boxty Scones

Boxty on the griddle, boxty in the pan,
If you can't make boxty you'll never get your man.

Boxty would be eaten at Lughnasa and was also traditional on St. Bridgit's Eve (Imbolc). This is a scone variation of the original Irish variety (which are thinner and fried in bacon fat).

1 c.	8 oz.	225 g	potatoes, peeled and diced
2 c.	½ lb.	225 g	self-raising flour
			Pinch of salt and black pepper
2½ tbsp.	2 oz.	60 g	butter
3 tbsp.	1 fl. oz.	25 ml	milk

Boil and mash the potatoes; allow to cool. Add salt and pepper to the flour and mix in the butter. Add the mashed potatoes and enough milk to make a soft, but not too moist and sloppy, dough. Turn the dough out onto a floured surface and roll it out to about ½-inch thickness (1.5 centimeters). Cut into 3-inch circles (8 centimeters) using a pastry cutter. Arrange on a lightly greased tray. Bake at 400 degrees F (200 degrees C/gas mark 6) for 20 to 30 minutes. Eat the boxty scones warm, split in half, and spread with butter. Makes about 9 or 10 scones.

Colcannon

This is another Irish potato recipe. Nowadays it is eaten throughout the year, especially on St. Patrick's Day and at Halloween, but was one of the most popular and traditional Lughnasa foods during the eighteenth and nineteenth centuries.

6 c.	1 lb.	450 g	cabbage or kale, chopped finely
½ pt.	7 fl. oz.	200 ml	milk or cream
2	2	2	small leeks or scallions, chopped
5 c.	2 lb.	900 g	potatoes, diced
			Pinch of salt and black pepper
			Pinch of ground nutmeg
4 tbsp.	3 oz.	80 g	melted butter

Cook the cabbage or kale in a pan of boiling water until it is tender. Drain and keep warm. Heat the milk or cream with the leeks or onions and gently simmer until soft. Boil the potatoes until tender, then drain and mash them. Mix in the other cooked ingredients and season with salt, pepper, and nutmeg. Drizzle the melted butter over the top and serve. Serves 4.

SOUPS AND SALADS

Three Sisters Soup

The Three Sisters—beans, corn, and squash—have traditionally been planted together by Native American gardeners throughout many regions of North America. This form of companion planting, where a beneficial mini-ecosystem is created, was invented by the Haudenasaunee ("People of the Long House").

> *We plant them together, three kinds of seeds in one hole. They want to be*
> *together with each other, just as we Indians want to be together with each other.*
> *So long as the three sisters are with us we know we will never starve.*
> *The Creator sends them to us each year. We celebrate them now.*
> *We thank Him for the gift He gives us today and every day.*
>
> —Chief Louis Farmer of the Onondaga

¼ c.	1½ oz.	40 g	butter
1	1	1	clove of garlic, grated
2 pt.	2½ pt.	1 l	stock, or a stock cube added to 2 pints water
			Pinch of salt and black pepper
			Pinch of nutmeg
3 c.	1 lb.	450 g	runner beans or French beans, sliced finely
4 c.	1 lb.	450 g	squash, diced into small pieces
3 c.	1 lb.	450 g	corn

Melt the butter in a large saucepan and add the garlic to soften. Pour in the stock and season with salt, pepper, and nutmeg. Add the vegetables and bring to a boil. Simmer until the vegetables are cooked.

Lughnasa Salad

This is a very colorful and attractive salad that uses several of the herbs and plants that are associated with Lughnasa. The edible flowers are a particular feature of this dish and both nasturtium and borage can be grown in large pots outside in your yard. Nasturtium is especially easy to grow; its large seeds make it ideal and great fun for children to cultivate.

Nasturtium is associated with the sun and with male strength — ideal for Lughnasa. Its Latin name *tropaeoleum* means "a trophy"; the flowers were said to represent the golden helmet of a Trojan warrior and the leaves his round shield. Borage is also associated with warriors and was one of the magical herbs of the ancient Celts. Its name is possibly derived from *borrach*, the Celtic word for a courageous person. Borage was widely cultivated during mediaeval times. There was a saying that "a garden without borage is like a heart without courage."

1 tbsp.	1 tbsp.	1 tbsp.	olive oil
1½ c.	8 oz.	225 g	cooked corn
½ c.	2 oz.	60 g	peas
½ c.	2 oz.	60 g	black olives, halved and pitted
1	1	1	large apple, diced
1 tbsp.	1 tbsp.	1 tbsp.	Finely chopped fresh herbs (basil, borage leaves, fennel)
			Pinch of black pepper
½	½	½	cucumber, finely chopped
			Nasturtium flowers
1 tbsp.	1 tbsp.	1 tbsp.	Borage flowers

Lightly toss all the ingredients in the olive oil, except the flowers. Pour into a bowl and decorate with the nasturtium flowers and sprinkle with the borage flowers. (Yes, they are edible!) The nasturtiums have a peppery taste rather reminiscent of watercress. This is a fairly strong-tasting salad, so it is best served with something bland.

FISH AND SEAFOOD

Scalloped Oysters

As well as Lammas being the start of the grain harvest, it was also seen as the commencement of the harvest of the sea. The traditional start of the oyster harvest was on St. James' Day, July 25. On the old calendar, St. James' Day would have been near to Lammas, on what we now know as August 5. Interestingly, St. James was the fisherman whose saint's day is celebrated in Spain at Compostela de Sagrado.

12	12	12	oysters
1 tbsp.	½ oz.	12 g	butter
1 tbsp.	½ oz.	12 g	flour
2 tbsp.	2 tbsp.	20 ml	cream
			Pinch of salt and black pepper
1/2 c.	2 oz.	50 g	breadcrumbs
1/2 c.	2 oz.	50 g	melted butter

Carefully open the oysters and remove them from the shells, saving the liquid. Remove the beards from the oysters. Simmer the oysters in the reserved liquid and a little water for around 10 minutes. Strain off the liquid and put it off to the side. Place the oysters in a dish. Melt the butter in a saucepan, add the flour and reserved oyster liquid and cook for 2 or 3 minutes, stirring constantly. Add the cream and the oysters; add salt and pepper to taste. Grease the empty shells with butter and fill with the oysters and sauce. Cover each with the breadcrumbs and pour on a little melted butter. Bake for 15 to 20 minutes at 200 degrees C (400 degrees F/gas mark 6), until brown and bubbling.

Baked Salmon with Cream and Hazelnuts

Fintan was the Salmon of Knowledge in Irish mythology. Originally human, he gained his wisdom by eating hazelnuts, and each nut gave him a red spot on his back and increased his wisdom. The hazel is the Celtic tree of wisdom, and its nuts represent this knowledge in its most concentrated form. Eventually, the Salmon of Knowledge was eaten by the legendary hero Fionn mac Cumhal. Fionn burnt his thumb on the magical salmon and, henceforth, had only to place the thumb in his mouth to foretell the future. Unfortunately we cannot guarantee similar results from this recipe, but who knows. It's certainly worth a try! Ideally this recipe should be made with freshly caught river salmon, but this may prove difficult, so farmed salmon is an acceptable substitute. Trout can also be used.

2–3 lbs.	2–3 lbs.	900–1500 g	fresh salmon, cleaned and skinned
3 tbsp.	2 oz.	60 g	butter
			Pinch of salt and black pepper
½ pt.	½ pt.	300 ml	heavy cream (or double cream)
1 tbsp.	1 oz.	25 g	melted butter
1 tbsp.	1 tbsp.	1 tbsp.	chopped fresh parsley
			Juice of 1 lemon
½ c.	2 oz.	55 g	crushed hazelnuts

Clean and scale the salmon and rub it all over with the butter. Place it in an ovenproof dish. Season with salt and pepper. Pour the cream around the fish and cover the dish with aluminum foil. Bake at 350 degrees F (180 degrees C/gas mark 4) for 30 to 45 minutes (depending on the size of the fish).

Remove from the oven and baste with more butter. Stir the parsley and half the lemon juice into the sauce. Sprinkle with the crushed hazelnuts. Leave the dish uncovered and gently broil (grill) for about 10 minutes. Squeeze the remaining lemon juice over the salmon.

Serve the fish by slitting along the spine with a sharp knife and cutting portions off each side. Lift each portion off the bone, turning the salmon over to repeat the process. Serves 4 to 6.

Fisherman's Pie

This dish is suitable for St. James' Day, as this festival on July 25 was dedicated to fishermen, whose boats would traditionally be blessed on this day. In fact, this recipe is fairly multicultural, as it also uses both potatoes and corn (maize/sweet corn), linking it with the Irish celebration of Lughnasa and the Native American Green Corn Ceremony.

1 lb.	1 lb.	450 g	cod, coley, or similar fish
			Juice of 1 lemon
			Pinch of salt and black pepper
1½ c.	8 oz.	225 g	corn
1½ c.	6 oz.	180 g	cheddar cheese, grated
			Pinch of mustard powder
4	4	4	hardboiled eggs, roughly chopped
2 c.	1 lb.	450 g	cooked mashed potatoes (with a touch of milk, butter, salt and pepper added)

Sauce:

½ stick	2 oz.	50 g	butter
½ c.	2 oz.	50 g	all-purpose flour
½ c.	1 oz.	25 g	finely chopped parsley
1¼ pt.	1 pt.	500 ml	milk
			Pinch of salt and black pepper

To make the sauce: melt the butter in a saucepan over low heat. Stir in the flour and cook for a couple of minutes. Add the parsley and a little of the milk. Gradually add the rest of the milk, stirring constantly until it comes to the boil. Reduce heat and gently simmer for a couple of minutes. Add the salt and pepper.

Put the fish on a buttered heatproof plate and season with the lemon juice, salt, and pepper. Cover the plate with aluminum foil and steam over a pan of boiling water until the fish is flaky; this should take about 10 to 15 minutes. Strain off any juice and add to the sauce, along with the corn. Blend in the cheese and mustard powder and gently heat the sauce. Flake the fish and toss with the eggs in an oven-proof dish. Pour on the sauce and spread the mashed potatoes on top. Bake in the oven at 400 degrees F (200 degrees C/gas mark 6) until the top is golden, approximately 20 minutes.

Berries and Fruit

Apple Jelly

Apples or crab apples
Water
Sugar

Peel and core the apples (use as many or as few as you like). Chop them roughly and put them in a large pan with just enough water to cover. Simmer gently for 10 to 15 minutes, until the fruit is soft and pulpy; remove from heat. Drain the liquid from the fruit by pouring the pulp through a jelly bag (muslin bag) or the knotted sleeve of an old cotton shirt. Allow to drain overnight, if possible, to extract as much liquid as you can. Do not squeeze the bag as solid pieces will be pushed out, and these will cloud the jelly.

The next day, discard the fruit pulp and measure the collected liquid. Return it to the pan and add 1 pound of sugar (500 grams) for every pint of liquid (500 milliliters). Boil until setting point is reached. (Use a sugar thermometer or test by dropping a little of the hot liquid onto a saucer. When the cooled drop of jelly wrinkles when it is touched, the jelly is ready.) Remove from heat and pour into warmed, clean glass jars. If you use crab apples rather than cultivated varieties, the resulting jelly will be an attractive bright pink color.

Summer Pudding

This easy-to-make traditional nineteenth-century English recipe is perfect for Lammas, combining bread with the summer berries that were traditionally picked at Lughnasa.

The Sunday of Lughnasa is known in many parts of Ireland as Bilberry Sunday, and it would be ideal to include this fruit in the recipe. Depending on where you live, this could prove impossible, but make every effort to include other small berry fruits that you have picked in your locality to retain the symbolism and the link with tradition (try and avoid imported "agri-business" produce). Despite this recipe's simplicity (or maybe because of it), we think it is wonderful. It is also great fun for children to lend a hand.

6 c.	2 lb.	1 kg	bilberries, blackberries, blueberries, black currants, cranberries, raspberries, red currants, or similar fruit
1 c.	6 oz.	180 g	sugar
			Good quality white bread, one or two days old

Wash the fruit and leave in a bowl with the sugar overnight. The next day, tip the contents into a saucepan and bring to a boil. Gently simmer for 2 or 3 minutes to lightly cook the fruit. There should be a fair amount of juice.

Cut the loaf into slices about ¼-inch thick (1 centimeter) and remove the crusts. Cut a circle from one slice of the bread slightly larger than the bottom of a 2½-pint (1 liter) pudding dish or similar bowl and place in position. Cut wedges of bread to fit around the sides of the bowl. If there are any gaps, push in small pieces of bread. Now pour in half of the fruit and juice mixture, cover with bread cut to shape, and add the remainder of fruit and juice. Cover the top with a couple of slices of bread, trimming off the excess to make a nice, neat finish to the pudding.

Put a plate on top and weight it down with two or three cans of food. Leave it in the refrigerator for a day or two, or at least overnight. If, by chance, there are any patches of bread not soaked in the fruit juice, boil a few more berries and pour the juice over the white bits.

When the pudding is taken out of the refrigerator, run a thin, flexible knife between the pudding and the bowl to loosen it. Place a serving dish or large plate, upside down, on top of the bowl. Quickly turn it over and remove the bowl. Serve with vast amounts of cream, as this is an intensely flavored pudding, and a little goes a long way. It should serve between 6 to 8 people (or, alternatively, one Anna Franklin).

YELLOWMAN

Did you treat your Mary Ann to dulse and yellowman,
At the Ould Lammas Fair at Ballycastle-O?

Dulse is a purplish-colored, edible seaweed that is stewed and eaten as a vegetable. It is virtually unknown outside of Northern Ireland, as it sounds disgusting; this is probably no great loss! Yellowman, on the other hand, is a sticky, honeycombed toffee that is traditional at fairs.

Yellowman Toffee

1½ c.	1 lb.	500 g	corn syrup
1½ c.	8 oz.	250 g	brown sugar
1 tbsp.	2 oz.	50 g	butter
2 tbsp.	2 tbsp.	25 ml	vinegar
1 tsp.	1 tsp.	1 tsp.	baking soda

Slowly melt all the ingredients together in a large saucepan, except the baking soda. Boil until a drop hardens in cold water or 240 degrees F (190 degrees C) on a sugar thermometer. Stir in the baking soda. The toffee will foam up as the gas from the soda is released by the vinegar. Pour into a tin greased with butter. When it is just cool enough to handle, fold the edges to the center and repeatedly pull the mixture until it is a pale yellow color. Allow it to cool and harden, and then break it into chunks with a small hammer.

BEVERAGES

Warrior's Cup

This drink is served at the Lughnasa games or during the ritual. It contains borage, the name being derived from *borrach*, the Celtic word for a courageous person.[2] It is also associated with warriors and was one of the magical herbs of the ancient Celts. Celtic ancestors would steep borage leaves in wine, and the mixture would result in a significant rise in the blood adrenaline level. To give courage to the Crusaders,

borage was added to stirrup cups drunk at their departure. It is believed that carrying borage flowers can bring you courage.

1 c.	6 fl. oz.	200 ml	white wine
3	3	3	fresh borage leaves
			Borage flowers for decoration

Steep the leaves in the wine for 4 hours. Strain and decorate with a few flowers.

Borage Tea

| 2 | 2 | 2 | borage leaves |
| 1 c. | 6 fl. oz. | 200 ml | boiling water |

Infuse for 10 minutes and strain.

Goldenrod Wine

1 gal.	1 gal.	4 l	water
1 gal.	1 gal.	4 l	goldenrod flowers
7 c.	3 lb.	1½ k	sugar
2	2	2	oranges and their grated rinds
2	2	2	lemons and their grated rinds
1 c.	6 fl. oz.	200 ml	black tea, cooled
			Yeast (follow manufacturer's directions)
			Yeast nutrient (follow manufacturer's directions)

Boil the water. Put the flowers in a jelly bag (muslin bag) or a cotton pillowcase.
Knot the top and drop it into the water and simmer for 20 minutes. Remove from
heat, and when cool enough to touch, take out the bag, squeezing it well to extract
all the liquid. Dissolve the sugar in this flower liquor. Add the juice from the
oranges and lemons and the grated rinds. Place in a brewing bin (large plastic bin
with tight-fitting lid). When cooled to lukewarm (70 degree F/20 degrees C), add
the tea, yeast, and nutrient. Cover and keep in a warm place for 3 days, stirring
daily. Strain into a 1-gallon glass brewing jar. Seal airtight. Keep in a warm place for

2 months. Rack off (syphon) into a clean glass brewing jar and put in a cooler place for another 6 months.

Beer

			Yeast (follow manufacturer's directions)
2 pt.	2 pt.	1 l	hops
2 c.	1 lb.	500 g	sugar
2 c.	1 lb.	500 g	malt
2 gal.	2 gal.	8 l	water

Activate the yeast. Put the hops in a large pan and cover with water. Boil for 15 minutes, then strain the liquid into a brewing bin. Add the sugar and malt and stir to dissolve. Add the rest of the water. When cooled to lukewarm (70 degrees F/ 20 degrees C), add the yeast. Cover and let stand for 5 days. Pour in screw-topped bottles and let sit for 7 days before drinking.

Lammas Wool

The apple harvest also begins at Lughnasa, the time of strength and fruitfulness, when the God prepares himself for his decline and death at Herfest. He is honored with Lamb's Wool, or Lammas Wool (from the Gaelic La Mas Nbhal, or "feast of the apple gathering"), a hot spiced drink of cider and ale, with toast or pieces of apple floating in it. Each person takes out a piece and wishes good luck to everyone before eating it and passing the cup on.

4	4	4	large cooking apples
2 tbsp.	2 tbsp.	30 g	honey
1 tsp.	1 tsp.	1 tsp.	ground nutmeg
12 c.	4 pt.	2 l	ale (or beer from previous recipe)

Core the apples and fill the centers with honey. Sprinkle with nutmeg and bake in the oven for 40 minutes in a deep baking dish. Remove from the oven and pour the ale over the apples. Heat gently over low heat for a few minutes, spooning the ale over the apples. Strain off the liquid and serve warm. The apples can be served separately.

Yard of Flannel

6 c.	2 pt.	1 l	ale
½ c.	3 fl. oz.	75 ml	rum
1 c.	¼ lb.	130 g	sugar
4	4	4	eggs
½ tsp.	½ tsp.	½ tsp.	ground nutmeg
½ tsp.	½ tsp.	½ tsp.	cinnamon

Warm the ale over low heat. In a bowl, beat together the other ingredients. Slowly add the ale to the mixture, stirring constantly. When the mixture is creamy, pour into warmed mugs.

Notes

1. K. Meyer, *Hibernica Minora*, 1894.
2. Anna Franklin and Sue Philips, *Pagan Feasts*, 1998.

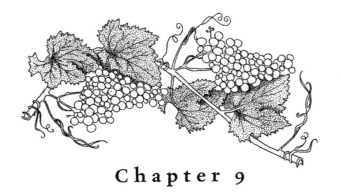

Chapter 9

Lammas/Lughnasa Rituals

O let me teach you how to knit again
This scattered corn into one mutual sheaf,
These broken limbs again into one body.[1]

PREPARATION FOR INDOOR RITUALS

The place in which you are to work should be cleared of as much furniture as physically possible. The room should be thoroughly cleaned and purified with cleansing incense, such as frankincense or rosemary.

The Altar

A low table or chest can be used as an altar. This should be placed on the north side of the room (you might need a compass to find the cardinal points). Cover it with a white cloth. On it place something to represent the Goddess and the God; what this might be is up to you. Some people have statues, but if you don't, think carefully about something natural that represents the deities to you. I have a pair of stag horns to represent the God, but it could be a pine cone or a pointed stone; use your imagination and what seems right to you. To represent the Goddess you might have a shell, a holed stone, or a mirror. The Goddess image is placed on the left, and the God image on the right.

Place three candles in holders on the altar. I use white, red, and black ones to represent the three stages of the Goddess — maiden, mother, crone — but you might like to use colors suitable to the occasion. For Lammas these would be orange, purple, or brown.

A dish of salt and a dish of water are placed near the front. A plate of bread or cakes and some wine in an open bottle or jug are placed to one side. You will need a cup or goblet for drinking the wine, and some people insist on a pentacle of clay or copper being placed on the altar. You will also need a knife that you keep for ritual

purposes, which some people call an athame. In the old days the cup was simply the best cup in the house, and the athame an ordinary knife just kept aside for ritual. These days people buy or make special equipment; this is nice but not necessary.

You can also decorate the altar with corn and grain, apples, grapes, bilberries, and blackberries. Place a dish of incense on it.

The Quarters

A candle is placed in each of the quarters. The colors chosen help to resonate with the vibration of that quarter: green for the north (earth), yellow for the east (air), red for the south (fire), and blue for the west (water). If you can't get these you can use white candles, but the more you can reinforce the imagery, the more it helps your visualization. Some people also like to place something that represents the elements in the quarters: a dish of earth in the north, the incense in the east, a flame or candle in the south, a dish of water in the west.

Check that you have everything you need within the circle (remember the matches!) before you start, as once the circle is cast, you will not be able to leave to get it.

CASTING THE CIRCLE FOR INDOOR RITES

Light the incense. The first act that must be performed is to establish the boundaries of the circle. Take the knife and, beginning in the north, draw the circle around the room. Remember where the point of the knife draws will be the edge of the circle. Include in the circle all the things and people you wish to be within the circle.

Take the knife and place the tip in the bowl of salt, saying:

> *Be this salt dedicated to the Lord and Lady to keep us from evil and*
> *protect us in this time.*

Take the knife again and place the tip in the bowl of water, saying:

> *Be this water dedicated to the Lord and Lady to keep us from peril*
> *and to purify this place.*

Tip the water into the salt and mix them together. Sprinkle clockwise (deosil) around the circle, saying:

> *May we cast from us all evil and darkness, viciousness and malice. May we become that which we must be before the Lord and Lady, seeking ill to no one. May we be clean within and without so that we are acceptable before them.*

Finish by sprinkling each person in turn.

Next connect the circle to all three realms. Take the knife and stand in the center of the circle. Point it above and say:

> *Powers of the worlds above, I do summon, stir and call you up to guard our circle and to witness our rites.*

Bring the knife down in a straight line and point it downwards. Say:

> *Powers of the worlds below, I do summon, stir and call you up to guard our circle and to witness our rites.*

The circle is then invoked. Take the knife and begin in the north. The casting of the circle is always begun in the north as this is the place of power that flows from north to south, so the power gateway is opened. Many people do not begin the invocations until reaching the east, as this is the direction of vocalization.

Draw a pentacle in the east, and say:

> *O mighty powers of the east, I do summon, stir and call you up to guard our circle and to witness our rites.*

Repeat this in the south, west, and north.

Return to the altar, and consecrate the altar candles with the words:

> *Be to me the fire of moon,*
> *Be to me the fire of night,*
> *Be to me the fire of joy,*
> *Turning darkness into light,*
> *By the Virgin, waxing cold,*
> *By the Mother, full and bold,*
> *By the Hag Queen, silent, old,*

By the moon, the one in three,
Consecrated, blessed be.

Light the candles, and take one around to light all the quarter candles. If you wish you can carry the dish of incense around the circle.

The God and the Goddess are then invoked:

(Goddess name²) I invoke and call upon thee, threefold Goddess of the moon, (goddess name), Queen of the moonlit sea, fairer than night and silver clad, thee I invoke. Mother of the moon and calm waters, let thy light fall upon us for thy hair is a pool of stars in the darkness. I call upon thee, widow of the waning moon whose children have left thee to sorrow. Guard us with learning and grant us a place in thy dark cloak of understanding. Thee I invoke. Descend I beseech thee and be with us now.

The God is then invoked:

(God name) Lord of the heaven and power of the sun. Lord of the hunt and forests. I invoke thee in thy secret name of (god name). Come unto us and honor our circle we beg of you. Mighty one, our Lord, all honor to thee, consort of the Goddess. Come, I call upon thee. Descend I beseech thee and be with us now.

The purpose of the ritual is then stated:

Lord and Lady, God and Goddess, sacred pair that were with us before the dawn of time and shall be till its dusk, hear now the purpose of this ritual and witness it. (State the purpose. On this occasion, the purpose of the ritual is to celebrate the Festival of Lammas.)

The circle dance is performed to raise power:

Thrice about the altar go
Once for Virgin pure as snow,
Once for Full Moon's soft sweet breath,
Once for Dark Moon, old as death.
Thrice about the altar spin
That the rite shall well begin.

The work of the ritual is now performed (see the Lammas rites below).

Ceremony of the Cakes and Wine

When the work of the ritual is accomplished, the cakes and wine are blessed and shared. Take the wine and pour it into the cup and say:

> *Lord and Lady, I call upon you to bless this wine, the blood of the earth pressed smooth. As we drink of thee may we learn of the wisdom of the Goddess.*

The wine is passed around clockwise. Take the cakes and say:

> *Lord and Lady, I call upon thee to bless these cakes, the fruit of the womb of the Goddess without which we would not live. As we eat of thee may we learn of the love of the Goddess.*

The cakes are passed around. Everyone takes one and eats it.

Dissolving the Circle

When all is finished, the circle is dissolved. Take the knife and cut through the boundary of the circle near the east and say:

> *Mighty powers of the east, thank you for guarding our circle and for witnessing our rites. I bless you in the name of the Lord and the Lady.*

Repeat in all the other directions. Cut through the center and thank the powers of above and below. The Lord and Lady are not dismissed but thanked, saying:

> *Companions, we have met together this night to celebrate the feast of Lammas. Together we have worked for our purposes. The God and Goddess have witnessed our workings and only they will measure our purposes and our hearts. Together we have invoked for power to accomplish our working, but it is not for us to command those whom we worship. Nor is it for us to bid them be gone. We cannot dismiss them. I ask instead of the Lord and Lady (God and Goddess names) that they are with us all our days, guiding our feet and lighting our paths. I ask that the Lord and Lady are with us in our*

lives and in our deaths, our true parents, even as we are their children.
Let the circle be extinguished but let us not forget the workings of this night.
Let the candles be put out but let us not forget what we have learned.
Let the rite be ended now in the knowledge we shall meet once more.

Before the Lord and Lady (God and Goddess name), God and Goddess,
the rite is ended. Blessed Be.

Put out the candles and dismantle the temple.

OUTDOOR RITUALS

When working indoors it is usual to incorporate a greater degree of ritual in order to build up the atmosphere. Outdoors it is much easier to feel the connections with the web, and usually the rituals are much simpler and often more powerful.

The altar may be a simple cloth on a tree stump, rock, or on the ground. Candles in jars can be placed on the altar and at the quarter points. The candles are lit and the axis mundi is invoked (see above). The circle is drawn with the knife, pausing to invoke the quarters at the cardinal points. The Lord and Lady are invoked, and the purpose of the ritual is stated. The circle dance is performed around the fire or cauldron in the center. The working of the night is then done. The cakes and wine are blessed and shared, and the circle is dismantled in the order it was created.

Everything should be collected and taken home with you. Do not leave candle stubs, crystals, or incense behind. The only thing I leave is some cake for the forest spirits, and I always pour a libation of wine on the ground.

RITE FOR LUGHNASA

In certain branches of the Traditional Craft, Lammas is celebrated as a festival of the God who, while at the height of his powers, must meet his death with the cutting of the corn. As a counterpoint to the Imbolc festival—celebrated by the women of the coven as a festival of the Goddess—Lammas is celebrated by the men as a festival of the God. However, they may decide to admit the women by consensus. If the women are permitted, then they must take part as warriors in the rough games that form part of the rite. The culmination of these games is the selection of the champion, who acts as sacred king in a marriage with the goddess of the land. He is marked with a tattoo that will last until Harvest Home at Herfest (September 21). He promises to sacrifice himself then for the good of the land. The sacrifice he makes is that of John Barleycorn, when he breaks the bread at the harvest feast, but the duty and honor of the role is very real; should he fail to keep his promise, the coven and the land will suffer.

The men proceed to the ritual site and set up the circle without the women. They may choose to dress as warriors with ritual woad or henna tattoos and animal totem masks or shields. The magister opens the circle wearing a stag mask.

Priest:

> *Lord of the Sun, the Hunt and Fire. . . .,[3] be with us now before the time of thy departure. We call upon thee this night for this is the time of thy festival. Come unto us we beg, and honor our circle. Come, before the time of departure is upon us, come and bless this rite.*

The men now perform any magic they wish to share between themselves. This may include secrets of hunting magic, stories of the god, dances, totem work, drumming, etc. The priest then steps forward.

Priest:

> *This is the festival of man, the hunt and the harvest which provide for the time of darkness. Yet the God stands alone without his proper consort. She must grieve for his departure and take him into the dark places. The women folk have been excluded on this night. How say you, servants of. . . .,[4] shall we let them enter?*

If the men decide to admit the women of the coven, each woman is challenged at the edge of the circle and asked what skills she brings to the assembly. She must reply according to her real skills, such as "I am a poet," or "I am an artist," or "I keep the hearth fire." Perhaps if she is a policewoman, soldier, or martial artist, "I am a warrior." If the men decide not to admit the women (though in practice it is virtually unknown for men to refuse them), they must continue the work of the night and close the circle alone.

The Warrior's Cup (for recipe, see chapter 8) is passed around, and the games are then celebrated with contests of skill and strength (for some ideas, see chapter 6.) Drumming, merriment, and calls of encouragement accompany all the games. When a champion has emerged, the atmosphere becomes solemn.

The champion is led to the coven's Fal Stone,[5] and if possible, is seated upon it or otherwise places his hand upon it. He is crowned with a wreath.

The champion swears:

> *My triumph I dedicate to the Goddess of the Land. With my strength and courage I will defend the land and all upon it. With my skill and knowledge I will protect and guide my brothers and sisters of the Craft. All this I swear in the name of the Goddess. This too I swear—that when the forces of dark and light stand in balance I will return and make sacrifice.*

Priest:

> *Witness now that our God is dying, but know that even in his death he gives his strength to the grain and his life to the harvest.*

The priest takes up the loaf and breaks it, saying:

> *The year did spin and spring come round*
> *While our dear Lord lay in the ground*
> *Till rain fell thick upon his bed*
> *And slowly then he raised his head*
> *And grew apace till Midsummer's Day*
> *When with his flowering bride he lay*
> *But the year spins round and he must die*
> *And as a seed must once more lie*
> *We hunt him down with sharpened sickle*
> *To pierce his heart and see blood trickle*
> *To flay his skin from off his bones*
> *And grind him up between two stones*
> *Our dying Lord has lost his head*
> *But with his death we have our bread.*

He takes four fragments of bread and places one in the north, one in the east, one in the south, and one in the west, saying at each:

Lord, give us your protection.

Each person present then eats part of the loaf. A cup of wine is blessed and passed around the circle.

The circle is closed, but feasting and storytelling follow.

Witch Rite for Lammas Eve

The place of meeting is decorated with ash boughs, apples, blackberries, grapes, and grain sheaves. The coveners should ride to the place of ritual on riding poles or hobbyhorses. Before the rite poems are read and songs are sung of sacrifice, of love betrayed, of parting and death. Any music and dancing should be slow and solemn. Games, wrestling, fencing, and footraces are traditional. The maiden crowns the winner.

The priestess casts the Great Circle. She stands before the north, arms outstretched, and invokes:

O Goddess, friend and sister to women, wife and mother to men, thou who art all woman, be among us as we learn the ancient sacred to thee.

She lowers her arms and rejoins priest.
Priest:

Throughout this world and others, and the many strange and the beautiful worlds of watersprites, nymphs, and woodsprites, creatures of earth and fire, in our many lives and the lives of others, in the great power of knowledge and in the magic of countless centuries of time it is known that all things are cyclic. Kingdoms rise and fall and others rise from them. Land come from the sea and to the sea return after aeons the mountains rise and sink into the waves and rise again in ages later. In all this the story remains the same, holding within it the greatest of truths and the greatest of magic.

The coven reflects on this.

Priest:

> The legends of this festival are clear: Isis, Osiris, and Set; Iduna, Bragi and
> Loki; Blodeuwedd, Lugh, and Gronw and others. As it is with the year's season
> it is with all things.

Priestess:

> Now does the Goddess turn away her face from the latest-born king of the
> golden cap, bright handsome and laughing, who dies today, and smiles instead
> her gaze upon his somber brother, the silent, hard, and clever king of the night.

Priest:

> As season follows season, as snow follows summer the change is made, for dark-
> ness must inevitably follow light.

Priestess:

> As the lady Ishtar did seal the doom of high Tammuz so also does she of the
> flowers require the life of the smiling king, wherefore from his blood do red
> flowers grow as his mortal soul journeys beyond

Priest:

> In time and in the midst of winter he will return and incarnate once again in
> his deep love of the Lady and decree fate on his brother. As day follows night
> this must come to pass. All things rise and fall and only the goddess remains
> the same.

Now is the rite of calling down the moon, cakes, and wine.
The Great Circle is closed.

A SAXON LAMMAS CELEBRATION

As everyone gathers for the festival, the Mead Bearer, with goblets of mead, greets
them. The altar is set up in the north and covered with a cloth.

The ceremony begins with a hammer-hallowing (equivalent to the Wiccan circle casting with an athame). The circle is invoked with Thor's hammer (a symbol in the shape of an inverted "T"), consecrating the place of ritual. First the circle is drawn on the ground with the hammer. It must be big enough to contain all the celebrants. It is usual to start in the east and work clockwise around the circle. A branch dipped in water is then used to sprinkle and purify the circle.

The quarters are then invoked with the hammer by the *gothi* (priest). Beginning at the east, the cardinal points are invoked:

East:

> *I invoke Austri, guardian of the east. Welcome spirits of the winds.*

South:

> *I invoke Sudri, guardian of the south. Welcome spirits of fire.*

West:

> *I invoke Westri, guardian of the west. Welcome spirits of the rivers and sea.*

North:

> *I invoke Nordri, guardian of the north. Welcome spirits of earth.*

The priest goes to the center of the circle and places the hammer there, saying:

> *I create here a link to Yggdrasil and the nine worlds. Welcome here all gods. Welcome here all spirits. Welcome here all men and women. Let no one disturb this sacred place hallowed with Thor's sign and now under the protection of the Thunderer.*

Priestess:

> *I welcome the spirits of this land here on Lammas Eve.*

She pours an offering of mead on the ground for the local spirits of the land.

Priest:

Now is the time when Loki's Brand rises each morning with the sun. The heat
of the Dog Days is upon us and the corn dries and ripens in its intensity. Sif's
hair is golden in the sunlight and ripe for shearing.

Priestess:

Erce, Erce, Erce, Earth Mother.,
May the almighty eternal lord
Grant you fields to increase and flourish
Fields fruitful and healthy,
Shining harvests of shafts of millet,
Broad harvests of barley,
Hail to thee, Earth Mother of Men;
Bring forth now in God's embrace,
Filled with good for the use of man.

Priest:

This is the season of sacrifice when the corn dies so that we might have bread.
This is the season when the dying god hangs on the tree to outface the abyss
and bring back knowledge. Odin hung upon the great ash tree Yggdrasil for
nine days and nine nights, pierced with a spear. He gave up one of his eyes for
the secrets of the runes.

Scald:

I declare I hung on that windy Tree
Nine full days and nights.
Pierced with a spear and offered to Odin:
Myself to mine own self given.
High on that Tree of which none know
From what roots it rises to heaven.

None refreshed me then with food or drink.
As I peered right down into the deep;
As crying aloud I lifted the Runes
Then fell back from the abyss.

Nine mighty songs I learned from the great
Son of Bale-thorn, Bestla's sire;
I drank a measure of the wondrous Mead
With the Soulstirrer's drops I was showered.

Ere long I bore fruit, and throve full well.
I grew and waxed in wisdom;
Word following word; I found me words.
Deed following deed; I wrought deeds.

Hidden Runes shalt thou seek and interpret,
Many symbols of might and power
By the Great Singer painted, by the High Powers fashioned.
Graven by the Utterer of gods.

For gods graved Odin, for elves graved Daïn,
Dvalin the Dallier for dwarfs,
All-wise for Jötuns, and I, of myself.
Graved some for the sons of men.

Dost know how to write, dost know how to read?
Dost know how to paint, dost know how to prove?
Dost know how to ask, dost know how to offer?
Dost know how to send, dost know how to spend?

Better ask for too little than offer too much
Like the gift should be the boon:
Better not to send than to overspend.

Thus Odin graved ere the world began:
Then he rose from the depths and came again.

The drinking horn is filled and passed again. As each person drinks, they may say something in praise of the season, about the nature of sacrifice, or share an insight about the runes.

Priestess:

> *On this Lammas Eve we give the gods thanks for the first fruits of the harvest.*
> *We break this loaf and offer it to them.*

Priest:

> *Thor, the Thunderer, we thank you for your protection.*

Priestess:

> *Sif, the golden haired, we thank you for the grain harvest.*

Priest:

> *Frey, we thank you for the beasts of the field.*

Priestess:

> *Freya, we thank you for your love and gentleness.*

Priest:

> *Odin, our father, grant us knowledge and justice.*

Priestess:

> *Frigga, our mother, grant that our lives may be fruitful.*

Priest:

> *All goodly powers grant us blessing!*

As each blessing is pronounced, the fragments of the loaf are thrown to the winds. Those present then solemnly consume the rest of the loaf.

Priestess:

> *The rite is over. Let the feasting begin!*

GROVE OF THE SILVER WHEEL: DRUIDIC RITE FOR LUGHNASA

The ceremony should be performed on the day of Lughnasa. The best place to perform it is on a hilltop or beside a holy well.

The acting chief druid or druidess and the bard, who is also responsible for blowing the horn and for drumming when it is needed, perform the rite. A man wearing royal purple robes and a corn mask represents the Corn Lord. A woman dressed in red and crowned with a wreath of wheat ears, poppies, and cornflowers represents the Harvest Goddess. She carries a sickle.

A circle is set up with the altar in the center, and the cardinal points of north, east, south, and west are marked. This is decorated with greenery including grain, ripe berries, apples, grapes, etc.

Everyone, led by the druid, processes around the outside of the circle three times before stopping at the northeast point of the circle, which is the entry point.
Druid:

> *I ask all ye here assembled — art thou ready to erect the sacred temple, and celebrate the rites of Lughnasa?*

Celebrants:

> *We are ready.*

All enter the circle and, walking sunwise, arrange themselves around it.
Druid: (Traces the outline of the circle with the ceremonial sword.)

> *I conjure thee O circle of power, that thou beest a meeting place of love, and joy and truth, a shield against all wickedness and evil, a bulwark that shall contain all the power we raise within thee. In the names of the gods and goddesses we worship so shall it be.*

Bard:

> *Spirits of this place, hear us! Spirits of this place, we honor thee and ask us to be with us in our rites.*

Celebrants:

> Be with us!

Druid:

> We are gathered here to celebrate the rite of Lughnasa as the time of the harvest
> approaches. The fields grow golden in the sun with ears of ripening grain. It is
> a time of rejoicing, for we see the fruits of our labors. It is a time of danger, for
> the wind and rain might still destroy the uncut crop. It is a time of death, for
> the Corn Lord sacrifices himself that we may have our bread.

Bard:

> Welcome O Corn Lord,
> Golden-haired son of Mother Earth and Father Sky,
> Lover of the sovereign goddess of the land,
> Sacred King who meets death at the Queen's hand.

The man playing the Corn Lord steps forward into the center of the circle.
Druid:

> Come Great Goddess,
> Spirit of the Earth, whose body supports us,
> Mother of the Universe, whose milk is the stars,
> Spinner of fate, who weaves and measures our lives
> Lady of Death, who cuts the thread,
> Be welcome here as Queen of the Harvest.

The woman representing the Harvest Goddess steps forward to face the Corn
Lord. She passes the sickle over his head, and he falls to the ground. The druid
picks up the Corn Lord's mask and chants:

> Each ridge, and plain, and field,
> Each sickle curved, shapely, hard.
> Each ear and handful in the sheaf,
> Each ear and handful in the sheaf.

Bless each maiden and youth,
Each woman and tender youngling,
Safeguard them beneath thy shield of strength,
And guard them in the house of the saints,
Guard them in the house of the saints.

Encompass each goat, sheep and lamb,
Each cow and horse, and store,
Surround Thou the flocks and herds,
And tend them to a kindly fold,
Tend them to a kindly fold.

For the sake of Llew, the many skilled,
Of Rhiannon fair-skinned branch of grace,
Of Arianrhod smooth-white of ringleted locks,
Of Gwyn ap Nudd of the graves and tombs,
Gwyn ap Nudd of the graves and tombs.[6]

The mask is passed around the circle, and each person holds it before their face and reflects on the nature of sacrifice. The man who portrayed the Corn Lord stands up and becomes an ordinary member of the circle.

The druid takes up a loaf of bread and offers it to the Harvest Goddess. She touches it with her sickle to signify her acceptance and blessing.

The bard says:

Mother of the Earth,
You gave us the new grain
Dried gently in the sun
Rubbed from the husks
Ground in the quern
Baked in the oven
To feed your people.

We walk sunwise round the circle
In your name, Great Mother
We ask that you preserve us

In peace, in plenty
In truth of heart.

Keep us in labor, in love
In wisdom, in mercy
For the sake of your Lord
Who dies with the harvest
Until he is reborn another day.

Great Mother preserve us!
Great Mother preserve us!

The druid leads the assembly in a sunwise procession three times around the circle. Only the woman playing the Harvest Goddess remains still at the center.

The bread is then broken by the druid and shared among those present. A goblet of wine or mead is passed around and everyone drinks.

The druid calls:

Let blessing be!

All:

Let blessing be!

Now follows any rites of divination the grove may wish to carry out, and storytelling, songs, and dancing.

When all is finished, the druid pours a libation of wine to the Earth Mother (i.e., he or she pours some wine on the earth), and says:

We give thanks to the Great Mother of the Earth. Mother, grant us your bless-
ings. Be with us in our lives, as you once were to those of old.
Grant us your love and blessings. Let blessing be!

Great Lord and consort of the Goddess. Grant blessing to this land, protect us
from the powers of blight and darkness. Be with us in our lives as you once
were to those of old. Grant us your wisdom. Let blessing be!

All:

Let blessing be!

The druid goes around the temple counterclockwise with the sword to wind down the power and close the temple.

Druid:

> *May there be peace in the North*
> *May there be peace in the East*
> *May there be peace in the South*
> *May there be peace in the West.*

All:

> *May peace reign everywhere!*

Druid:

> *Together, brothers and sisters, we have met together to celebrate the rite of Lughnasa. We have witnessed the harvesting of the grain and the sacrifice of the Corn Lord. We have honored the Lady and her Lord. The rite is ended, let us go in peace until we meet again.*

All:

> *Go in peace!*

Notes

1. William Shakespeare, *Titus Andronicus.*
2. Insert here the goddess name your coven uses, or the name of the goddess you feel closest to.
3. Insert the name of the godform your coven uses.
4. Insert the name of the godform your coven uses.
5. A consecrated stone that stands in the north of the circle.
6. A Gaelic version might be:
   For the sake of Lugh, the many skilled,
   Of Macha fair-skinned branch of grace,
   Of Tailtiu smooth-white of ringleted locks,
   Of Crom Dubh of the graves and tombs,
   Crom Dubh of the graves and tombs.

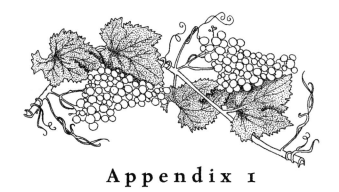

Appendix 1

Lughnasa Calendar

July 15

- Greek Olympic New Year.

- Festival of Rauni. Rauni is the Finnish rowan goddess associated with spells and runes.

- St. Swithin's Day. Lore has it that if it rains today, then it will rain for the next forty days:

St. Swithin's Day if thou be fair
For forty days 'twill rain no more.
St. Swithin's Day if thou bring rain
For forty days it will remain.

Farmers anxiously watched the skies, as too much rain at this time of year would ruin the harvest. St. Swithin was a ninth-century English bishop. When his bones were removed from the churchyard into the cathedral, he seems to have objected, as a thunderstorm broke out and went on for forty days. He was weeping at the moving of his grave.

July 16

- Birth of Set in Egyptian lore.

July 18

- Birth of Nepthys, Egyptian death goddess.

July 19

- Marriage of Isis and Osiris (Egyptian).

- Festival of Astarte (Canaanite).

- Festival of Mut (Egyptian).

- Marriage of Aphrodite and Adonis (Greek).

July 20

- St. Margaret's Day. Margaret was a shepherdess who became a saint. In Gloucestershire, it was traditional to serve Heg Peg Dump (a plum pie) on this day in her honor.

- Festival of Freya (Norse).

- Festival of Inanna (Sumerian).
- Festival of Carman (Irish).

July 21

- Mayan New Year.

July 22

- Choctaw Festival (Native American).
- Feast Day of La Maddelaine.

July 23

- An ancient festival was held in Rome in honor of Salacia, goddess of saltwater and inland mineral springs.
- Festival of Sul (or Sulis), patron goddess of the famous mineral springs at Bath in England. Such mineral springs have healing properties.
- Roman Festival of Neptunalia.
- Festival of Sophis.
- Festival of Athene (Greek).

July 24

- A festival in honor of Isis-Neith.
- A festival of lamps was held in Egypt at Sais. Lamps were carried in procession around the coffin of Osiris, the corn god.

JULY 25

- St. James' Day.

- Feast of St. Christopher, patron saint of travelers.

- In Pondevedra, the first bunch of grapes and the first ear of corn are offered to Santiago.

- Festival of Naga Panchami (Hindu Snake God).

- Festival of Salacia.

- Feast of Furrina, in honor of the Roman goddess Furrina, patroness of freshwater springs. She was invoked to prevent water drying up at this hot and dry time of year.

JULY 26

- St. Anne's Day. The mother of the Virgin Mary in Christian lore.

- In Santiago de Querétaro, the Santa Ana festival is celebrated with a fair and traditional Spanish-style bullfight.

- Festival of Sleipnir, shamanic steed of Odin.[1] (Horses are a common theme of Lughnasa).

JULY 27

- Start of Dog Days.

JULY 28

- St. Botvid's Day.

JULY 29

- St. Martha's Day. Along with her sister Mary, Martha served Jesus Christ.

- Festival of Thor, the Thunderer (Norse), who has aspects as a god of agriculture. He is invoked for fertility and asked for good weather for the harvest.

- St. Olaf's Day.
- Festival of Ra (Egyptian).
- Festival of Mercury (Roman).
- Festival of Pan (Greek).
- Festival of Tammuz (Akkadian).

JULY 30

- Micmac Festival (Native American).

JULY 31

- Lammas/Lughnasa Eve New Style.
- Sacred to Loki, the Trickster (Norse), and his consort Sigyn, who unlike her husband was famous for her constancy.
- St. Neot's Day: The saint who was invoked in Cornwall for good fishing catches.

AUGUST 1

- Lammas/Lughnasa New Style.
- Feast of Tailtiu: Earth goddess and foster mother of Lugh (Irish).
- Festival of the goddess Carman (Irish).
- Festival of Macha of the Golden Hair (Irish).
- Festival of Bloduewedd: Flowering earth goddess (modern Wiccan-invented feast).
- Festival of Demeter (Greeks) or Ceres (Roman), goddess of corn and harvest, who rules the entire month of August.
- In Norse lore, it is Sif of the Golden Hair (i.e., the corn) who rules the month.
- In Brythonic Celtic lore, Ceridwen is the goddess of the harvest.

- Rhiannon, the Great Queen (corresponds to the Gaelic Macha), is honored at this time (British).

- The month of August is named after the deified Roman emperor Augustus who reformed Roman paganism.[2]

- Originally this was the feast of St. Catherine, now moved to November 25. Like other Christian saints, she is either a thinly disguised Pagan goddess or has accrued some of the attributes of an older goddess.

- Festival of Crom Dubh, a Celtic or pre-Celtic god associated with the mounds. He causes the crops to ripen at Lughnasa.

- Aztec festival of Xiuhtecuhtli, the fire god and ruler of the year. Human sacrifices were thrown into the flames for him.

AUGUST 2

- In some localities, this was the day on which Lammas was celebrated. On this day William Rufus, perhaps the last sacred king of England, may have been killed in a ritual hunt.

- St. Sidwell's Day. This day commemorates a supposed saint who had a chapel and well in Exeter dedicated to her. She is said to have been murdered on the instructions of her stepmother who was jealous of her lands and who hired killers to cut off Sidwell's head. As was the case with Sir Bevercote (see entry for St. Catherine in appendix 4), a spring gushed forth. As the name Sidwell is thought to derive from "scythe" and "well," it is highly likely that the "saint" postdates the story and is a Christianization of an earlier legend related to sacrificial victims of the harvest rituals.

- Costa Rican festival of Our Lady of the Angels.

AUGUST 3

- Festival of Diana.

- Festival of Brighid.

- Festival of Minerva.

- Festival of Cybele.

- Festival of Artemis.

AUGUST 4

- Festival of Aphrodite.

- Festival of Ishtar.

- Festival of Isis.

- Festival of Inanna.

- Feast of the Blessed Mary (European Catholic).

AUGUST 5

- Shoshone Bannock starts (Native American).

- Festival of Tiamet.

- Festival of Ishtar.

- Festival of Venus.

- Old St. James' Day.

AUGUST 6

- In England, this is the traditional day of the Tan Hill fair, commemorating the sacred fire of the Celts called *teinne*.[3]

- Festival of Thoth (Egyptian).

- Cherokee Green Corn Dance (Native American).

AUGUST 7

- Festival of Hathor (Egyptian).

- Festival of Neith (Egyptian).

- Festival of Yemaya.

- Russian festival of Zaziuki. The first sheaf of corn, the *zazhinochnyl* or *zazhinnyi*, was taken into the farmhouse and threshed separately. In some areas it would be blessed and mixed in with the seed corn.

AUGUST 8

- Shoshone Bannock ends (Native American).

AUGUST 9

- Chinese Milky Way festival.

- Vinalia Rustica, Roman wine festival.

- Festival of Venus.

AUGUST 10

- St. Lawrence's Day. He was martyred by being cooked on a gridiron, his last words being, "This side is toasted, so turn me, tyrant, eat, and see whether raw or roasted I make the better meat." With somewhat black humor he has become the patron saint of cooks and bakers, highly appropriate for Lammas.

- Festival of Nuit.

- Festival of Hathor.

- Festival of Sothis.

AUGUST 11

- Old Lammas Eve.

AUGUST 12

- Old Lammas/Lughnasa.

- Dog Days end.

- Feast of St. Claire of Assisi.

AUGUST 13

- Old Lammas Day in some areas.

- Festival of Hecate. In Greece the festival was to invoke her aid in preventing storms from ruining the harvest. In Rome it was the slaves' holiday and women processed to Diana's temple in Aricia to ask her to avert any autumn storms that might destroy the harvest. Hunting dogs were crowned, wild beats were free from hunting, and young people were purified. A feast was served consisting of cakes served on leaves, apples still hanging on their boughs, and a goat kid.

- Festival of Vertumnus. Roman festival in honor of Vertumnus, god of the autumn winds.

- In Norse lore, this day is sacred to gods of stability and order.

AUGUST 14

- Festival of Hathor.

- Festival of Hera.

- Festival of Selene.

- Feast of the Assumption of the Virgin Mary celebrated in Spain and Portugal.

AUGUST 15

- St. Mary's Day. Feast of the Assumption of the Virgin Mary taken into heaven.

- In Rome, the day was sacred to Diana.

- Birth of Isis.

- Festival of Sophia.

- Festival of Diana.

AUGUST 16

- Festival of Chan-go (Chinese moon goddess).

AUGUST 17

- Odin's ordeal on Yggdrasil begins.

- Amenartus Festival (Egyptian).

- Festival of Isis.

- Festival of Ishtar.

- Festival of Selene.

AUGUST 18

- Feast of St. Helen. She was born during the third century and was the mother of Constantine, the first Roman emperor to be a Christian. Many wells are named after her, and in this aspect, she may have usurped the Celtic Pagan goddess Elen.

- Festival of Zeus (Greek chief god).

- Festival of Thor (Norse thunder god).

- Festival of Jupiter (Roman chief god).

AUGUST 19

- Rustica Vinalia. At this Roman festival, Venus and Minerva were called upon as patrons of gardens and olive groves, respectively. The festival was a holiday for kitchen gardeners.

AUGUST 20

- Hopi spider woman flute ceremony.

AUGUST 21

- Heraklia (Greek festival in honor of Herakles).

- Festival of Inanna.

- Festival of Beltis.

- Festival of Ishtar.

- Festival of Isis.

- Festival of Kore.

AUGUST 22

- Festival of Isis.

- Festival of Tara.

- Montu Festival (Egyptian).

AUGUST 23

- Festival of Juturna.

- Festival of Nemesis, Greek goddess of divine vengeance, earlier perhaps a goddess of the wheel of the year.

- Festival of Moira, Greek goddess of fate.

AUGUST 24

- Festival of Ceres.

- Festival of Nuit.

AUGUST 25

- Feast of St. Maelrbha. He was an Irish saint who seems to have become confused with the Celtic deity Mourie, a water god associated with Loch Maree and its holy island. The first fruits ceremony would have been later this far north, so this probably marks a first fruits ceremony. Those wishing to be cured of lunacy should visit the island at Lughnasa and go to the wishing tree and oracular well that lies beneath it and make offerings.[4]

- Odin's ordeal ends. Discovery of the runes.

- Festival of Ops.

- Festival of Nuit.

Notes

1. Nigel Pennick and Helen Field, *The God Year*, 1996.
2. Ibid.
3. Ibid.
4. David Clarke, *A Guide to Britain's Pagan Heritage*, 1995.

Appendix 2

Names of the Festival

In modern Irish, the name of the old festival is preserved in the Gaelic name for August, Lúnasa. The festival is generally given as Lughnasa, though an older spelling is Lughnasadh.

In Scots-Gaelic, the name is Lughnasair. In Manx, Lhuany's Day.

According to the Gaulish Celtic Coligny calendar, Lughnasa would have fallen during the month called Elembios, meaning "claim time," perhaps referring to the tribal gatherings at this time where claims would have been resolved. This month corresponds to our late July, early August.

In Anglo-Saxon, the festival is called Lammas, from *hlaef-mass* meaning "Loaf Mass." Saxons called the month of August *woedmonath*, meaning "the weed month," named after the fast-growing weeds at this time of year.

In mediaeval England, the festival was called "the Gule of August," which has caused problems for the linguists. Some say it was "Yule of August," but it is more likely to be an Anglicization of the Welsh *gwyl*, which translates as "feast." It fell between Hey Monath (Hay Month–July) and Barn Monath (Harvest Month–August).

In Welsh August is called *awst*, and the first of August is *gwyl aust*, "the feast of august."

The month of August was named in honor of the Roman emperor Augustus (63 B.C.E.–14 C.E.)

In Ireland folklore, survivals of the ancient festival have a number of names, according to locality:

- Crom Dubh Sunday (Domhnach Chrom Dubh)
- Domhnach Lughnasa (Lughnasa Sunday)
- Garland Sunday
- Garlic Sunday
- Garden Sunday
- Sunday of the New Potatoes
- Colcannon Sunday
- Black Stoop Sunday
- First Sunday in August
- Harvest Sunday
- First Sunday of the Harvest
- Donagfh Sunday
- Last Sunday of Summer
- Last day of Summer
- Bilberry Sunday
- Blaeberry Sunday
- Heatherberry Sunday
- Mulberry Sunday
- Whort Sunday
- Hurt Sunday
- Fraughan Sunday
- Big Sunday
- Mountain Sunday

- Height Sunday
- Rock Sunday
- Lough Sunday
- Glen Sunday
- Wood Sunday
- Pilgrimage Sunday
- Pattern Sunday
- Papish Sunday
- Cullen Well Day

- Owna Day
- Peakeen Sunday
- Rann Sunday
- Reek Sunday
- Skein Sunday
- Skelp Sunday
- Steeple Sunday
- Scabby Friday

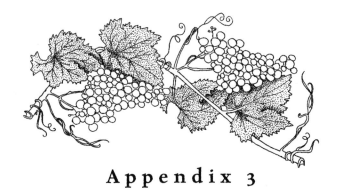

Appendix 3

Symbols for Lughnasa

COLORS

Royal purple or heather purple

Gold and yellow (for the ripening
   corn)

Brown (for the earth)

Red (for blood)

PLANTS

Alder

Apple

Arum lily

Ash

Basil

Borage

PLANTS CONTINUED

Daisy
Fennel
Gorse
Grain
Hazel
Heather
Honeysuckle
Oak
Poppy
Reed
Rush
Vine
Woad

GEMS

Tigers-eye
Amber
Rutilated quartz

TOOLS

Staff
Stang
Sickle
Flail

BASIC ENERGIES

Sacrifice
Harvest
Redemption
Renewal
Death
Mourning
Protection

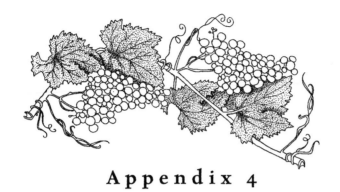

Appendix 4

Gods and Goddesses of Lughnasa

Adonis: His name means "Lord," and another of his titles was Christos, or "anointed one." He was a vegetation god mourned during the Dog Days, when plants withered and died in the heat.

Anu/Ana: (Irish) A ninth-century glossary describes Anu as "the mother of the Irish gods," and here she seems to have been confused with Danu. However, while Danu is a goddess of water, Anu is derived from the old Gaelic word *anai*, which meant "wealth," connecting her with the earth and its minerals. Various sites in Ireland are sacred to Anu; an early text describes the country as *iath nAnann*, the Land of Anu. Perhaps the most famous location sacred to this goddess are the two mountaintops near Killarny called Dá Chich nAnann, which are still known today as "the Two Paps of Anu."

Arianrhod: ("Silver Wheel") This Welsh goddess is the mother of Llew (see chapter 3 for the full story). She has aspects as a moon, initiation, and spinning goddess. She lives in the Castle of the Silver Wheel, where souls go at death, and where poets travel in trance to be initiated.

Artemis: Greek maiden goddess of the moon and hunt. She haunts the forests with her silver bow, accompanied by her dogs.

Aset: See Isis.

Attis: Called "anointed one" (Christos), a vegetation god similar to Adonis.

Blodeuwedd: (Welsh) This goddess was formed by two magicians from flowers as a bride for Llew. Her name means "flower face." She betrayed Llew by falling in love with Gronw, and the pair plotted Llew's murder. When the plot failed and Llew returned, she fled from him and was changed into an owl as punishment. She is the summer goddess of the flowering earth who becomes the winter crone goddess represented by the owl.

Bran: A number of giants appear at Lughnasa including the god Bran ("Raven"), who was the guardian of all Britain. While avenging the ill-treatment of his sister in Ireland, Bran was poisoned in the foot and knew he was dying. He instructed his companions to cut off his head and carry it home. All the time the head continued to speak. Eventually they came to the White Mount where the head was buried and magically continues to guard Britain against invasion. This is the present site of the Tower of London. The presence of ravens, Bran's totem birds, at the Tower confirms its association with the god. It is still said that as long as the ravens remain at the Tower, then Britain is safe from invasion; if they should ever leave, disaster will follow. They are still carefully looked after. Bran is associated with the alder tree. In Ogham, the Celtic tree alphabet, the alder is *fearn;* the Brythonic spelling of which is Gwern, who is described as Bran's nephew. Bran's singing head may refer to the top-most branch of the alder, called "the head," which was used to make magical flutes and whistles through which the god was thought to speak; one of the old names for the alder is "whistlewood." The top-most branches of the alder move when the wind blows, and the leaves rustle more musically than any other tree — the tree seems to sing.

Carman: (Irish) The goddess Carman is said to have come from Athens in Greece to Wexford in Ireland with her three sons. A seasonal festival was held in her honor at Carman in Leinster once every three years at Lughnasa. Those who visited the fair were considered to be blessed and would enjoy prosperity, plenty, corn, milk, and fruit.[1] Women played an important part in the festival and held special councils to discuss women's affairs.

Cerberus: The three heads of Cerberus, the dog guardian of the Underworld in Greek myth, refers to the tri-partite year.[2] Cerberus was the child of Echidne and Typhon. He may be associated with the Dog Star, Sirius, which rises with the sun at Lammas to guide the soul of the sacrificed corn lord to the Underworld.

Ceres: Roman goddess of corn. Equivalent to the Greek Demeter.

Ceridwen: British harvest goddess with aspects as moon goddess, crone, and initiatrix.

Chicomecoatl: Aztec maize goddess of plenty, known as "Seven Snakes."

Corn Maiden: Native American corn goddess. A warrior dreamed of a golden-haired woman who ordered him to burn the grass-covered prairie. He should then take her by the hair and drag her across the ground. Each time he stopped, ears of maize grew. The corn silk is the hair of the corn goddess.

Cotys: Thracian fertility goddess, worshipped at night with orgiastic rites.

Crom Dubh: The Irish Crom Dubh is the "Black Crooked One" or "Black Bowed One," also called Crom Cruach or Cenn Cruaich ("the Bowed One of the Mound") and was a sacrificial god associated with the beginning of August. The eleventh-century *Book of Leinster* states: "In a rank stand twelve idols of stone; bitterly to enchant the people the figure of Crom was of gold."

This is thought to refer to a circle of standing stones at Magh Sléacht near Killycluggin (the plain of Tullyhaw in County Cavan). It may be that in ancient times a human sacrifice was made here, perhaps selected during special games. Crom Dubh is thought to belong to the religion of the ancient Irish, before the time of the Celtic invaders. The earliest written account of him refers to an idol at Magh Sléacht worshipped by King Tignermas and his followers, at which human sacrifices were made. This statue is said to have sunk into the ground after St. Patrick demolished it, and indeed, the stone circle stands in ruins. In most of the folklore he is called Crom Dubh, characterized as the "dark croucher" or the "old bent one" and was identified with the devil. It seems that after the sacrifice, the victim was identified with the god, also becoming a "crooked one" and believed to be dwelling in the mound with the god as king of the dead.

In later ages, Crom Dubh's human sacrifice was substituted with a bull. On the north shore of Galway, there is still a tradition that a beef animal must be roasted to ashes in honor of Crom Dubh on his festival day. In various versions of the story, Patrick is said to have overcome or converted a Pagan called Crom Dubh by resuscitating his dead bull.

According to another Lughnasa story, Crom Dubh was buried up to his neck for three days and only released when the harvest fruits had been guaranteed. Crom is associated with the ancient mounds as an old agricultural god of the earth who caused the crops to ripen, as are the *sidhe* ("people of the mounds") or fairies of Celtic lore who are the descendants of such gods. They also have to be offered regular sacrifices in the form of milk. Crom is possibly an Underworld god, like the Greek Hades (Roman Pluto) who captured Persephone (Proserpina). Hades/Pluto was both the guardian of Underworld treasure (the minerals of the earth) and grain, which sprouts in the Underworld.

Cronos: At Lughnasa, the alder and the ash are seen to be in conflict, and many tales relate how alder gods and giants are defeated by ash gods. Among the Greek alder gods was Cronos, who, like Bran, was a Titan, or giant figure with a raven totem. One of his titles may have been Phoroneus, who was said to be the first to discover the use of fire after Prometheus stole it from the gods. In *The Greek Myths*, Robert Graves suggested that his name may be derived from *fearinus* ("of the dawn of the year"), a variant of Bran, Gwern, or Fearn, making him an alder god. His mother was the ash nymph Melia because, Graves suggests, the ash courts lightning, man's first source of fire. There is an ancient association of the alder and the ash, and they are sometimes seen as opposites. In the Celtic poem "The Battle of the Trees" (Cad Goddeu) from the "Romance of Taliesin," the alder is in the front line on one side and Gwydion's ash on the other, the ash defeating the alder, perhaps denoting a change of season.

Cybele: Phrygian goddess whose relationship with Attis parallels that of Ishtar and Tammuz. She was an earth and bee goddess, depicted wearing a crown and flanked by lions.

Damara: British fertility goddess.

Dana: Wife of Balor, sometimes given as Ceithlenn.

Danae: Pre-Greek barley goddess. In classical myth, she was seduced by Zeus in the form of a shower of gold.

Danu: Celtic mother goddess. Danu was worshipped throughout the ancient Celtic world. Several European rivers are named after her, the most famous being the Danube. There is a Welsh equivalent called Dôn; mediaeval texts describe her as the mother of a family of mythical wizards. Mediaeval Irish literature identifies Danu with Anu. The name Danu is most often come across in the description of a race called the Tuatha Dé Dannan ("People of the Goddess Danu"), where she is described as the mother of all the gods.

Demeter: Greek goddess of corn and harvest. Demeter is possibly a triple goddess with Kore, or Core, as maiden and Perspehone as Queen of the Underworld. According to the story, Kore (or Persephone) was picking poppies when Hades, King of the Underworld, abducted her. She was taken to his realm and forced to stay there. Demeter sought her all over the land while the world became barren and sterile. Winter ruled. Then at last, overcome with weariness, she sat down for nine days and nights, and the gods caused poppies to spring all around her feet. Breathing in the soporific perfume, she fell asleep and rested. The gods ruled that Persephone could return to her mother providing she had not eaten anything while in the Underworld. Unfortunately she had eaten six seeds from a pomegranate. She would have to stay in the Underworld for six months of the year, and this is why we have winter. When she returns to earth, her mother rejoices and the earth blooms. Poppies, which grow along with corn, are an emblem of Demeter, goddess of the harvest, and Persephone is the seed corn in the earth, which grows in the spring and returns to the Underworld at the harvest.

Diana: Roman goddess of the moon and hunt, cognate with the Greek Artemis.

Dionysus: The Greek god of wine. The start of the grape harvest is around Lammas. Dionysus is a savior god, titled Christos ("anointed one"), Dendrites ("god of the tree"), and acts as a scapegoat as Dionysus Melanaigis ("of the black goat skin").

Dôn: (Welsh) This Welsh goddess is described as the mother of the gods and equates to the Irish Danu. She is the grandmother of Llew.

Elen: Elen is the Brythonic patron goddess of wells, pathways, and streams. Her name is also linked to known ley lines and other paranormal activity. In some places, Elen is known by the diminutive Nell. "Peg o'Nell" is a popular local name for a water spirit or fairy. Elen was one of the patron deities, or *genius loci*, of London. The Christian saint Helen seems to have usurped many of her sites. Elen/Helen/Nell is associated with several wells sited along the River Fleet in London. Both Nell and Elen have been depicted in the form of a beautiful young woman holding a basket of fruit and accompanied by a small dog. Nell is supposed to have lived near the Bagnigge Wells in London, probably indicating an earlier link between the wells and the Celtic water deity. The Bagnigge Wells were a popular meeting place in the eighteenth century. The pastimes indulged in were far from sacred. According to a contemporary verse, Bagnigge Wells were often the scene of amorous encounters where "the sons of lawless lust conven'd, where each by turns his venal doxy woo'd."

Epona: Gaulish goddess of sovereignty. One of the more important Celtic deities, Epona is always depicted with horses, either riding sidesaddle or sitting or standing between two or more mares. She is very closely associated with several of the main themes of Lughnasa. Her horse is sometimes shown with a foal, symbolizing regeneration and fecundity. Other symbols of fertility often appear in representations of Epona, usually baskets of corn or fruit. Another clear link between Epona and the festival of Lughnasa was her association with healing wells and springs in ancient Gaul. These links between horses, water, and healing are clearly related to the practice of horse-swimming at Lughnasa.

Faula: Roman goddess of animal life. She is the female equivalent of the horned god of the wild, Faunus (the Roman Pan), though she is sometimes identified with Ops.

Formori/Formorians: These are often described as a race of sea monsters, but this is the result of a confusion between *mor* (meaning "phantom") and *muir*, the word for sea. Further confusion crept in when they were described as living far to the north of Ireland and thus became wrongly identified with Viking raiders and described as sea pirates. Their name actually means "underworld-phantom"; they were the demonic element in the Irish retelling of the Indo-European myth of a titanic struggle between an underworld and a divine race. They are often depicted as grotesquely deformed and monstrous, although in the story of the Battle of Moytirra they are given a somewhat more salubrious appearance, probably because Lugh is descended from them on his mother's side of the family! A later portrayal of them, the *Lebor Gabala* (a medieval pseudo-historical compilation), describes them as having only one arm and one leg. This is very similar to the Fachan, a rather sinister fairy or goblin of the Scottish Highlands. Such creatures may be a folk-memory of the practices of Celtic seers, who stood on one leg with one arm extended and one eye closed when casting spells or practicing divination. In this rather awkward stance they stood not entirely in this world nor out of it; the closed eye was focused on the inner world and the extended arm directed toward the Otherworld. Some folklore states that this is the position in which to see fairies or enter fairy realms. In addition, there is one theory that associates one-legged, one-armed, one-eyed beings with psychotropic mushrooms. A pretty certain means of being "away with the fairies!"

Furrina: Roman goddess of springs and freshwater, honored with a festival on August 25.

Gilgamesh: Hero god, perhaps the Sumerian equivalent of Herakles. They both slay monstrous lions, wear their pelts, and seize a sky bull by its horns to overcome it. Both visit hell and discover a secret herb of immortality.

Gofannon or Govannon: Welsh smith god. Equivalent of the Irish Goibhniu. See *Smith gods.*

Goibhniu: ("Smith") Irish Divine Smith. Blacksmith to the Tuatha Dé Danann, he fashioned the spear of Lugh and the spears used at the Battle of Moytirra. Any spear made by him would never miss its target. He served a marvelous ale feast to the gods, and those who drank would never age or die. He had a marvelous cow, which gave neverending supplies of milk. He is sometimes known in folklore as Gobán Saor.

Hades: The Greek god of death and the Underworld, who abducted Persephone, causing winter. He wears as dog skin.

Hephaestus: In Greece, the smith god was lame Hephaetus. He presided over the magical craft of metalworking, and his temples overlooked the streets of the craftsmen and smiths. He was a fire god of Lycia, the son of Hera. He was born lame and ugly, and, in disgust, she threw him out of heaven. He fell into the sea and was fostered by Thetis and Euronyme, two sea goddesses. He forged many marvelous gifts for these two goddesses and eventually became the smith and craftsman of the gods. So valued was he that the beautiful goddess of love, Aphrodite, became his wife. It has been suggested that he was originally a dangerous fire demon whose power had to be contained, so his legs were twisted. Others say that he was lame, because smiths are often maimed by accidents in the forge; others say that they suffer deformity due to arsenic poisoning. Whatever the reason, we again have the theme of the lame god/king expelled from home and fostered only to return later and marry the daughter of the king.

Herakles: (Greek; Hercules in Latin). As a warrior, Herakles is a suitable icon for Lughnasa, but there is another link—Lughnasa occurs when the sun is in Leo. This constellation is associated with the Nemean lion that Herakles killed as the first of twelve labors, afterward wearing its skin. His labors may be considered as the journey of the solar hero around the zodiac, others include being nipped by a crab and overcoming a sky bull. At his death he was cremated on an alder wood pyre, and his remains were floated away on a river in an alder wood boat, probably symbolic of the sun passing through the Underworld river at night on the sun barge. Floating on alder wood boats or arks occurs elsewhere in myth. A solar eclipse marked his death. He was titled "Only Begotten Son" and "Prince of Peace." He was the son of the virgin Alcmene and the chief god, Zeus.

Inanna: Sumerian earth/mother goddess called "the green one" and "she of the springing verdure" after the rippling green corn that was her mantle in spring. The rainbow is her necklace, and the lunar horns are on her head. She was queen of the earth, goddess of grain, vine, date palm, cedar, sycamore, fig, olive, and apple trees. One of these trees was always planted in her temple as a symbol of her power. A kind of bread was baked on her altars, called the "baked cakes of the goddess, Inanna," symbolizing the body of the goddess herself feeding her children.

Isis: Egyptian mother goddess. Isis is the Greek form of her Egyptian name Aset ("throne"). She is the chief mourner of her husband, Osiris, whom she brings back to life with magic, after he is murdered by her brother, Set. She is the mother of Horus, the falcon-headed god, and protects him from Set until he is old enough to avenge his father's death. Her importance grew during the Greek and Roman periods of Egyptian history, and her cult spread to the Mediterranean and as far west as Oxford in England. She was the patroness of magic, motherhood, life, nature, healing, protection, the dead, and seafarers, and called Queen of Heaven and Star of the Sea—titles usurped by the Virgin Mary in later days. As a goddess of this time of year she is associated with the Dog Star, Sirius (or Sothis), the heliacal rising of which heralded the welcomed annual Nile inundation. It is considered to be the goddess coming to mourn her husband and raise him from the dead.

Leo: Lughnasa falls in the constellation of Leo the lion. Lions are associated with sun gods and lionesses with lunar goddesses, depicted drawing their chariots or supporting their thrones. Cybele, lover of Attis (a death and resurrection god in the manner of Tammuz), was depicted riding in a chariot drawn by lions. She also changed the two lovers Hippomenes and Talanta into lions. A nymph called Cyrena overcame a lion that was terrorizing Libya with her inner strength, now depicted on the tarot card "Strength." The lion is considered a guardian, standing at temple gates and palaces as a symbol of kingship, heraldry, etc. The Egyptians reverence Leo because the rise of the Nile coincided with the entrance of the sun into the constellation of Leo. There are many lion-headed fountains, with water flowing from the mouth in consequence. The Great Sphinx has the body of the lion Leo and the head of Virgo, though perhaps later carved into the head of a king.

Llew: (Welsh) See chapter 3.

Loki: (Norse) The Dog Star is called "Loki's Brand" (Lokabrenna), and he steals the hair of Sif, a kenning for corn. These two things associate him with the time of Lammas. Loki was a trickster god, a practical joker. His temperament was mercurial, sometimes helpful, and sometimes malicious. He was very clever and cunning. He is a god of wildfire, son of Farbauti, who engendered fire, and Laufrey ("wooded isle"), who provided fuel for the fire. He seems to have had no shrines of his own, thought he was of the company of the ruling gods the Aesir. He was the father of the Fenris wolf, who will devour the gods at the end of the world.

Lugh: (Irish) See chapter 3.

Macha: An annual fair was held at Armagh in Ireland to honor Queen Macha of the Golden Hair at Lughnasa. Her golden hair, of course, is the golden corn. She has aspects as a horse goddess and sovereign goddess of the land.

Mithras: He is a Persian god of light whose cult spread with the Roman Empire. He was the favorite god of the soldiers, and Mithraism almost became the state religion in place of Christianity. He killed a bull whose blood fertilized the earth. According to D. J. Conway (*Lord of Light and Shadow*), he was born on December 25, met with his twelve disciples for a last supper, died, and ascended to heaven. His followers celebrated a ritual, which shared bread marked with a cross. He carried the Keys of Heaven, raised the dead, healed the sick, and was called "the Savior," the "Light of the World." Followers were baptized in bull's blood, which removed their sins. He was born at a rock called Petra, adopted as Peter.

Morrigan (or Mór-ríoghain, Mórrigu): (Irish) "Great Queen." She is an Irish battle goddess and a triple deity with three aspects. The ravens are her birds and feast on the slain. She fought alongside the Tuatha Dé Danann during the first battle against the Fomorians. As with Anu, she also has two hills named after her breasts, *dá chich na Mórrigna*, near the great burial mound of Newgrange in the Boyne Valley.

Mourie: An ancient Scottish god of lochs and lakes whose feast day was August 25, perhaps a Lughnasa ceremony, held later as the harvest ripened later so far north. Well into the seventeenth century C.E., people sacrificed bulls, adored wells and monuments and stones, and made offerings of milk upon the hills. He was connected with the island of St. Ruffus, commonly called Ellan Moury. The name of the island may be a corruption of *Eilean a Mhor Righ*, meaning "Island of the Great King"; perhaps a sacred king who stood for the god and ruled on the island.[3] The local people used to speak of "the god Mourie" well into the seventeenth century, much to the disgust of the church.[4]

Ninurta: A Sumerian god, also titled Lugalbanda, whose exploits are detailed in the *Lugal-e*. He was lord of the plow and master of the fields, also the young warrior and champion of the gods, as well as being an ancient thunder god who brought the storms that gave life to the land. The *Farmer's Almanac* (1700 B.C.E.), an instructive manual on how to grow barley, praises him as "the life giving semen."[5]

Odin: Scandinavian chief god, patron of war, poetry, magic, and the dead. He rode an eight-legged horse called Sleipnir and had a magic spear called Gungnir. In the month of August, he hung on Yggdrasil, the world tree, for nine days and nights to gain the secrets of the runes, losing one of his eyes in the process.

Ops: Ops was the Roman goddess of the harvest, fertility, and sowing. She was the wife of Saturn. Her festivals were the Opeconsiva August 25, when she was worshipped by touching the ground, and the Saturnalia, when she was worshipped with her consort December 17–23. The Opalia was on December 17.

Orpheus: Lughnasa sees the battle of ash and alder, fought between gods connected with the ash and decapitated giants and gods allied with the alder. As well as being associated with Bran, the alder is associated with another "singing head," that of Orpheus in Greek mythology. His name is derived from *orphruoesis*, which means "on the river bank," i.e., the alder tree. He could charm both men and beasts with his music. After failing to rescue his wife from the Underworld, he wandered the earth until the maddened Maenads, followers of Dionysus, tore him limb from limb. His head was laid to rest in a cave by the Muses, where it continued to prophesy day and night, until Apollo himself ordered it to be silent.

Orthus: In Greek myth, he is the two-headed hound of Geryon. He fathered Chimaera, the sphinx, the hydra, and the Nemean lion on Echidne. He was Sirius, the Dog Star, that inaugurated the Athenian New Year. The reformed year had two seasons, and his son, the lion, represented the first half and his daughter, the serpent, the second. The reformed New Year began when the sun was in Leo and the Dog Days had begun. Orthus, like Janus, looked in two directions, past and future.

Osiris: (Egyptian) Osiris became king of Egypt after his father, Geb, retired into heaven. He married his sister Isis. Their brother, Set, was jealous and tricked Osiris into getting into a coffin and killed him. Later he cut the body of Osiris into fourteen pieces and scattered them throughout Egypt. Isis found them all, apart from the phallus. Isis turned herself into a falcon and mated with the corpse, conceiving the falcon god, Horus. Osiris decided to remain in the Underworld as receiver of the dead, and this is how he is pictured in the tombs of the pharaohs. At the sowing festival, the priests buried effigies of Osiris made of earth and corn. These were dug up again after a year, when the corn would have sprouted. Thus the corn god produced corn from his own body—his sacrifice to feed his people. His followers ate wheat cakes marked with a cross, believed to contain the spirit of Osiris. He granted eternal life to the righteous. His symbol was a shepherd's crook, and he was called "the good shepherd."

Persephone: Greek underworld and corn goddess, the daughter of Demeter and wife of Hades. She is the Underworld/crone aspect of the Kore-Demeter-Persephone triad, and represents the seed corn in the earth.

Pomona: The Roman goddess of fruiting trees, she protects the fruits, trains, and prunes the vines, and brings fresh water to the roots of trees and vines. She was the bride of Vertumnus, the autumn wind that marked the ripening of fruits on August 13.

Prometheus: This Greek god sacrificed himself to bring fire to humankind, stealing it from the forge of the smith god Hephaestus. For this he was condemned to be chained to a rock on a mountain, where a bird would eat out his liver every day. It would grow back during the night, and then the torment would begin again. Prometheus was one of the Titans — early gods or giants — overcome by the Olympian pantheon. The overcoming of giants or primordial gods is another theme of Lammas, possibly symbolizing winning the harvest from them.

Proserpina: The Roman equivalent of Persephone.

Rhiannon: ("Great Queen") A Welsh sovereign goddess, with fertility and Other-world aspects. The wife of the Otherworld god Pwyll.

St. Anne: St. Anne was said to be the mother of the Virgin Mary and hence the grandmother of Jesus Christ. She is associated with a number of holy wells and her feast day is celebrated just before Lammas on 26th July. In parts of France her feast day is a first fruits festival. The similarity of her name to that of Anu or Danu was most likely part of this attempt to Christianize ancient holy places, especially the wells associated with the goddess. One of the best-known wells dedicated to St. Anne is that of the spa town of Buxton in the English Peak District.

St. Catherine: Although now celebrated on November 25, St. Catherine's Eve has been moved all around the calendar by the Roman Catholic Church, before being finally removed from its official list of saints. She was originally associated with Lammas, and a highlight of the festivities was the "Catherine Wheel." Nowadays, the name is given to a small firework, but the original Catherine Wheel provided a far more impressive spectacle, consisting of a large, tar-covered wagon wheel, which would be lit and rolled down a hill. St. Catherine is often shown with a wheel and was the patron saint of spinners; there are clear similarities with the spinning and weaving goddesses who spin the cosmos, though her legend says that she was martyred on a wheel before being beheaded.

St. Helen: Her feast day is on August 18. She was born during the third century and was the mother of Constantine, the first Roman emperor to be a Christian. She was the daughter of Coel, the "Old King Cole," who was the "merry old soul" of the well-known nursery rhyme. Her claim to fame is that she is said to have discovered the cross on which Christ was crucified. The similarity of her name to that of Elen, a Celtic water goddess, led to several British Pagan wells being renamed after her. St. Helen is said to have founded a church on a Romano-British site near the ancient wells known as Pancras Wells. Nell Gwynne, the mistress of King Charles II, took on many of the characteristics of Elen in popular imagination; she acquired various symbolic details that made her a kind of living representation of the goddess.

St. James: The traditional start of the oyster harvest was on St. James' Day, July 25. In the old calendar, St. James' Day would have been near Lammas, on what we now know as August 5. One of the disciples of Jesus, he was martyred in Jerusalem in A.D. 43 but somehow managed to be buried at Santiago de Compostella in Spain. In his honor, pilgrims carried scallop shells on their travels. On St. James' Day, many British and Irish parishes celebrate the blessing of the seas and fisheries. The fishermen, boats, nets, and the sea itself is blessed. On Old St. James' Day (August 5) shell grottoes were built, though given the date this may be the remnant of an older festival in honor of the sea god. Oysters are traditionally eaten on this day, and it is the start of the oyster season. It is said that those who eat oysters on this day will not be in want for the rest of the year.

St. Lawrence: St. Lawrence's Day is celebrated on August 10. He was martyred by being cooked on a gridiron, his last words being, "This side is toasted, so turn me, tyrant, eat, and see whether raw or roasted I make the better meat." With somewhat black humor he has become the patron saint of cooks and bakers, highly appropriately for Lammas.

St. Oswald: The feast of St. Oswald is on August 5. Though he is ostensibly a Christian saint, killed in battle with the Pagan king of Mercia in 642 C.E., there are two wells dedicated to him, one in Lancashire and one in Shropshire. The Shropshire well is a healing and wishing well. At the back of it is a stone that used to have a crowned head carved upon it. St. Oswald's head is supposed to be buried there. This resembles the head of the giant Mimir buried at a well near Yggdrasil in Norse myth.[6] After death his body was dismembered, and parts of it were hung from a tree and other parts scattered across the land, a tale told of many sacrificed corn gods and sacred kings.

St. Patrick: (Ireland) St. Patrick is well-known as the national saint of Ireland. Although St. Patrick's Day is celebrated in March, his victory over the Pagan Crom Dubh is commemorated at Lughnasa. Patrick lived during the fifth century C.E., and although he was not the first Christian missionary to visit Ireland, he is considered to be the most important and influential in introducing and spreading Christianity throughout the country. He was born in western Britain to a family of Romanized Celts and was kidnapped and taken to Ireland as a slave during his youth. He eventually escaped to continental Europe where he studied and was ordained as a priest. He is said to have had a vision in which he was asked "to come back and walk once more" among the Irish. Many stories are told of his mission and victory over Paganism; the best known of these is, of course, that he drove all the snakes out of Ireland. In fact, as Ireland was separate from the rest of Europe before the last Ice Age, there were no snakes to begin with. Similar stories tell of Patrick banishing various monsters into lakes at many different locations throughout Ireland. These folktales symbolize the supposed victory of the new Christian religion over the older Pagan deities. The other well-known story about St. Patrick is that he illustrated the three persons in one god of the Christian Trinity by using a shamrock. This would hardly have been a novel concept to the ancient Celts; the triple leaves of the shamrock had probably been associated with their own threefold goddess. The main Lughnasa traditions associated with Patrick at Lughnasa are his victory over Crom Dubh and various pilgrimages to hilltops, lakes, and caves, etc., the most important being that at Mount Croagh, Patrick in County Mayo. In England, St. Michael is his nearest counterpart. Churches on hilltops and/or Pagan sites are often named after Michael, who is usually shown fighting a dragon as a symbol of Paganism. Michaelmas is celebrated at the end of the harvest on September 29. Until the early twentieth century, St. Patrick's Well and Chair in County Tyrone, Ireland, were the scene of riotous Lughnasa celebrations. St. Patrick, or St. Bright in some accounts, is said to have driven a herd of devils over a nearby cliff. St. Patrick's Chair itself is thought to have been an inauguration throne, and the site remained more or less unaltered by Christian practices, Patrick's name being merely a thin disguise over the earlier Pagan customs.

St. Sidwell: St. Sidwell's Day on August 2 commemorates a supposed saint who had a chapel and well in Exeter dedicated to her. She is said to have been murdered on the instructions of her stepmother, who was jealous of her lands and hired killers to cut off Sidwell's head. As in other tales of decapitated heads, both Pagan and Christian, a spring gushed forth where the head fell. As the name

Sidwell is thought to derive from "scythe" and "well," it is highly likely that the "saint" postdates the story and is a Christianization of an earlier legend related to sacrificial victims of the harvest.

Salacia: Roman goddess of freshwater springs. Such water goddesses are honoured at the hot, dry time of Lammas to ensure there is enough water for the harvest.

Set: This Egyptian god was crucified on a fork. His blood and death were said to make the yearly renewal possible. Before his sacrifice he was wounded in the side and his reed scepter was broken. He is only one of many sacrificed gods associated with the Lammas period.

Sif: Scandinavian wife of the thunder god, Thor. Her golden hair is the corn, cut by Loki at Lammas.

Smith gods: There are many legends of smith gods associated with the Lammas time of year, including Lugh, perhaps because they are connected with the constellation of Cancer, the crab. After the summer solstice in June, which occurs in the constellation of Cancer, the sun appears to be moving backward, southward again, signaling the decline of the year after its zenith. Like the sacrificed sacred king, smith gods are described as lame or crooked, and sometimes as walking like crabs. Some even have the word as part of their names. The sons of Hephaestus were lame, as were his grandsons, the Kabeiroi, described as dwarf smiths or crabs. The sons of Carcinos ("crab") were dwarf smiths. The hard-tailed crab has crooked legs, the twisted limbs of Hephaestus, and their pincers resemble those used by smiths. The penis of Osiris was eaten by a crab, i.e., the generative power of the corn god was destroyed by the hot, sterile part of the year in Cancer.

Sul/Sulis: Goddess of the mineral springs at Bath, in southern England.

Tailtiu: Lugh is said to have established games in honor of his foster mother, Tailtiu, the earth goddess, at Lughnasa. It marked the beginning of the harvest and the end of summer. She was a chieftainess of the Fir Bolg.

Thor: Scandinavian thunder god, husband of Sif, bringer of fertilizing rain. His symbol is the hammer.

Vertumnus: The festival of this Roman god is celebrated on August 13. He is the autumn wind that bring change to the land. At his touch grapes ripen and the grain swells. In time he will bring the snow and rain, but now he is said to be the first to taste the fruits of Pomona, the goddess of fruiting trees.

Vulcan: Roman equivelent of Hephaestus, a very ancient Stone Age god, originally Volcanus, a fire, thunderbolt, and sky god, a god of volcanic fire who became associated with forges "and the dawn of the metal age." In later myth he took on many of the same attributes as Hephaestus, marrying Venus, the Roman equivelent of Aphrodite.

Wayland: The British smith god lamed by a king, who avenged himself on the king by taking his daughter. Wayland is said to live in a chambered Neolithic long barrow in Berkshire, England. If a horse should be tethered there under a full moon, the owner returning in the morning would find it newly shod. It is said that he shoes the nearby chalk horse on the hill at Uffington. (See *Smith gods.*)

Notes

1. Patrick Joyce, A *Social History of Ireland*, London, 1903.
2. Robert Graves, *The Greek Myths*, 1955.
3. Lewis Spence, *The Minor Traditions Of British Mythology*, Benjamen Bloom, 1972.
4. David Clarke, A *Guide to Britain's Pagan Heritage*, London: Hale, 1995.
5. Http://www.gatewaystobabylon.com
6. Yvonne Aburrow, *The Sacred Grove*, Chieveley: Capall Bann, 1994.

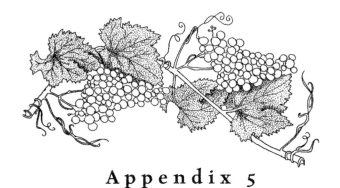

Lughnasa Songs and Chants

IT WAS UPON A LAMMAS NIGHT

It was upon a Lammas night,
When corn rigs are bonnie,
Beneath the moon's unclouded light,
I held awa to Annie;
The time flew by, wi' tentless heed,
Till, 'tween the late and early,
Wi' sma' persuasion she agreed
To see me thro' the barley.

Corn rigs, an' barley rigs,
An' corn rigs are bonnie:
I'll ne'er forget that happy night,
Amang the rigs wi' Annie.

The sky was blue, the wind was still,
The moon was shining clearly;
I set her down, wi' right good will,
Amang the rigs o' barley:
I ken't her heart was a' my ain;
I lov'd her most sincerely;

I kiss'd her owre and owre again,
Amang the rigs o' barley.
Corn rigs, an' barley rigs (etc.).

I lock'd her in my fond embrace;
Her heart was beating rarely:
My blessings on that happy place,
Amang the rigs o' barley!
But by the moon and stars so bright,
That shone that hour so clearly!
She aye shall bless that happy night
Amang the rigs o' barley.
Corn rigs, an' barley rigs (etc.).

I hae been blythe wi' comrades dear;
I hae been merry drinking;
I hae been joyfu' gath'rin gear;
I hae been happy thinking:
But a' the pleasures e'er I saw,
Tho' three times doubl'd fairly,
That happy night was worth them a',
Amang the rigs o' barley.

—Robert Burns

JOHN BARLEYCORN

The old ballad of John Barleycorn relates the widespread and ancient belief in a corn god or spirit in the form of a colorful and imaginative narrative. There are several versions of the ballad, but all tell of the sacrifice of John Barleycorn. He is the spirit of the vegetation that is "sacrificed" to harvest the food (or, in this particular case, the beer or whiskey) that will sustain the people throughout the dark winter months and will be reborn with the next growing season. The name "John Barleycorn" has now become synonymous with—and sometimes a euphemism for—alcoholic drink, generally.

There were three men came out of the West
Their fortunes for to find,
And these three men made a solemn vow,
"John Barleycorn must die."

They've ploughed, they've sown, they've harrowed him in
Through plods of barley's head,
And these three men made a solemn vow,
"John Barleycorn is dead."

They let him lie for a very long time,
'Til the rains from heaven did fall,
And little Sir John sprung up his head
And so amazed them all.

They've let him stand until Mid-Summer's Day
'Til he looked both pale and wan,
And little Sir John's grown a long, long beard
And so become a man.

They've hired men with the scythes so sharp
To cut him off at the knee,
They've rolled him and tied him by the way
Serving him most barbarously.

They've hired men with the sharpest hooks
Who've pricked him to the heart,
And the Loader, he has served him worse than that,
For he's bound him to the cart.

They've wheeled him around and around a field
'Til they came unto a barn,
And there they made a solemn oath
On poor John Barleycorn.

They've hired men with the [crofting] sticks
To cut him skin from bone,
And the Miller, he has served him worse than that,
For he's ground him between two stones.

And little Sir John and the nut brown bowl,
And he's brandy in the glass,
And little Sir John and the nut brown bowl
Proved the strongest man at last.

The huntsman he got off the fox
Oh so loudly to blow his horn,
And the tinker he can't mend kettle nor pots
Without a little Barleycorn.

WHO KILLED COCK ROBIN

This old song is said to commemorate the death of red-headed King William Rufus on August 2, thought by many to have been the Lughnasa killing of a sacred king. This version dates from 1788.

"I," said the sparrow,
"With my little bow and arrow,
I killed cock Robin."

Who saw him die?
"I," said the pie,
"With my little eye,
I saw him die."

Who caught his blood?
"I," said the fisher,
"With my little dish,
I caught his blood."

Who'll make his shroud?
"I," said the eagle,
"With my thread and needle,
I'll make his shroud."

Who'll dig his grave?
"I," said the owl,
"With my little trowel,
I'll dig his grave."

Who'll be the parson?
"I," said the rook,
"With my little book,
I'll be the parson.

Who'll be the clerk?
"I," said the lark,
"If it's not in the dark,
I'll be the clerk.

Who'll carry the link?
"I," said the linnet,
"I'll come in a minute,
I'll carry the link."

Who'll be the chief mourner?
"I," said the dove,
"I mourn for my love,
I'll be chief mourner."

Who'll carry the coffin?
"I," said the kite,
"If it's not through the night,
I'll carry the coffin."

Who'll bear the pall?
"We," said the wren,
"Both cock and hen,
We'll bear the pall."

Who'll sing a psalm?
"I," said the thrush,
As she sat in a bush,
"I'll sing a psalm."

Who'll toll the bell?
"I," said the bull,
"Because I can pull,
I'll toll the bell."

Who'll lead the way?
"I," said the martin,
"When ready for starting
I'll lead the way."

All the birds of the air
Fell sighing and sobbing,
When they heard the bell toll
For poor cock Robin.

In the Brythonic Celtic tongues, *coch* means "red" and *rhi-ben* means "chief king." The sparrow is "Bran's Sparrow," i.e., the goldcrest wren, ruler of the winter half of the year.[1] The arrow is shot at Lammas when the magpie of ill omen appears. The kingfisher catches his blood, and his soul departs as an eagle. The owl is Blodeuwedd in her winter aspect. The rook is considered an unlucky bird. The lark is sacred to the goddess of death in life. The linnet is connected with flax, from which the torch is made, sacred to Arianrhod. The kite is a carrion bird, but also associated with goddesses, such as Isis, who revive the king. The thrush is connected with the holly at the midwinter solstice, when the sun is reborn. The bull is the bullfinch; the martin leads in the year. At Midsummer is An Fheill Eoin, the festival of birds[2] who fall silent in August.

Iolach Buana or "Reaping Salutation"

This is a traditional Scottish Marymass chant.

> *Each ridge, and plain, and field,*
> *Each sickle curved, shapely, hard,*
> *Each ear and handful in the sheaf,*
> *Each ear and handful in the sheaf.*
>
> *Bless each maiden and youth,*
> *Each woman and tender youngling,*
> *Safeguard them beneath Thy shield of strength,*
> *And guard them in the house of the saints,*
> *Guard them in the house of the saints.*
>
> *Encompass each goat, sheep and lamb,*
> *Each cow and horse, and store,*
> *Surround Thou the flocks and herds,*
> *And tend them to a kindly fold,*
> *Tend them to a kindly fold.*

For the sake of Michael head of hosts,
Of Mary fair-skinned branch of grace,
Of Bride smooth-white of ringleted locks,
Of Columba of the graves and tombs,
Columba of the graves and tombs.

LAMENT FOR ADONIS

In ancient Greece, when the slopes blossomed with the red anenomes that were the blood of Adonis, the cries went up from the women, mourning the death of the vegetation god.

At his vanishing away she lifts up a lament,
"O my child," at his vanishing away she lifts up a lament
"My Damu" at his vanishing away she lifts up a lament
"My enchanter and priest!" at his vanishing away she lifts up a lament
At the shining cedar, rooted in a spacious place,
In Eanna, above and below, she lifts up a lament
Like the lament that a house lifts up for its master, lifts she up a lament,
Like the lament that a city lifts up for its lord,
Her lament is the lament for the herb that grows not in the bed
Her lament is a lament for the corn that grows not in the ear,
Her chamber is a possession that brings forth a possession,
A weary woman, a weary child forspent.
Her lament is for a great river, where no willows grow,
Her lament is for a pool, where fishes grow not.
Her lament is for a thicket of reeds, where no reeds grow.
Her lament is for a wilderness where no cypresses grow.
Her lament is for the depth of a garden of trees, where honey and wine grow not.
Her lament is for meadows, where no plants grow.
Her lament is for a palace where length of life grows not.

TRADITIONAL IRISH LAMENT

My treasure and my love
My little dark headed boy,
Whom I thought whiter than new milk
Or than water on a summer's day!

HOMERIC HYMN TO GAIA

Her I praise, the mother of all
The foundation, the oldest one
I sing to the mother of the Earth
The nourisher, she upon whom everything feeds.
Of Gaia I sing.
Wherever you are on her sacred ground
She feeds you, nourishes you from her treasure store.
Through her bountiful harvests, beautiful children come
The giving of life, the fullness of life
The taking of life, these are hers.
Praise her.

Notes

1. Michael Bayley, *Caer Sidhe, The Celtic Night Sky*, 1997.
2. Ibid.

GLOSSARY

Anima Loci: The soul or spirit of a place.

Athame: A witch's black-handled knife, used in ritual to invoke the circle.

Avalon: "Apple Land," a Celtic paradise.

Axis mundi: "Axis of the world," an imaginary or magically invoked pole that links a place or person to the realms of heaven, earth, and Underworld.

Cailleach: A Scottish word for the hag/winter aspect of the Goddess.

Corn: A generic word for grain crops in the Old World, though specifically referring to maize in the New World.

Coven: A group of witches or Wiccans.

Covener: A member of a coven.

Dog Star: The star Sirius that rises with the sun in the morning during late July and early August. This period is called the dog days.

Druid: A priest or priestess of the ancient Celts.

Hag: The crone or old woman aspect of the Goddess, often representing winter.

Handfasting: A Pagan wedding that binds a couple for "a year and a day."

Heliacal: Rising with the sun.

Lustral: Consecrated water used for rituals of purification.

Mumming: A folk play acted out by people in traditional costumes.

Ogham: A magical alphabet, based on tree lore, of the ancient Celts.

Otherworld: The realm where the gods and the dead live in Celtic lore, otherwise known as Fairyland, Elfhame, or Avalon.

Precession of the equinoxes: Because the earth wobbles on its axis, the stars at certain times are year are not fixed, but appear to move backward through the zodiac. Thus the spring equinox now occurs in Aries, but formerly appeared in Taurus, etc.

Rath: An earthwork or mound, otherwise called a fort.

Rune: A magical alphabet of the Saxons and Norse.

Sacred king: A king chosen by lot or contest to embody the fortune of the land, and be sacrificed when his powers fail.

Sidhe: Gaelic for "fairy."

Sirius: See *Dog Star*.

Tuatha Dé Danann: "People of the Goddess Danu," a god-like race said to have dwelled in Ireland, until driven underground by the invading Celts.

Web: A magical concept that proposes that all things are linked in some way. Any action will resonate throughout the entire web.

Wiccan: A person who follows one of the magical traditions originating from Gerald Gardner, based on ancient witchcraft.

Wildfolk: British Craft term for fairy folk.

Witch: A practitioner of an ancient Pagan religion and magic

World tree: A mythical tree that links all the planes of existence.

SELECT BIBLIOGRAPHY

Bailey, Jaqui (ed.). *Five Minute Faces*. Kingfisher Books, 1991.

Bauval, Robert and Adrian Gilbert. *The Orion Mystery*. Arrow, 1998.

Bayley, Michael. *Caer Sidhe*. Chieveley: Capall Bann, 1997.

Bell, Brian (ed.). *Insight Guide: Ireland*. APA Publications (HK) Ltd., 1991.

Beresford, Ellis Peter. *Dictionary of Celtic Mythology*. London: Constable, 1992.

Briggs, Katherine M. *The Folklore of the Cotswolds*. Batsford, 1974.

Cambrensis, Giraldus. *The Historical Works*. Thomas Wright (ed.). Bohn, 1863.

Campbell, Joseph. *Oriental Mythology*. Penguin, 1962.

———. *The Hero with a Thousand Faces*. Princeton: Princeton University Press, 1968.

Carmichael, Alexander. *Carmina Gadelica*. Edinburgh: Oliver and Boyd, 1928.

Chadwick, Nora. *The Celts*. Penguin Books, 1997.

Cheney, W. *The Cult of Kingship in Anglo-Saxon England*. Manchester University Press, 1970.

Clarke, David. *A Guide to Britain's Pagan Heritage*. Hale, 1995.

Cockayne, T. O. (ed.). *Leechdoms, Wortcunning and Starcraft of Early England*. Rolls Series, 1866.

Conway, D. J. *Lord of Light and Shadow*. St. Paul, MN: Llewellyn, 1997.

Cooper, Quentin and Paul Sullivan. *Maypoles, Martyrs & Mayhem*. Bloomsbury, 1994.

Cotterell, Arthur. *Encyclopedia of World Mythology*. Parragon, 1999.

Crowley, Vivianne. *Principles of Wicca*. London: Thorsons, 1997.

Dames, Michael. *The Silbury Treasure*. London: Thames and Hudson, 1976.

Detienne, Marcel. *Gardens of Adonis*. Princeton: Princeton University Press, 1977.

Devereux, Paul. *Symbolic Landscapes*. Gothic Image, 1992.

Dineeen, P. *An Irish-English Dictionary*. Dublin, 1975.

Dixon, Hardy Phillip. *The Holy Wells of Ireland*. Hardy & Walker, 1840.

Durdin-Robertson, Lawrence. *The Year of the Goddess*. Aquarian Press, 1990.

Egan, Patrick. *The Torch and the Spear*. Chieveley: Capall Bann, 1996.

Farrar, Janet and Stewart Farrar. *Eight Sabbats for Witches*. Robert Hale, 1981.

_____. *The Witches' Goddess*. Robert Hale, 1987.

Feest, Christian F. *Native Arts of North America*. London: Thames and Hudson, 1980.

Franklin, Anna. *Familiars: Animal Powers of Britain*. Chieveley: Capall Bann, 1997.

Franklin, Anna and Sue Lavender. *Herb Craft: A Guide to the Shamanic and Ritual Use of Herbs*. Chieveley: Capall Bann, 1996.

Franklin, Anna and Sue Phillips. *Pagan Feasts: Seasonal Food for the Eight Festivals*. Chieveley: Capall Bann, 1997.

Frazier, Sir James. *The Golden Bough: A History of Magic and Religion*. Macmillan & Co., 1922.

Graves, Robert. *The Greek Myths*. Penguin, 1955.

_____. *The White Goddess*. London: Faber and Faber, 1961.

Gray, Louis Herbert (ed.). *The Myhology of All Races*. Vol. 3. Marshall Jones Company, 1918.

Grigson, Jane. *English Food*. Penguin Books, 1997.

Grimassi, Raven. *Hereditary Witchcraft*. St. Paul, MN: Llewellyn, 1999.

Gwyn. *Light From The Shadows*. Chieveley: Capall Bann, 1999.

Hesiod. *Works and Days*. T. Dane (ed.). Private edition, 1957.

Hole, Christina. *Saints in Folklore*. London: G. Bell & Sons, 1965.

Hone, William. *The Every Day Book and Table Book*. 1832.

Hunt, Robert. *Popular Romances of the West of England*. Chatto and Windus, 1923.

Hutton, Ronald. *Stations of the Sun*. Oxford: Oxford University Press, 1996.

Jacobson, Thorkild. *The Treasures of Darkness*. New Haven, Conn.: Yale University Press, 1976.

Jennings, Pete. *The Norse Tradition*. Hodder & Stoughton, 1998.

Jones, Julia and Barbara Deer. *Cattern Cakes & Lace: A Calendar of Feasts*. Dorling Kindersley, 1987.

Joyce, Patrick. A *Social History of Ireland*. London: Bohn, 1903.

Julius Caesar. *The Conquest of Gaul*. S. A. Handford (trans.). Penguin Classics, 1951.

Jung, Carl. G. *Man and His Symbols*. Aldus Books, 1964.

Keating, G. *General History of Ireland*. Dublin, 1859.

Kelly, Eamonn P. *Sheela-na-Gigs: Origins and Functions*. Dublin: Country House, 1996.

Kondratiev, Alexi. *Celtic Rituals*. Ireland: Collins Press, 1998.

Laing, Lloyd and Jennifer Lloyd. *Art of the Celts*. London: Thames & Hudson, 1992.

Lambeth, M. A *Golden Dolly: The Art, Mystery and History of Corn Dollies*. John Baker, 1969.

Macaulay. *History of St. Kilda*. n/d.

Manilus. *Book 5 of the Astonomica*.

Meyer, K. *Hibernica Minora*. 1894.

Murray, Margaret. *The Divine King in England*. n/d.

Naddair, Kaledon. *Keltic Folk and Fairy Tales*. Century Books, 1987.

Ó hÓgáin, Dáithí. *Myth, Legend and Romance: An Encyclopaedia of the Irish Folk Tradition*. Prentice Hall Press, 1991.

_____. *The Sacred Isle*. Cork: The Collins Press, 1999.

Ogden, Daniel. *The Crooked Kings of Ancient Greece*. London: Duckworth, 1997.

Palmer, Roy. *The Folklore of Warwickshire*. Batsford, 1976.

Pennick, Nigel. *Crossing the Borderlines*. Chieveley: Capall Bann, 1998.

Pennick, Nigel and Helen Field. *The God Year*. Chieveley: Capall Bann, 1996.

_____. *The Goddess Year*. Chieveley: Capall Bann, 1996.

Pliny. *Natural History II*.

Porter, Enid. *The Folklore of East Anglia*. Batsford, 1974.

Reader's Digest Family Book of Things to Make and Do. Reader's Digest, 1997.

Reed, Lori. *Hidden Knowledge*. Bodmin: Bossiney Books, 1988.

Ross, Anne. *Pagan Celtic Britain.* Sphere Books, 1974.

Rundle, Clark R. T. *Myth and Symbol in Ancient Egypt.* London: Thames and Hudson, 1959.

Simpson, Jaqueline. *The Folklore of the Welsh Border.* Batsford, 1976.

Spence, Lewis. *The Minor Traditions of British Mythology.* Benjamen Bloom, 1972.

Squire, Charles. *The Mythology of the British Isles.* Bohn, 1905.

————. *Celtic Mythology.* Geddes and Grosset, 1999.

Summers, Montague. *The History of Witchcraft & Demonology.* Castle Books, 1992.

Walshe, John G. and Shrikala Warrier. *Dates and Meanings of Religious and Other Festivals.* W. Foulsham & Co., 1993.

Waring, Philippa. A *Dictionary of Omens and Superstitions.* Souvenir Press Ltd., 1978.

White, Emmie. *Corn Dollies: From the Start.* G. Bell & Sons, 1978.

Index

The Sacred Circle Tarot
A Celtic Pagan Journey

ANNA FRANKLIN
ILLUSTRATED BY PAUL MASON

The Sacred Circle Tarot is a new concept in tarot design, combining photographs, computer imaging, and traditional drawing techniques to create stunning images. It draws on the Pagan heritage of Britain and Ireland, its sacred sites and landscapes. Key symbols unlock the deepest levels of Pagan teaching.

The imagery of the cards is designed to work on a number of levels, serving as a tool not only for divination but to facilitate meditation, personal growth, and spiritual development. The "sacred circle" refers to the progress of the initiate from undirected energy, through dawning consciousness, to the death of the old self and the emergence of the new.

The major arcana is modified somewhat to fit the pagan theme of the deck. For example, "The Fool" becomes "The Green Man," "The Heirophant" becomes "The Druid," and "The World" becomes "The World Tree." The accompanying book gives a full explanation of the symbolism in the cards and their divinatory meanings.

1-56718-457-X
Boxed Kit: 78 full-color cards; 288 pp. book, 6 x 9   **$29.95**